W9-BRH-368

COMPARATIVE EDUCATION
SOME CONSIDERATIONS OF METHOD

Unwin Education Books

Education Since 1800 IVOR MORRISH
Moral Development WILLIAM KAY
Physical Education for Teaching BARBARA CHURCHER
The Background of Immigrant Children IVOR MORRISH
Organising and Integrating the Infant Day JOY TAYLOR
The Philosophy of Education: An Introduction HARRY SCHOFIELD
Assessment and Testing: An Introduction HARRY SCHOFIELD
Education: Its Nature and Purpose M. V. C. JEFFREYS
Learning in the Primary School KENNETH HASLAM
The Sociology of Education: An Introduction IVOR MORRISH
Developing a Curriculum AUDREY and HOWARD NICHOLLS
Teacher Education and Cultural Change H. DUDLEY PLUNKETT and JAMES LYNCH
Reading and Writing in the First School JOY TAYLOR
Approaches to Drama DAVID A. MALE
Aspects of Learning BRIAN O'CONNELL
Focus on Meaning JOAN TOUGH
Moral Education WILLIAM KAY
Concepts in Primary Education JOHN E. SADLER
Moral Philosophy for Education ROBIN BARROW
Beyond Control? PAUL FRANCIS
Principles of Classroom Learning and Perception RICHARD J. MUELLER
Education and the Community ERIC MIDWINTER
Creative Teaching AUDREY and HOWARD NICHOLLS
The Preachers of Culture MARGARET MATHIESON
Mental Handicap: An Introduction DAVID EDEN
Aspects of Educational Change IVOR MORRISH
Beyond Initial Reading JOHN POTTS
The Foundations of Maths in the Infant School JOY TAYLOR
Common Sense and the Curriculum ROBIN BARROW
The Second 'R' WILLIAM HARPIN
The Diploma Disease RONALD DORE
The Development of Meaning JOHN TOUGH
The Countesthorpe Experience JOHN WATTS
The Place of Commonsense in Educational Thought LIONEL ELVIN
Language in Teaching and Learning HAZEL FRANCIS
Patterns of Education in the British Isles NIGEL GRANT and ROBERT BELL
Philosophical Foundations for the Curriculum ALLEN BRENT
World Faiths in Education W. OWEN COLE
Classroom Language: What Sort? JILL RICHARDS
Philosophy and Human Movement DAVID BEST
Secondary Schools and The Welfare Network DAPHNE JOHNSON *et al.*
Educating Adolescent Girls E. M. CHANDLER
Classroom Observation of Primary School Children RICHARD W. MILLS
Essays on Educators R. S. PETERS
Comparative Education: Some Considerations of Method BRIAN HOLMES

Comparative Education: Some Considerations of Method

BRIAN HOLMES
Professor of Comparative Education, University of London

London
GEORGE ALLEN & UNWIN
Boston Sydney

First published in 1981

GEORGE ALLEN & UNWIN LTD
40 Museum Street, London WC1A 1LU

British Library Cataloguing in Publication Data

Holmes, Brian
Comparative education
1. Comparative education — Methodology
I. Title
370.19'5'018 LA133 80–41625

ISBN 0-04-370101-9
ISBN 0-04-370102-7 Pbk

Set in 10 on 11 point Times by Inforum Ltd, Portsmouth
and printed in Great Britain
by Billing and Sons Ltd, Guildford
London and Worcester

Contents

Acknowledgements *page* ix
Introduction 1
1 Cultural Borrowing – Misconceived Comparative Education 19
2 Comparative Education, Scientific Method and Educational Planning 36
3 The Positivist Debate in Comparative Education – an Anglo-Saxon Perspective 57
4 A Framework for Analysis – 'Critical Dualism' (Conventionalism) 76
5 The Collection and Classification of Data – National Profiles 89
6 Ideal-Typical Normative Models 111
7 Plato's Just Society 133
8 Dewey's Reflective Man in a Changing Scientific Society 142
9 The Ideal-Typical Soviet Man 162
Select Bibliography 176
Published Works by the Author 181
A Selected Guide to Ancillary Reading 188
Index 191

Acknowledgements

It has been my good fortune to work closely, for long or short periods of time, with Joseph Lauwerys, Nicholas Hans, Robert King Hall, George Bereday, Gerald Read, Saul Robinson and Philip Idenburg. I am grateful to them all, and indeed to countless comparativists all over the world who have stimulated my thinking in participating in the development of their subject.

This contribution will be apparent to some extent from the content of this book. Less evident, but gratefully acknowledged, is the help given by Thelma Bristow, for many years our specialist comparative education librarian at the University of London, Institute of Education, and the many students I have been privileged to teach. Coming from every corner of the globe they have taught me a great deal in seminars, discussions and through their own research theses.

I wish to thank Miss Barbara White for preparing the manuscript for press.

Most of all I am indebted to my wife, Margaret, and my daughter, Ruth: to Margaret for criticism and encouragement, and to both for their inexhaustible patience.

BRIAN HOLMES
London

Introduction

Nicholas Hans introduced me to comparative education when in 1945–6, as a recently 'demobbed' RAFVR radar officer and a student at the University of London, Institute of Education, I was fascinated by his extremely coherent lectures at King's College London to those of us who had chosen comparative education as our foundations option in an initial training course. Hans had just returned to King's after war service and in retrospect it is surprising that he could lecture without reference to notes and with a wealth of up-to-date information about education at home and abroad. What impressed me most, perhaps, was the relevance of comparative evidence to on-going English debates. If Hans inspired me, it was Joseph Lauwerys, as my physics method tutor, who stimulated my ambition to make a career in comparative education.

In working towards the achievement of this ambition in 1950–1 I attended the comparative education course as part of the Academic Diploma in Education of the University of London. Hans gave the general lectures and provided a framework within which he consistently worked. He classified the factors influencing educational provision as 'natural' and 'secular'. For him an 'ideal' nation was one in which the people occupying a well-defined territory, enjoyed political sovereignty, spoke the same language, shared the same religious beliefs and came from the same race. These factors were basically historical, operated through the exchange of ideas and were the antecedent causes of present practices. For Hans religion and nationalism were the most powerful ideological traditions against which enlightened men had to struggle. His best-known book, *Comparative Education*,[1] was based on these lectures and quickly became a standard work and then a classic. It has been reprinted several times and translated into many languages including Italian, Japanese, Portuguese and Spanish. No review of the literature in comparative education fails to refer to it. *Comparative Education* remains an extremely useful analytical tool and its continued popularity among students is well deserved.

Lauwerys had an even greater influence on my thinking. He stimulated my interest in scientific method, introduced me to the progressive education movement and made me want to know more about the American and French systems of education. During the year 1945–6 his course included lectures in the history and philosophy of science, methods of teaching science, the philosophy of John Dewey and comparative education. Under his charismatic guidance the books which contributed most to my conceptual position were H. E. Armstrong's *The Teaching of Scientific Method*, J. S. Mill's *System of Logic*, John Dewey's *How We Think* and Karl R. Popper's *The Open Society and its Enemies* and *Logik der Forschung*[2] (a second-hand copy of which I chanced upon at G. K. Lewis's for four old shillings). Armstrong's heurism and Mill's logic were frankly part of an older, nineteenth-century, tradition of learning by discovery. Dewey's book presented a different approach to the teaching and learning of science and his other writings inevitably drew my attention to curriculum theory and progressive education in the USA and elsewhere. Popper's *Open Society*, which had just been published, his seminars which I attended as an occasional student at the London School of Economics and his articles in *Economica*[3] subsequently published as *The Poverty of Historicism*[4] gave direction to my understanding of the methods of science and piecemeal social engineering.

As a comparative educationist Lauwerys shared the methodological assumptions exemplified by Hans. Unlike the latter, however, who was a historian-philosopher, Lauwerys was trained as a scientist and brought his analysis of scientific method and the role of science in society to bear on the study of comparative education. His prewar knowledge of American education, the growth of progressive education and the development of social science research in that country made it possible for him to introduce a sociological perspective not only into comparative education but into studies of British education. Indeed *The Content of Education*,[5] published in 1946, which he helped to prepare, was years ahead of its time. In addition to the contribution he was making to educational theory, his work with the Committee of Allied Ministers of Education[6] in exile during the war and his significant role in the establishment of Unesco and the definition of its objectives enabled him to establish a worldwide network of connections on which the growth of comparative education was very dependent.

Lauwerys introduced me to the debates which were going on in the immediate postwar period about the reconstruction of British society. Popper's *Open Society*, which embodied many of Lauwerys' anti-Platonic and anti-Hegelian views about society, made a major contribution to debates which in academic terms centred on Friedrich von Hayek and Karl Mannheim.[7] Mannheim's charisma was enormous. He was appointed professor of education at the London Institute in 1945 and in a series of lectures at King's College and seminars at the Institute he inspired war-weary veterans and young graduates to believe that a future generation of teachers, under his leadership, could help to build a totally planned, free and democratic society. Parenthetically this message appealed to the social reconstructionist professors of education at Teachers College, Columbia, and elsewhere in the USA and helps, perhaps, to explain the vogue enjoyed by Mannheim in these quarters for some time. Popper, of course, shared von Hayek's doubts about total planning and offered his theory of piecemeal social engineering as an alternative.

Thus in very early days I was offered a choice between two methods of scientific inquiry and between two theories of societal planning. I rejected Mill's inductive method in favour of Dewey's reflective thinking (or problem-solving) approach and rejected Mannheim's notion of total planning and accepted Popper's theory of piecemeal social engineering. But the charisma of Mannheim touched me and the intellectual stimulus provided by Lauwerys, Hans and Popper during that year at the Institute has sustained me throughout my subsequent career.

SCIENCE EDUCATION AND THE PHILOSOPHY OF SCIENCE

To date my career falls rather neatly into three periods. Between 1946 and 1953 I taught physics, mathematics and general science in a grammar and in a public school. Then for two years I was a lecturer in methods of teaching science at the Durham Colleges and inevitably my major preoccupation was the teaching of science. During this period, apart from those of Mill, Dewey and Popper, among the books which absorbed my attention those of F. A. Lange, William Whewell, Ernst Mach, Arthur Eddington, Susan Stebbing, Morris Cohen and Ernest Nagel, and Bertrand Russell placed the debates among philosophers of science in perspective. Several of these authors accepted induction as the method of science and Stebbing, and Cohen and Nagel, spelled out in detail the implications of the canons of induction, that is, the methods of agreement, difference, concomitant variation and residues. Russell offered a classical account of the roles played by induction and deduction in scientific method.

Mach and Eddington, however, threw a somewhat different light on science and the nature of the physical world. Mach's phenomenalism and Eddington's conventionalism anticipated among natural scientists the position taken up much later by phenomenologists and ethnomethodologists among the social scientists. Their views should be seen against the impact Einstein's theories had on the philosophers of science and the abandonment, in important respects, of paradigms derived from Newtonian physics. It was undoubtedly Herbert Dingle, however, as professor of the history and philosophy of science at University College London who impressed on me the need to assess the impact of Einstein's achievement on attitudes towards the nature of scientific laws and the objectivity of data and measuring instruments. One consequence was that discussions among the logical positivists of the Vienna Circle and particularly the work of Otto Neurath became relevant in my search for a viable position. A. J. Ayer in *Language, Truth and Logic*[8] offered a clue when he suggested that it was possible to draw distinctions between analytic and empirical modes of verification and between normative and factual statements even though these were often taken to be the same. These commentaries on the nature of science and Popper's criticism of Mill's position in the *Economica* articles served to reinforce my early rejection of induction and positivism as satisfactory accounts of scientific method, as approaches to our understanding of our physical and social worlds and as the bases on which societal planning can legitimately rest.

Since the appearance of *The Open Society* Popper's influence among philosophers of science has been very great and through the writings of R. B. Braithwaite, P. H. Nidditch, Dudley Shapere, Israel Scheffler and Carl Hempel I have tried to keep in touch with some of the debates.[9] Thomas S. Kuhn's[10] position, however, threw most light on a dilemma I faced when I began to apply systematically the methods of science as I understood them to the study of comparative education. While agreeing to a considerable extent with him, Kuhn drew a distinction between Popper's view of science as necessarily a process of refuting or falsifying hypotheses and normal science as common sense. This distinction was useful in clarifying for me the different social functions comparative education can perform.

Distinguished natural scientists such as Peter Medawar and John Eccles have, of course, accepted Popper's account of how scientists proceed.[11] Until recently, however, 'established' social scientists failed to grasp the challenge presented to the natural scientists at the end of the nineteenth century. Now some of them take a view of the social world similar to that taken by Eddington of the physical world, namely, that it was a world of convention or 'mind stuff.'[12] Some of the debates which turn on Popper's radical initiative in discussing the philosophy of the natural and social sciences are well illustrated in the two volumes edited by Paul Arthur Schlipp on *The Philosophy of Karl Popper*.[13] Many of them are relevant to the development of comparative education as a social science.

THE (WORLD) YEAR BOOK OF EDUCATION[14]

The second period of my career started in 1953; the chance to work in the field of comparative education came when I was invited to join the University of London, Institute of Education, as assistant editor of *The Year Book of Education* and tutor in the advanced studies department. For some five years my major responsibility was to help prepare volumes, sub-edit them and see them through to press. Each year a new theme was taken, analysed in comparative perspective and discussed in invited articles from scholars from all over the world. These years were among the most demanding, enjoyable and formative of my life. They brought me into daily contact with Hans and Lauwerys and regular contact with Robert King Hall of Teachers College, Columbia, when with Lauwerys he became a joint editor of the *Year Book*. These pioneers put me in touch with all the established figures in the field who contributed regularly to the *Year Book*. It was an excellent apprenticeship.

The Year Book of Education was founded in 1932 by the chairman of Evans Brothers, Sir Robert Evans, and for the first four years (1932–5) its editor-in-chief was Lord Eustace Percy, formerly president of the Board of Education. Both these men wanted the *Year Book* to provide a forum for the discussion of educational issues in the United Kingdom, the British Commonwealth and elsewhere. The decision to make it lively and stimulating by including non-official impressions of opinion on contemporary subjects was deliberate and found favour with Donald McLean from the Board of Education, who wrote in the foreword to the first volume:

> In compiling a yearbook two alternatives at any rate are possible. One may be content with the safe but somewhat unambitious course of compiling a volume of the principal facts and figures relating to education: or, on the other hand, one may go further and adopt the more venturesome and interesting alternative of endeavouring to bring these facts and figures into some sort of perspective and to suggest underlying principles and lines of development.[15]

The bolder course was chosen and followed throughout the prewar and postwar periods when it was published eventually in association with the University of London, Institute of Education, and then after 1953 jointly with Teachers College, Columbia University.

Percy also wanted to use the Year Book as a way of illustrating problems by viewing them comparatively. He wrote: ‘If the common features of British education at home and overseas are to be intelligently observed it is also necessary to study British education against the background of the educational systems of other nations’.[16] This objective, namely, the illumination of national problems by examining them in comparative perspective, has remained a major aim among comparative educationists regardless of the theoretical position adopted by them.

Percy held that to achieve it and to help the authorities to formulate policy they should be provided with facts and figures and consequently he argued that the methods of inquiry used to prepare the *Year Books* should be strictly empirical. In the 1930s, in working towards the achievement of this aim, Hans and Harley V. Usill tackled the task of establishing a taxonomy for the collection, classification and comparison of statistical and narrative data about education in the Commonwealth and wanted to extend this service and keep the data up to date on an annual basis. They recognised the difficulties of standardising methods of collecting material but with the co-operation of Commonwealth countries were eventually able to present 'a few comparative tables of the British Commonwealth of Nations'.[17] Graphs and block diagrams were introduced to facilitate comparisons and in using these techniques Hans and Usill anticipated the subsequent work of Unesco on a worldwide scale. The provision of this service by Unesco and the resources required to ensure that relevant data were identified, collected and classified persuaded Lauwerys and Hans, and finally the editorial board of *The Year Book of Education*, that it was not possible after the war to do this and the annual collection of statistics was abandoned in 1952.

The statistical or empirical method did not command universal acceptance. After the *Year Book* became associated with the London Institute Fred Clarke, who succeeded Percy Nunn as its director, took the view that 'The real objection to a statistical method, from the present point of view, is that it must fail to exhibit those differences and resemblances that are truly significant'.[18] Clarke did much to promote comparative education in the Institute and to give it a sociological flavour. The *Year Books* reflected this emphasis and in the late 1930s research theories were examined in comparative perspective but not statistically. Hans and Reinhold Schairer gave the *Year Book* a European flavour and links were established with the USA when Isaac Kandel was invited to become a member of the editorial board. These features, non-statistical or non-empirical analysis and worldwide cover, characterised the volumes from 1947 to 1973.

These postwar volumes owed much to Lauwerys, who was joint editor until he retired in 1970. The first task undertaken by the editors was to review the postwar reconstruction of school systems. In the early 1950s a decision was reached to select for comparative analysis a new theme or problem each year. This policy was maintained during the period after 1953, when Teachers College, Columbia, shared editorial responsibility for *The Year Book of Education* (subsequently renamed *The World Year Book of Education*). Many of these volumes anticipated research in the sociology and economics of education, innovation studies, educational planning and into higher education and teacher training.

For example the 1956 *Year Book of Education* explored almost virgin land and Friedrich Edding[19] and John Vaizey,[20] subsequent pioneers in the economics of education, acknowledged the contribution made by this volume. Early on, in 1950, in the volume to which Jean Floud contributed,[21] the relationship between educational opportunity and social mobility was examined. The 1957 *Year Book of Education: Education and Philosophy* anticipated the flood of innovation studies in the 1960s. Teacher training and higher education were analysed in comparative perspective in the 1953 and 1959 volumes. All these *Year Books* not only provided a forum for international debate, but made a major and original contribution to the development of comparative education research and stimulated social science investigation into aspects of education.

To the best of my knowledge, however, it was King Hall who first made explicit to me how Dewey's 'problem-solving approach' could be systematically applied to comparative education. For a short time (1953–6) I listened in admiration to the way he analysed problems, placed them in context and discussed ways of tackling them in a rigorous and systematic manner. In particular he brought this kind of approach to bear on the preparation of the 1954 *Year Book of Education: Education and Technological Development*[22] which dealt with the moral, cultural, economic, political and technical problems associated with the introduction of new technologies in a variety of national contexts. The analysis turned on the impact of technical innovations (and the hopes and aspirations associated with them) when confronted by traditional beliefs and practices. In this volume the role, successes and failures of bilateral and multilateral technical aid and assistance programmes were discussed by scholars deeply interested in the planned development of education and its contribution to economic growth. Undoubtedly this was a pioneering comparative study, the quality of which has rarely been surpassed in the subsequent literature dealing with educational planning in what we choose to call developing countries or countries of the Third World. Indeed, I find it rather tragic that so little progress has been made since that time to solve the theoretical and practical problems associated with technical assistance programmes in education. From my point of view the study of educational planning and development persuaded me, if any persuasion was needed, that the 'problem(-solving) approach' was the most appropriate way of tackling comparative education research. I have not changed my mind.

THEORIES OF SOCIAL CHANGE

Indeed, my confidence in problem-solving was strengthened and the ways I could use it were developed as a consequence of my studies in the evolution of American education and in particular in the role played by Dewey and faculty members at Teachers College, Columbia, in the progressive education movement. Dewey's *How We Think*[23] remains, for me, the single most useful rationale for activity and discovery methods of teaching and learning and indeed for many other slogans which inform child-centred, informal and other kinds of non-traditional proposals about schools in the USA and Britain. Slogans and misguided practices apart, distortions of Dewey's central epistemological position, described as 'reflective thinking', should not be used to discredit the educational practices which have been attacked from time to time by those who advocate as the school's role a return to the basic three Rs. Nor should criticism of instrumentalism or any cavalier dismissal of pragmatism as a viable and coherent philosophy persuade comparative educationists to dismiss as useless or misconceived the problem(-solving) approach which I have tried to develop with some success. Indeed, Dewey's work and that of other early pragmatists can be seen as an attempt to formulate a new and more appropriate rationale for American life in a period of rapid and radical change towards the end of the nineteenth century. Philip P. Wiener's *Evolution and the Founders of Pragmatism*,[24] to which reference will be made later, throws light on the relationship between the theories of Herbert Spencer and Charles Darwin and those of pragmatists such as Chauncey Wright, C. S. Peirce, William James, George Herbert Mead, Oliver Wendell Holmes, Jnr, Nicholas St John Green and of course Dewey himself. Each of these men in discussions with each other was trying to make sense, in his chosen sphere of professional or academic life, of the commercial, industrial and urban nation that was rapidly emerging from an agrarian, rural American society. In the face of a prevailing Hegelianism, best exemplified by educationist William Torrey Harris, the pragmatists adapted Darwinism to provide a new intellectual framework for Americans. As an educationist and philosopher Dewey's seminal analysis of conditions in a Chicago growing at an unprecedented rate and the role he ascribed to schools as vicarious communities in inner cities set the stage for a great deal of subsequent research into urban education and fathered the community school movement in the USA and Britain.

Basic to his analysis of societal problems was the concept of change. Fundamental to his proposals about how problems should be solved was his faith in the intelligence of individuals and their ability collectively to resolve their difficulties by thinking reflectively. It was central, therefore, to Dewey's educational philosophy that above all schools should educate children to tackle and resolve confused situations according to his problem-solving techniques. A case could be made that these techniques are now widely used in the USA among businessmen, military leaders and research workers and that pragmatism is indeed the philosophy of Americans.

A key to the perjorative view taken of pragmatism is found in Bertrand Russell's assessment of Dewey as a defender of American commercialism and industrialism. My judgement, on the contrary, is that through the schools Dewey hoped to perpetuate those worthwhile values that were part of the frontier spirit of rural America. Be this as it may, more favourable assessments have been made of the early pragmatists among whom Peirce has been described by Popper as 'one of the greatest philosophers of all time'.[25] Mead is now revered by ethnomethodologists but the individual contributions made by members of this 'club' to the philosophy of mathematics, science, psychology, education and law have yet to be fully recognised outside the USA.

What is certain is that the progressive education movement in the USA (and in England, perhaps influenced by J. J. Findlay in the first instance) developed under the acknowledged leadership of Dewey, first at Chicago University along with Jane Addams and then at Teachers College, Columbia, where John Childs, Harold Rugg, George Counts, William H. Kilpatrick and others constituted a galaxy of stars during the 1930s. At Ohio State University Boyd H. Bode[26] provided leadership in another centre in which H. Gordon Hullfish[27] as a devotee of Bode contributed greatly to the progressive education movement. Innumerable professors of education throughout the USA were trained at Teachers College and Ohio State. Among this generation B. O. Smith, W. O. Stanley, Harry S. Broudy, Archie Anderson and Theodore Brameld[28] influenced me most. In particular as a visiting professor on several occasions at the University of Illinois at Urbana-Champaign I participated with Smith and Stanley in a compulsory seminar for doctoral candidates in which the theories of social change of Marx, Myrdal, Mannheim, Mosca, Ogburn, Pareto, Sorokin, Sumner and Toynbee were analysed and compared.

The relevance of these theories to research based on the 'problem approach' in comparative education was immediately apparent. Commentaries on the work of European writers by Talcott Parsons in *Structure of Social Action*[29] added substantially to the analysis made in the Smith–Stanley seminars. William F. Ogburn's theory of social or cultural lag certainly influenced progressive educationists such as Rugg, who ascribed to traditional schools responsibility for cultural lag in a technological society. Gunnar Myrdal's analysis was based on his distinction between 'higher' and 'lower' valuations and the internal tensions these create in individuals. Vilfredo Pareto's purpose was to describe the conditions under which a society can change from one state (of equilibrium) to another, different state without violent revolution. The analyses made by Karl Marx and Karl Mannheim took as their points of departure changes in technology and the organisation of industry. Generally speaking, however, most of these theorists assumed that change takes place first in one aspect of society and that problems are created because individuals or other aspects of society fail to respond immediately to such change.

For a time Ogburn's theory which asserts that change takes place first in the material culture, that the adaptive non-material culture responds slowly and that the non-adaptive, non-material culture changes extremely slowly in spite of change elsewhere influenced my analysis of change most. Subsequently I accepted that any one of these theories permits problems to be analysed in comparative perspective, and that a choice should be made in the light of the research worker's interest. Any one of them, on a continuum from consensus-evolutionary to conflict-revolutionary, makes it possible to operationalise problem analysis in a way that can be replicated.

My own theory of social change is consequently rather eclectic and has its origins in the societal taxonomy derived, as I shall discuss later, from critical conventionalism and the distinctions I draw for the purpose of classifying societal data between normative patterns, mental states, institutional patterns and man's natural environment.

In Dewey's scheme problem analysis is a process in the stages of reflective thinking (or problem-solving). Each of these stages is implicit in Popper's hypothetico-deductive method of scientific inquiry. He claimed, for example, that inquiry starts from pure or practical problems which arouse interest in data of a certain kind. Both Dewey and Popper regard hypotheses as tentative solutions to identified problems and consider that in order to test hypotheses the circumstances (specific initial conditions) should be identified and described. Testing involves comparing outcomes predicted from general hypothetical statements under specified conditions with observable events. If events confirm prediction for Dewey the problem has been solved and the hypothesis verified. Verification is consequently an important feature of problem-solving. Popper, on the other hand, has stressed the need for scientists to try to refute or falsify hypotheses.

The similarities and differences between the two positions are important among philosophers of sciences. They have implications for comparative educationists who wish to identify the social functions they can legitimately perform, but for my purposes Dewey's problem-solving approach and Popper's hypothetico-deductive method and critical dualism (conventionalism) can be reconciled and I brought them together into a working paradigm for comparative education research which I chose to call the 'problem approach' or 'problem

(-solving) approach'. It was first exemplified in the first section of *Problems in Education: A Comparative Approach*[30] which appeared in 1965.

PROBLEM–SOLVING AND POSITIVISM IN COMPARATIVE EDUCATION

The development of my position during the 1960s and early 1970s should be seen against a background of growing interest in the role of education to solve the world's economic and social problems. *The World Year Book of Education* continued to provide me with the chance to give substance to the theoretical models I had accepted. Throughout the 1960s topics were selected for comparative analysis and commissioned articles provided information on a worldwide basis. Some of the topics – such as teacher education (1963), the economics and planning of education (1967) and higher education (1971/2/3) – had been dealt with earlier and these volumes were consequently prepared on the basis of more substantial research. On other occasions, however, the editors broke new ground by selecting topics and issues on which there were few comparative research data. Church and state in education was regarded as a particularly controversial issue to be tackled in a volume to which authors from all over the world would contribute. It was presented in the 1966 *World Year Book*. Less controversial but equally relevant were questions relating to the education explosion, and in the 1965 *World Year Book* the editors assembled a great deal of carefully prepared data from a variety of sources on the topic. New issues considered in comparative perspective included the growing use of new media of communication in education (1964), examination systems (1969) and education within industry (1968) and education in cities (1970).

Some of these volumes took up original themes which had not previously been analysed in comparative perspective and most of them initiated further research. By the 1960s, however, the virtual monopoly enjoyed by *The World Year Book of Education* as the source of analytical comparative studies was a thing of the past. Up to then international agencies such as Unesco, the International Bureau of Education in Geneva and the Council of Europe had been content, for the most part, to build up information about school systems in the light of models derived from the United Nations Declaration of Universal Rights and European–North American prototypes. The IBE *International Year Books* brought together statements prepared by member governments about the aims of policy, the present state of their own school systems and trends in their development. Selected aspects of these systems were described in greater detail from time to time. Unesco meanwhile had built up statistical data and in a series of *World*

Surveys of Education[31] had reviewed legislation and brought together in a systematic manner information about the school systems of member states. Introductory articles described in turn trends of development in primary, secondary and tertiary education and in administrative systems.

The creation in 1961 of the Organisation for Economic Co-operation and Development brought new resources and a new dimension to research in education.[32] One of the main tasks of the OECD was to assist member countries to adapt their policies to changing circumstances in the modern world. Its Committee for Scientific and Technical Personnel took up aspects of educational policy. At first OECD comparative studies of education paid great attention to issues which had been raised in the 1956 *Year Book of Education*, namely, the extent to which education could be regarded as a form of economic investment (rather than as a 'human right') and how educational systems should figure in the planned allocation of economic resources. In this phase of the OECD's work economists and social scientists who favoured this approach dominated the comparative methodology. This was a period during which cost-benefit studies and analyses of education as the residual cause of economic growth occupied the attention of research workers. They concluded that investment in education would bring its own economic rewards not only to individual recipients but to the society in which they lived and worked.

The methods of comparative study adopted by the economists of education were similar to those used by sociologists who wanted to show that there was a close relationship between the social class position of young people and their chances of gaining access to prestige secondary schools and institutions of higher education. Hans and Lauwerys had initiated comparative research into this phenomenon. It was taken up by sociologists and other social scientists who came into comparative education who were in favour of reorganising secondary education along comprehensive lines. In other words the economists and sociologists sought to justify a normative or ideological commitment to educational expansion and its reorganisation by using evidence from comparative studies.

The assumptions on which the economists and sociologists based their inquiries were the same, namely, that relationships between education and the socioeconomic aspects of society could be established and measured. A further assumption was that by changing one of the variables – the provision of education – the other variable, that is, economic levels and social class divisions, would be changed. The resulting methodology, as I discuss in Chapter 3, was positivistic. It informed the research of comparative educationists who followed up an initiative taken by the Unesco Institute for Education in Hamburg in a series of studies of education achievement on an international basis. The Ford Foundation generously financed the International Association for the Evaluation of Educational Achievement (IEA) during the 1960s. Its first study compared achievements in mathematics on the grounds that mathematics was not culture-specific, used a universal language and levels of achievement in it would measure the productivity of an educational system in a technological world. Subsequent research was undertaken in science, literature, reading comprehension, English and French as foreign languages and civic education. Over a period of seven years or so some twenty countries were covered and more than a quarter of a million students in nearly 10,000 schools were involved.

Members of the Association claim that these series of studies represent the most extensive empirical study ever carried out in comparative education and indeed that they broke new ground. The overall aim was to 'relate student competence as measured by international tests of achievement to instructional, economic and social factors which account for differences between students, schools, and national systems of education'.[33]

Undoubtedly the techniques used in all these studies were brought to a high level of sophistication. Unfortunately they were derived from a traditional approach to social scientific research, the failures of which have their origins in the failure of many social scientists to seek new ways of understanding society. Until recently, when Alvin Gouldner's *The Coming Crisis of Western Sociology* received considerable attention in the USA and Britain, 'established' social scientists failed to grasp the challenge presented to natural scientists when an accumulation of inexplicable experimental results brought into question the conceptual framework of Newtonian physics. The crisis produced a paradigm shift among social scientists who came to question the value of positivism as a framework within which 'normal social science' could proceed.

My study of Dewey, Popper and Dingle had, as I have said, persuaded me that positivism was not a framework within which I wished to develop research methods in comparative education. The apparent success of those comparativists who developed techniques within this frame of reference did not persuade me to abandon my commitment to Dewey's method of reflective thinking and to Popper's critical dualism (conventionalism) which as far as I am concerned anticipated and adequately took into account the anti-positivist arguments raised by sociologists. Unfortunately Popper's critique of Marx in *The Open Society* made him the object of neo-Marxist criticism. The failure of members of the Frankfurt school of sociologists to make him a positivist is plainly shown in the volume *The Positivist Dispute in German Sociology* which includes papers by Theodor Adorno, Hans Albert, Ralf Dahrendorf, Jürgen Habermas, Harald Pilot and Popper himself.[34] Nevertheless it is against this background of involvement in comparative education by social scientists committed to an approach which was accepted by the academic pioneers of comparative education – Kandel, Schneider and Hans – that my desire to provide an alternative paradigm should be judged.

In the event, universal macro-solutions drawn from positivist empirical research or supported by it have met with varied success in countries around the world. Results have hardly justified the confidence shown by governments in this kind of social science research. Indeed in human terms we have yet to count the full cost of 'experimenting' on a grand scale with the lives of children throughout the world.

Let me, however, be charitable by taking a leaf out of David Riesman's book *Constraint and Variety in American Education*[35] where he writes that Americans have had a hundred years to learn that economics 'hasn't done anything worse than raise the national debt – dreadful as that is! . . .'[36] by taking a reasonably optimistic view of recent developments in the traditional approach to comparative education. Over the past quarter of a century (because remember that the 1956 *Year Book of Education* virtually initiated the comparative study of the economics of education) economists of education who have flirted with comparative education have done nothing worse than raise wastage and stagnation rates in education throughout the world by convincing governments that there were sound economic reasons for doing what they had already decided to do on the grounds of expediency, political necessity, or ideology. Comparative psychometric studies of achievement have probably done no harm at all because in the absence of any real analysis of national attitudes towards education they have influenced national policies hardly at all. Comparative sociologists have identified to their own satisfaction the residual 'causes' or educational disadvantage and underachievement and its influence on life chances. Perhaps the only harm such studies have done is to raise aspirations throughout the world which either cannot be satisfied or at best can only be satisfied if the 'causes' of socioeconomic disadvantage are removed by political action.

A good deal of work remains to be done on the alternative paradigm derived from Dewey's method of reflective thinking and Popper's hypothetico-deductive method of scientific inquiry and his critical dualism (conventionalism). A unique opportunity presented itself when in 1973–4 I was awarded a personal research grant by the Social Science Research Council to develop models and techniques for the purpose of comparative education research. Those I presented in the final report were designed to operationalise the following processes:

1 the identification and analysis of problems to which at least some of the assumed solutions are educational;

2 the classification of educational data and information about its associated infrastructure;
3 the establishment of ideal-typical normative models designed to facilitate some understanding and comparison of overt aims and internalised attitudes which influence the way national school systems are run;
4 the analysis and comparison of the ways in which policies are formulated, adopted and implemented;
5 the prediction, under known circumstances, of the outcomes of adopted policy or of possible outcomes of proposed policies.

My intentions were, and are, twofold. In the first place I hope to provide a theoretical framework which takes account of debates in the philosophy of science and more recent in the philosophy of the social sciences. Secondly, within this paradigm I hope to show how comparative education research can contribute to the planned reform of education. In the collection of revised articles which follows I have therefore placed the debates among non-Marxist comparative educationists in the perspective of recent disputes among sociologists. In order to identify more precisely the social functions comparative educationists can perform I have drawn a distinction between comparative education as a 'pure' and as an 'applied' social science. In these chapters considerations of method are placed in the context of the traditions out of which comparative education has grown. Then follow chapters in which I discuss the principles on the basis of which I suggest problem identification and analysis should be made, the principles of classifying relevant data in comparative education, and the possibilities of anticipating the outcomes of policy using a systems analysis approach. Finally examples are given of ideal-typical models that inform major systems of education throughout the world and focus attention on on-going debates about the aims and organisation of school systems.

The articles on which this volume is based have been prepared and published over a period of some twenty-five years. They are not presented in historical sequence and for the most part they have been rewritten or heavily edited in order to avoid repetition and in order to give the volume greater coherence. I hope it will stimulate discussion and promote co-operation. Much still needs to be done to improve techniques and models of analysis if the social functions of comparative education are to be performed adequately.

NOTES AND REFERENCES: INTRODUCTION

This introduction is based largely on Brian Holmes, 'A postscript', in *Education and Rural Development: The World Year Book of Education, 1974* (ed. P. Foster and J. R. Sheffield), Evans, London, 1973. See also Brian Holmes, *Ivory Towers, the Glass Bead Game and Open Societies* (an inaugural lecture), University of London, Institute of Education, London, 1979.

1 Nicholas Hans, *Comparative Education,* 3rd edn, Routledge & Kegan Paul, London 1958.
2 H. E. Armstrong, *The Teaching of Scientific Method,* Macmillan, London, 1903.
J. S. Mill, *A System of Logic,* 8th edn, Longman, London, 1970.
John Dewey, *How We Think,* D. C. Heath, Boston, Mass., 1910.
K. R. Popper, *The Open Society and its Enemies,* Routledge & Kegan Paul, London, 1945.
K. R. Popper, *The Logic of Scientific Discovery,* Hutchinson, London, 1959.
3 K. R. Popper, *Economica*, n.s., vol. XI, nos. 42 and 43, 1944, and vol. XII, no. 46, 1945.
4 K. R. Popper, *The Poverty of Historicism*, Routledge & Kegan Paul, London, 1960.
5 Council for Curriculum Reform (chairman: J. A. Lauwerys) *The Content of Education*, University of London, Bickley, Kent, 1945.
6 For an account of the origins of Unesco see Philip W. Jones, 'Literacy education for national development in the program of Unesco 1946–1970', unpublished PhD, University of Sydney, 1976.
7 F. von Hayek, *The Road to Serfdom*, University of Chicago Press, Chicago, 1944. Karl Mannhiem, *Man and Society in an Age of Reconstruction*, Routledge & Kegan Paul, London, 1941 and *Diagnosis of our Times*, Routledge & Kegan Paul, London, 1941.
8 A. J. Ayer, *Language, Truth and Logic*, Gollancz, London, 1946.
9 See Brian Holmes, 'Concepts of culture and society in educational research', in *Philosophical Redirection of Educational Research,* NSSE, Chicago, 1972, pp. 193–216.
10 Thomas S. Kuhn, *The Structure of Scientific Revolutions,* University of Chicago, Chicago, 1962.
11 See P. A. Schlipp (ed.) *The Philosophy of Karl Popper* (2 vols), La Salle, Illinois, 1974; see particularly J. C. Eccles, 'The world of objective knowledge', pp. 349–70, and Peter Medawar, 'Hypothesis and imagination', pp. 274–91.
12 Arthur Eddington, *The Nature of the Physical World,* Everyman Library, Dent, London, 1935.
13 Schlipp, op. cit.
14 *The Year Book of Education,* published by Evans Brothers, first appeared in 1932. Some years later editorial responsibility for these annual volumes was taken over by the University of London, Institute of Education. After a period during the Second World War when it was not published the *Year Book* reappeared in 1948. The last volume to appear under the auspices of the Institute came out in 1974. *The World Year Book of Education* has been revived under a new publisher (Kogan Page, London) and different editors.
15 Foreword, *The Year Book of Education*, 1932, Evans, London, 1932.
16 Introduction, *The Year Book of Education, 1932,* Evans, London, 1932, p. xiv.
17 Editors' introduction, *The Year Book of Education, 1937,* Evans, London, 1937, p. 80.
18 Fred Clarke, *The Year Book of Education, 1933,* Evans, London, 1933.
19 See Friedrich Edding, *Internationale Tendenzen in der Entwicklung der Ausgaben für Schulen and Hochschulen,* Universität, Kiel, 1958, and *Ökonomie des Bildungswesens*, Rombach, Freiburg, 1963.
20 See J. Vaizey, *The Costs of Education,* Allen & Unwin, London, 1958.
21 Jean Floud, 'Educational opportunity and social mobility', in *The Year Book of Education,* Evans, London, 1950.
22 The sections in this 1954 *Year Book of Education* were: I Aims, objectives and implications of technological development, II Cultural change, III Planning and education, IV Techniques and methods, V The agencies of administration, VI The impact of Western culture.
23 Dewey, op. cit.

24 Philip P. Wiener, *Evolution and the Founders of Pragmatism,* Harvard University, Cambridge, Mass., 1949.
25 K. R. Popper, *Objective Knowledge,* Clarendon Press, Oxford, 1972, p. 212.
26 Boyd H. Bode, *Progressive Education at the Crossroads,* Newsom, New York, 1938; see also Brian Holmes, *American Criticism of American Education,* Ohio State University, Columbus, Ohio, 1957. Bode was one of the best-informed and most sympathetic critics of some aspects of the progressive education movement.
27 See H. Gordon Hullfish and Philip G. Smith, *Reflective Thinking,* Dodd, Mead, New York, 1961, and H. Gordon Hullfish (ed.), *Educational Freedom in an Age of Anxiety,* Harper, New York, 1953. I met Hullfish when we were both visiting professors in the social foundations department at the University of Illinois at Urbana-Champaign. He wrote a great deal, but impressed me most as a teacher.
28 Among the works I most enjoyed were: Harry S. Broudy, *Building a Philosophy of Education,* Prentice-Hall, New York, 1954; W. O. Stanley, *Education and Social Integration,* Teachers College, Columbia, New York, 1953; and B. O. Smith *et al.* (eds), *Social Foundations of Education,* Dryden, New York, 1956.
29 Talcott Parsons, *The Structure of Social Action,* The Free Press, Glencoe, Ill., 1964, summarises the positions of well-known social theorists such as Pareto, Durkheim and Weber.
30 Brian Holmes, *Problems in Education: A Comparative Approach,* Routledge & Kegan Paul, London, 1965.
31 Unesco, *World Survey of Education,* Unesco, Paris: Vol. 1, 1955; Vol. 2, *Primary Education,* 1958; Vol. 3, *Secondary Education,* 1961; Vol. 4, *Higher Education,* 1966; Vol. 5, *Administration,* 1967.
32 The OECD was established in 1961 as a successor to the Organisation for European Economic Co-operation (OEEC), set up in 1948. Its *Catalogue of Publications,* Paris, shows the range of its work.
33 The International Association for the Evaluation of Education Achievement (IEA) published its first report on mathematics in 1967. Since then studies on science, languages and civics have been prepared.
34 Theodor W. Adorno *et al., The Positivist Dispute in German Sociology,* Heinemann, London, 1976.
35 David Riesman, *Constraint and Variety in American Education,* University of Nebraska, Lincoln, Nebr., 1958.
36 ibid., p. 50.

Chapter 1

Cultural Borrowing – Misconceived Comparative Education

The nineteenth-century pioneers or precursors of comparative education were men whose task was to develop their own national system of education. Almost without exception they were members of a new class of officials appointed to take a special interest in education. Many of them were scholars in their own right. Victor Cousin (1792–1867), for example, was a professor of philosophy at the Sorbonne before becoming Minister of Education in France in 1840. Matthew Arnold (1822–88) is as well known as a littérateur as for his activities as an inspector of English schools. William Torrey Harris (1839–1909) was the leader of the American Hegelian school of philosophy as well as a distinguished superintendent of St Louis schools and later US Commissioner of Education. It is hardly surprising, therefore, that their contribution to educational reform, though principally practical, had a theoretical component.

As administrators they wanted to know if anything of practical value could be learned from the study of foreign systems of education. Their answers differed. Some of them were prepared to take over from foreign systems these features which would benefit but not harm their own schools. During a period of growing nationalism in Europe rivalry and competition between nations encouraged imitation. National sentiments which included feelings of special national virtues discouraged it. The question these administrators asked was: how can we select from foreign systems what is good, and perfect it? The answer was that foreign systems should be studied, preferably at first hand by visits and observation. Such men represent a strong (but in my view mistaken) tradition among comparative educationists who consider that comparative education can, and should, serve a useful function by making possible more discriminating choices when reformers propose to copy features from another system.

Other administrators were much more sceptical. They were unwilling to concede that much of value could be borrowed from a foreign system but they were prepared to compare their own systems unfavourably in order to persuade their fellow countrymen to mend their ways. The 'comparative argument' has a long history and it is still used today. It is dangerous because at best the comparative argument constrains or promotes action. At worst it diverts attention away from a serious analysis of national problems and careful consideration of alternative solutions.

Towards the end of the nineteenth century a new generation of administrators, seeking to plan the development of secondary education, viewed cultural borrowing with grave suspicion. They made explicit their theoretical and practical objectives to it as a function to be served by comparative educationists and returned to earlier proposals that the purpose of comparative education should be to establish principles of policy and general theories of education from which sound practice could be deduced. They laid the foundations of method on which my own approach to comparative education is based. At the same time they have also been the source of inspiration for other comparative educationists with whose accepted methodological assumptions I basically disagree – but more about this in Chapter 3.

Thus in spite of their practical concerns administrators throughout the century made some contribution to the theory and methods of education. In this chapter I propose to examine the role played by comparative educationists who favoured cultural borrowing and to comment on its misuse in the post-Second World War period.

FOREIGN TRAVEL, CULTURAL BORROWING AND THE COMPARATIVE ARGUMENT

Cultural borrowing has a long history. Among its exponents Plato is the most famous. As an observer of Sparta, he then incorporated all that he thought best in that city-state in his description of his ideal republic. For this he has been regarded as a pioneer of comparative method. To be sure his willingness to adopt a Spartan model exemplifies a most radical form of cultural borrowing in that a foreign system is accepted by an observer as better than his own.

The fact that Plato built the *Republic* into a universal model does not deny his aim was to observe *one* foreign system and transplant major features of it into his own. This approach has relatively few present-day adherents except perhaps among communists who look to the USSR for a model.

Erasmus had a different purpose in mind and used comparative studies in a somewhat different manner. As an itinerant scholar he studied in England, France, the Netherlands, Switzerland and Italy and enunciated principles which influenced virtually all the educational leaders and school reforms in the sixteenth and seventeenth centuries. His ideal was to establish a common culture throughout

Europe. This aim represents the universal model building aspect of comparative education which finds expression today in the work of some international agencies.

An early example of a third type of practical activity may be cited. Comenius, to some extent through force of circumstances, worked in Poland, England, Sweden and Hungary after leaving his native land. In modern parlance he was invited as a 'technical assistant' by Samuel Hartlib to come to London in 1641 and advise the government of the day on how to establish a pansophic college. After returning to Poland he went on to Hungary to establish a school at Savos Patok. He hoped that an international centre for the study of education could be established. In these activities he anticipated the 'technical assistants' of today and the creation of international centres.

Some decades later Peter the Great of Russia sent officials to study the Royal Mathematical School at Christ's Hospital in England with the intention of setting up similar institutions in Russia to train naval personnel and engineers. The assessment by Henry Barnard (1811–1900) of Peter's aim was that he 'desired to transplant Western culture to Russia, and for this purpose sent Russians to foreign countries and called foreigners to Russia . . .'[1] Of equal interest is the procedure adopted by Maria Theresa[2] in her attempts to develop a comprehensive plan of educational reform. Her Imperial Chancellor, Prince Kaunitz, was given the task of collecting useful information on foreign improvements in education. In 1774 Kaunitz sent a circular to the Austrian embassies abroad asking for information about various aspects of educational systems which might be useful in the reorganisation of education at home. Some time later in 1801 the government of Prussia sent a school inspector to study the work of Pestalozzi in Burgdorf[3] and young men of promise were also encouraged to study there so that they might return to Prussia better equipped as teachers and administrators.

During the first half of the nineteenth century when national systems of elementary education were being established the flow of travellers abroad increased.[4] The implicit and frequently explicit purpose of these visits was to observe foreign schools to see what could be borrowed from them and transplanted into the visitor's own system of education. Often such travellers were commissioned by their governments to report on schools abroad. Many of them prepared reports which became widely known but, while they are carefully written, it is not possible to detect in them any conscious desire to collect comparable observed data and to classify them or indeed to discuss the problems of classifying educational data. Documentary evidence and information derived from direct observation were the bases on which their recommendations were made. As foreign observers they were free to recommend to their governments whatever they thought would improve their own system and to reject whatever would be harmful.

The period between, let us say, 1810 and 1880 was one in which governments in Europe and North America were seeking to set up national systems of elementary or primary schools. Some eighteenth-century models were available and some national governments had proposed or enacted legislation designed to create systems of universal elementary or primary schools. For the most part during the early part of the nineteenth century governments in Europe and North America (whether local or national) were breaking new ground in attempting to reduce or eliminate the monopoly of a church or churches in the running of schools and to reach the mass of young children. Administrators were more willing to copy emerging systems of elementary education than they were later to adopt foreign models of secondary schooling when the expansion of secondary schooling occupied the attention of governments. Roughly by 1880 in many Western European countries and in the USA universal, compulsory elementary education under lay control had been achieved in theory and was on the way to being realised in practice. Post-1880 debates turn on the expansion of post-primary or second-stage education. Post-1945 debates are about the reorganisation of secondary education and educational expansion includes the rapid growth of universities and institutes of higher education.

The first half of the century, when observers were interested in foreign systems of elementary or primary instruction, can be more accurately described as one of 'selective cultural borrowing' because while Prussian legislation, schools and teacher training attracted much attention not all aspects of this system found favour with foreign observers. Moreover some visitors were principally interested in the work of European educators whose fame had spread. Among the Americans who came to Europe between 1810 and 1850 to learn something of value about schools and educators, Benjamin Silliman, John Griscom, Calvin Stowe, Alexander Dallas Bache, William C. Woodbridge, and Horace Mann are cited by Stewart Fraser.[5]

The influence of these men had on developments in the USA is not so clear. In 1815 Griscom visited educational institutions in Great Britain, France, Switzerland, Italy and Holland and he published *A Year in Europe* in 1818–19. He visited Pestalozzi and was impressed by his methods of teaching. Hans[6] claims that as a result he influenced American education but it is difficult to find in standard histories the extent of this influence except that, in spite of his reservations about Lancaster's mechanical methods, he established a private Lancastrian high school in New York City. Silliman, too, merits little attention except as editor of the American *Journal of Science* and as a teacher at Yale. Woodbridge also is known as the editor of the *American Annals of Education* (1830–9) and did much of the visiting in Europe to make known the methods of von Fellenberg and Pestalozzi. At the request of the Ohio legislature Calvin Stowe reported on *Elementary Education in Europe* in 1837 and several states reprinted his report in official documents.[7] Stowe was impressed by Pestalozzi and by the efficient and enriched curriculum in Prussian schools. There is little evidence that his report had much effect on American education. The same cannot be said of the use made by Horace Mann[8], as Secretary to the Massachusetts Board of Education, of his report on the schools of Europe. In his seventh report in 1844 he praised Prussian methods of teaching the three Rs and the way teachers kept discipline without resorting to corporal punishment. There is little doubt that he wished to stir up the teachers of Massachusetts and he succeeded. The Boston schoolmasters reacted violently and there followed a long and acrimonious debate.[9] It demonstrated, in a rather dramatic fashion, one of the ways in which comparative arguments were and are used. Today unfavourable comparisons with other countries are frequently used by politicians to exhort people in their country to work harder or improve their standards of educational achievement.

All the 'cultural borrowers' wanted to be sure that their own system would not be harmed by innovations taken over from elsewhere. Three examples of the cautious attitude adopted by Americans who were undoubtedly impressed by the Prussian schools may be mentioned. A digest of Victor Cousin's *Report on the State of Public Instruction in Prussia*[10] was published in the USA in 1836. In the preface to this edition J. Orville Taylor welcomed the report and stated that many lessons would be learned from the Prussian system but warned that 'Many parts of this system of public instruction are not adapted to the spirit and feelings of the American people nor to their form of civil government'.[11] Horace Mann's expressed admiration for the Prussian methods of teaching was modified by the hope, however, that if Prussians had used education to support arbitrary power Americans could use similar methods of instruction to support republican institutions.[12] Henry Barnard, who also admired Prussian methods of teaching, was more forthright. He did not consider the German model one that should be imitated.[13]

Victor Cousin, who at the request of the French government studied primary schools and teachers' colleges, had more confidence in the unity of French national traditions. He wrote:

> The experience of Germany ought not to be lost upon us. National rivalries and antipathies would be completely out of place. The true greatness of a people does not consist in borrowing nothing from others, but in borrowing from whatever is good, and in perfecting whatever is appropriate.

He was confident that the French would assimilate all that was good 'without fear of ceasing to be ourselves'.[14] His reports received a good deal of attention in England and Leonard Horner, who translated Cousin's report on education in Holland, went so far as to urge his fellow Englishmen to 'take a lesson from a neighbour'.[15]

It is not surprising that this period of 'cultural borrowing' is associated with the development of elementary schools and methods of teaching in them. In most countries these schools represented innovations, few possessed a long or any history and consequently, for the most part, less concern was shown about the difficulties and dangers of cultural borrowing than later in the century when the problems of expanding secondary education were discussed. By that time in many countries elementary schooling had been made compulsory but the type, content and administration of non-compulsory schooling were issues which faced national governments. The place of technical training in a system of education was debated; so too was the private or public nature of academic pre-university provision. Reform and expansion touched on institutions in most countries with long and distinguished histories. Under these circumstances the notion of 'cultural borrowing' was viewed with more caution and the comparative argument in favour of reform was used less confidently.

Among this new generation of administrators Michael Sadler (1861–1943) in England and Harris in the USA agreed that selective cultural borrowing was neither viable nor desired. At the time many Englishmen were aware of the growing challenge of Germany to their industrial and commercial supremacy and favoured educational growth along German lines. Sadler said 'No!'. He recognised the skill with which the Germans had geared their education to serve commerce and industry. He admired much in the German system and conceded that a great deal could be learned from it, but he wrote:

> No other nation, by imitating a little bit of German organisation, can thus hope to achieve a true reproduction of the spirit of German institutions. The fabric of its organisation practically forms one whole. That is its merit, and its danger. It must either be taken in all, or else left unimitated.[16]

As part of any education system there was, he argued, a 'living spirit . . . All good and true education is an expression of national life and character.'[17] It was this about schools, and the national character that informed them, that educationists were not, and are not, willing to abandon when building up a national system of education. In other words they are not willing either to take over the 'living spirit' or 'national character' of another country or to abandon their own traditions.

Harris shared Sadler's views. Each nation, he appreciated, 'stamps upon its system its own ethical character and, consciously or unconsciously, perpetuates its own institution by its schools'.[18] The ethos of a nation informed its educational system. Harris considered that an investigation of the relationship between the training of children in schools and habits in harmony with a nation's laws would form the basis of 'a science of comparative pedagogy'. He went further. Since he recognised that a multiplicity of 'educative values' and 'special fruits' grows out of any educational system he hoped that before assessing relative merit 'a more discriminating comparison may be made in regard to the methods of education abroad, so that we may know the entire scope of the problem. We must count without omission all the educative values before we weigh the products of our schools against those of other nations.'[19]

He stressed the uniqueness of each system but advocated the separation of 'what is peculiar and incidental to local needs from what is of universal application and useful to all educational systems'. He held that the comparative study of foreign systems of education would make possible the formulation of certain general principles about the operation of education which could be applied everywhere. He concluded: 'And this sort of knowledge it is that gives directive power.'[20] With quite remarkable insight Harris touched on two features – reliable predictions in unique circumstances – which are regarded by modern philosophers as extremely important in scientific work. They are central in my own approach to the scientific study of education.

NATIONAL CHARACTER

The uniqueness of national systems of education as expressions of national life and national character was well understood by K. D. Ushinsky (1824–70) who compared science and education. 'Science is science', he wrote, 'precisely because it accepts only those conclusions which are consistent with the laws of general human thinking.'[21] Education is different. 'Education takes the whole man as he is, with all his national and individual characteristics – his body, soul and mind – and above all addresses itself to a man's character; and character is that very soil in which national characteristics are rooted.'[22] So while Ushinsky was prepared to concede that 'the public systems of all European nations appear at first glance, to be quite similar . . .'[23] and had their origins in the spiritual life of Europe, under this homogeneous armour 'are conceded the most heterogeneous personalities of a completely different age'.[24] Each European nation, he maintained, had its own unique national system of education, its own goals and its own ways of attempting to attain these goals. The notions of science and unique national characteristics are not however antithetical. For example, among the academic pioneers of comparative education the notion that 'national character' could be used to explain differences between systems having the same origins found a good deal of favour. Both Kandel and Hans took nationalism and national character as explanatory 'causes' or 'factors'. Kandel devoted the first chapter of his *Comparative Education*[25] to 'Education and nationalism', claiming that the growth of national self-consciousness gave to educational systems their unique characteristics, and interpreting nationalism to mean either more state control or more community participation in the running of schools. Hans followed Kandel's analysis of the factors which contribute to national self-consciousness and explained the differences between national systems in terms of the factors he regarded as making up an ideal nation.

Among comparative educationists who have built on this notion of national character, Vernon Mallinson (1910–) has made much of it. He has rejected some of Hans's necessary categories and hinged his comparative study of national systems of education on a definition of national characters derived from Morris Ginsberg. It is for Mallinson 'the totality of disposition to thought, feeling and behaviour peculiar to and widespread in a certain people, and manifested with greater or less continuity in a succession of generations'.[26] More succinctly, he regarded national character as equivalent to a collective fixed mental constitution that guarantees a common purpose and forms of behaviour on the part of those who share it. These deeply held sentiments may, as in Europe, inhibit certain kinds of change or, as in the USA, encourage change. As well as explaining differences between school systems, national character can be used to explain change and no-change in societies. For this reason I find it a useful concept and in subsequent chapters I have tried to show how it can be operationalised in comparative education research.

Of course familiarity with the history and literature of a country is important if its 'living spirit' or the 'fixed mental constitution' of its citizens is to be understood. There is a great deal of literature on the subject of natural character and Juan Tusquets, in his account of the Spanish contribution to comparative education, does not fail to mention José Ortega y Gasset (1883–1955) and Salvador de Madariago. The former's theory of knowledge was that the world can be interpreted by alternative systems of concepts each of which is unique but equally true. This position can be reconciled with that held by comparative educationists who wish to use national character to explain national and cultural differences. Ortega himself was an important interpreter of Spanish national character and contributed greatly to Spain's cultural and literary life during his lifetime. Madariago's discussion of national characteristics in *Englishmen, Frenchmen, Spaniards,* published in Spanish in 1928, is a classic in the field of comparative studies. So too is André Siegfried's *The Character of Peoples,* first published in English in 1952.[27] Both are well worth studying as examples of the light that can be thrown on national character by impressionistic studies based on profound insights. They are, nevertheless, highly individualistic. I have suggested ways of establishing ideal-typical models which can be replicated and used to compare national ideals, desires and ambitions and, by inference, to compare the mental states that motivate human behaviour.

The presumption that out of a common European heritage emerged sovereign states and national self-consciousness explains why cultural borrowing has played a less important role in the evolution of educational systems than some of the precursors of comparative education expected. The similarities between these systems can be examined in the light of normative models proposed, for example, by Condorcet (and others) in France and Jefferson in the USA. Differences in organisation, curricula, methods of teaching and the ways teachers are prepared should be examined against national normative patterns derived from selected philosophers and national constitutions and legislation.

MISSION SCHOOLS, COLONIALISM AND CULTURAL BORROWING

If the strength of national sentiments gave unique features to the character of secondary schools and institutions of higher education in Europe and North America during the period from, let us say, 1880 to 1940, the extent to which the history of education since about 1800 in Asia, Africa and to some extent, Latin America has been dominated by cultural imperialism should be noted. Traders, missionaries, military personnel and colonial officials with somewhat different aims in mind could do little else but set up in the territories in which they worked schools fashioned in the image of those at home. The models taken over from Europe were no doubt modified by local traditions and prevailing attitudes. Moreover, it should not be supposed that these systems were simply imposed on powerless people. Negotiations between factions at home and the missionaries, local officials and teachers of the indigenous peoples overseas were complex and turned on the extent to which the colonial powers should transplant their own systems of schooling regardless of circumstances.

The conviction with which the colonial powers carried out their educational policies varied. The French were in no doubt that what was good for France was good for the colonial peoples. Mission and colonial schools in the French Empire were as much like the schools in metropolitan France as possible. Colonial officials were quite prepared to support any of their missionaries who set out to bring the benefits of French culture and Catholicism to Muslims, Jews, Buddhists and pagans. A useful case-study of French colonial policy is made by Gail Kelly in *Education and Colonialism*.[28]

Rather surprisingly American colonial educational policy in the Philippines was pursued with the same kind of conviction. Attempts were made to introduce universal primary education with a vocational, pragmatic bias in a cluster of islands in which Spanish traditions ran deep. A thoughtful comparison of American and British colonial policies was made by S. Jayaweera in her unpublished PhD thesis.[29]

British policy and the officials responsible for it were more ambivalent. For many years the object of British imperial policy was to prepare each of the dependent territories for self-government and eventual independence. Yet throughout the history of imperial education there was a debate between those who held that schemes for the improvement of education should be based on existing institutions and those like Macaulay who rejected as worthless the study of Eastern classics and the vernacular languages. In his famous minute of 1835 he claimed that the main objective of British policy in India was to form a class of persons who would be 'Indians in blood and colour' but 'English in tastes and opinions, in morals and in intellect'.[30] In India at least this view prevailed, but elsewhere this assimilationist policy was pursued with less vigour.[31] Whenever and wherever the missionaries translated the Bible into vernacular languages, proposed to teach in these languages, and tried to set up vocational schools they were unsuccessful. Parents and pupils wanted European-style schools.

Nevertheless, British officials at home and abroad were sensitive to the political implications of setting up Christian schools. In the West Indies local planters had a great deal of political autonomy. Their concern was that missionary activity and schools would create unrest and resistance to them among the slaves. A Bill passed in Jamaica in 1802 restricting the activities of priests among the blacks was thought too harsh by the British government – eventually the Act was disallowed. The abolition of the slave trade in 1808 and the emancipation of the slaves in 1834 indicate the extent to which political pressures affected these colonies and the provision of education by the missionaries.

Elsewhere where the majority of people were Muslims or Buddhists British officials took a firm line. Missionaries were told not to penetrate into northern Nigeria where political power was in the hands of Muslim sheikhs. In Mohammed Ali's Egypt they were warned not to try to convert Muslims, though they could convert Jews.[32] In Kashmir the Church Missionary Society could not at first set up a school and had to be content with a hospital. In Ceylon an agreement was reached with the King of Kandy in 1815 designed to protect Buddhism from the threat of Christianity. In all these territories, of the communities who took advantage of the missions schools – the Ibos in Nigeria, the Copts in Egypt and the Tamils in Ceylon – there was a disproportionately high number with a Western European-type education. When these and similar territories became independent the advantages of education and the administrative power enjoyed by minority groups gave rise to serious political conflict.

Few of Britain's colonial territories were populated by people who all spoke the same language, accepted the same religion, or indeed came from the same ethnic group. Resistance to European-type education varied. One or two principles may be stated. In India members of the higher castes – the Brahmins and Kshatriyas – were conscious of their Hinduism, were not easily converted to Christianity but took advantage of English secondary education. In Ceylon the mission secondary schools, which charged fees, appealed to Buddhists and Hindus in the urban areas, and many of the latter were converted and went into government offices, the liberal professions, or politics. In Kashmir many distinguished political leaders were educated at mission schools. All these educated leadership groups promoted national consciousness before independence and their members were in the forefront of anti-British activity. After independence unity gave way to conflict amongst the different groups.

In short, by design or by chance European schools and much of their ethos were taken over in the colonial territories. They promoted forms of nationalism which were antithetical to the persistence of political imperialism and certainly were important agents in its overthrow. Their cultural impact is less clear. Evidently some members of the scheduled castes – low-status artisans – were converted to Christianity. A tiny elite in many colonial territories learned to speak English rather better than they spoke one of the vernaculars. Many acquired tastes, manners and opinions similar to those of British missionaries and officials. It is doubtful, however, whether the 'living spirit' of either the English or the Scottish systems of education was taken over and certainly the schools in Nigeria, the Indian subcontinent, the nations which formed Malaysia, or indeed the islands of the British West Indies failed to instil a permanent national self-consciousness which would ensure the persistence after independence of national goals which could unite peoples living in a sovereign territory, speaking different languages, with different religious beliefs and different communal and kinship relationships.

POST–SECOND WORLD WAR TECHNICAL ASSISTANCE PROGRAMMES

The problems associated with cultural imperialism and cultural borrowing were not solved when after the Second World War previously dependent countries gained their independence. Most of them were not industrialised, had very low per capita incomes and GNP, had little or no experience of government except under the tutelage of a colonial power, and no system of universal education. Tiny elites trained in mission schools or by the armed services faced the tasks of raising standards of living, creating democratic forms of government and expanding education.

Some of the founders of Unesco who met in London in 1945 took the view that it should advance civilisation and find a philosophical basis for world peace. Others involved in the early stages of Unesco's life regarded this moral force as impractical, doubting that Unesco could reconcile the communist and non-communist worlds, Western and non-Western men and the rich and poor nations. They wanted the organisation to perform a limited service function. While this latter view prevailed, the moral tone found expression in the preamble to Unesco's constitution. Participating governments, it said, 'do hereby create the United Nations Educational, Scientific and Cultural Organisation for the purpose of advancing, through the educational and scientific cultural relations of the peoples of the world, the objectives of international peace and the common welfare of mankind for which the United Nations Organisation was established and which its Charter proclaims'.[33]

In an early publication, *Fundamental Education*,[34] methods of achieving these goals were discussed. Many participants at the conference suggested that Unesco should first tackle the task of reducing and finally eliminating illiteracy. Lauwerys pointed out that it was not the illiterate nations which had waged war and suggested that an attack of illiteracy along the lines followed in the industrial nations should not receive top priority. In the event a scheme which for non-industrialised countries has its origins in Mahatma Gandhi's Wardha Plan of 1938 was given high priority. Basic or fundamental education has as its central point the proposition that a sound general education should be provided through the vocational activities of the community – in Indian village crafts.

Georg Kerschensteiner had advocated something similar, so had Dewey. Basic or fundamental education offered an alternative to the kind of education offered in the elementary schools of Europe – namely, the three Rs. But at the time, 1945, there were virtually no successful basic schools. Unesco set up pilot projects with the idea of testing out the feasibility of this type of education. Fundamental or basic education was soon more than an experiment; it became a panacea. As other attempts to reduce illiteracy and to provide universal primary education in the low-income countries falter or fail, fundamental education is revised as a universal solution to the problems of education.

As a model for developing countries it has been in competition with a more obviously European model. In the United Nations Declaration of Universal Rights, approved unanimously with some abstentions, Article 26 stated:

1 Everyone has the right to education. Education shall be free, at least in the elementary and fundamental stages. Elementary education shall be compulsory. Technical and professional education shall be made generally available, and higher education shall be accessible to all on the basis of merit.
2 Education shall be directed to the full development of the human personality and to the strengthening of respect for human rights and fundamental freedoms. It shall promote understanding, tolerance and friendship among all nations, racial or religious groups and shall further the activities of the United Nations for the maintenance of peace.
3 Parents have a prior right to choose the kind of education that shall be given to their children.

The model of universal primary schools and selective secondary schools and institutions of higher education was the same as that proposed by Condorcet to the French Legislative Assembly in 1792,[35] and by Jefferson for his own state of Virginia first in 1799 and then in 1817. Both men failed to see their plans put into practice, but against the background of their proposals the history of European and American education can be explained. Differences between the national systems that emerged are broadly speaking within the model and represent national interpretations of it. The model was first modified in the USA when, after the Supreme Court of Michigan ruled in 1874 in the Kalamazoo case that communities could legally support high schools from public funds, high school enrolments increased throughout the USA at a phenomenal rate and continued to do so, so that by 1940 virtually all students in America attended high school. Secondary education for all was proposed in England by R. H. Tawney in 1923[36] and by Paul Langevin in France in 1932, but it was not until after the Second World War that real progress towards its achievement was made. In the Soviet Union the communist government set out from the start to equalise provision throughout its vast country. The level of provision inherited from the tsars was so low that it was not until 1958 that eight years of compulsory school attendance was effectively achieved; by the late 1970s ten years schooling for all was on the horizon.

These movements should be seen against models which have gained universal credence. They were normative, derived from ideology and presented as plans long before there was any chance that they could be realised in practice. They were, in short, goal-setting and in the post-war period became models on which educational legislation was based and towards the achievement of which newly independent governments strove. Fundamental or basic education and its alternative universal primary and selective secondary and higher education have both been accepted as normative frameworks within which Unesco technical assistance programmes have been conceived. In many ways UPE and basic education are incompatible, yet at a series of conferences in Karachi, Santiago and Tokyo[37] the goal of universal primary education within an impossibly short time was accepted as the basis of policy on the advice of experts. Doubtless the public relations success of the policy of self-reliance in Tanzania helped to persuade the World Bank to promise financial aid to governments which adopted basic education as a central plank in their policy.

Two things should be noted. First, postwar international or multinational aid has been provided on the assumption that a universal world model is viable under all circumstances. In *Learning To Be*,[38] a report prepared for Unesco under the chairmanship of Edgar Faure, this model was spelled out. It is undoubtedly a consensus model and consequently includes internal inconsistencies and contradictions. Hints of the particular philosophy or 'living spirit' which informs the systems known to committee members can be discerned. They are not sufficiently strongly stated, however, to prevent agreement among the members. The second feature of international models, clearly connected with the first, is that they are described in the most general terms, leaving in effect plenty of room for field workers to interpret principles of policy as they think fit.

Bilateral aid programmes give a clue to how this is done. In the absence of a sound background in comparative education, experts from Britain, France, the USA, the USSR, Sweden and elsewhere could, in the early days, do little more than advise governments as best they could how to achieve in practice an idealised universal model – let us say basic education – of which they had no experience. Or as experts they could advise governments to adopt aspects of the only system they knew anything about – namely, their own. They could also help their local counterparts to run institutions created in the image of those they knew. It is not surprising to find that British and American experts almost always favour, regardless of circumstances, the introduction of a decentralised system of educational administrators. Kandel, alas, maintained that they were more democratic.[39] He was a member of the American Education Mission[40] which visited Japan shortly after the Second World War and recommended that a previously powerful Ministry of Education should simply have advisory power and that real power should be given to local authorities. One consequence was an upsurge in the influence of the communist-dominated Japanese

Teachers' Union.[41] British advisers invariably assume that teachers in Africa and Asia should have a very large say in what should be taught and how it should be taught. Paradoxically they have also recommended that the latest Nuffield and PSSC science education syllabuses should be adopted. Soviet and German Democratic Republic experts always recommend the introduction of polytechnical education in countries they advise.

Such technical advisers are neo-colonialists. Unwittingly they are cultural imperialists imposing, with the best will in the world, models of educational provision which may be ill-adapted and indeed not capable of adaptation by the nations whose governments have asked for help and advice. The difference between present-day technical experts (whether under contract to an international agency or on a bilateral programme) and the missionaries and former colonial officials is that the modern adviser rarely stays long enough in any country to be held personally responsible for either success or failure. There is no doubt that the development of education on the basis of rather crude cultural imperialism which frequently involves rather crude cultural borrowing still includes many unanticipated and unwanted consequences. Because technical assistance frequently takes no account of the 'living spirit' of the host countries there are as many failures as successes. Doubtless these considerations influenced the growth in Latin America of debates about 'dependence' theories. These considerations and the threat of neo-colonialism combine to make wholesale borrowing from Europe and North America quite unacceptable to many intellectuals in these countries which, we choose to say, constitute the Third World.

Comparative educationists should, it seems to me, ask themselves, in spite of its long history, whether selective cultural borrowing is theoretically justified and practically feasible. If it is, then much more than at present needs to be known about the value systems that motivate the outlook and behaviour of the recipients of foreign innovations. For this reason I consider the establishment of useful ideal-typical models in the light of which a clash of cultures can be analysed constitutes a major research task for comparative educationists. Such ideal-typical models would serve to show what can be borrowed and what cannot be taken over. If, as Sadler maintained, educational systems can be transplanted only if the ethos or living spirit which informs them is taken with then, then comparative educationists need to understand the implications for host countries of proposed innovations which carry with them unique characteristics. For this reason we need techniques and models which will give us some understanding of the mental states of technical assistants and local counterparts. We need appropriate normative patterns, which will permit us to weigh all the fruits and educative values of innovation and which will enable us to predict in known circumstances the outcomes of policy. We need, as Harris said, theories with predictive value if we are to plan education. The successful planning of educational development depends upon the care with which we refine techniques and models to describe local needs and conditions and to formulate generalisations from which predictions can be made.

NOTES AND REFERENCES: CHAPTER 1

Material in this chapter is drawn from Brian Holmes, 'Some considerations of Method', unpublished PhD thesis, University of London, 1962, and 'Los precursores de la educación comparada', *Educación comparada, Revista de Educación,* no. 260, January–April, 1979.

1 Henry Barnard, *National Education, Systems, Institutions and Statistics of Public Instruction in Different Countries,* Steiger, New York, 1872, pt II, p. 515.
2 See Joseph Alexander Freeherrn von Helfert (Baron), *Die Östereichische Geschichte System Statistik,* Vol. 1, *Die Gründung der österreichischen Volkschule durch Maria Theresia,* Prague, 1860, pp. 285–7.
3 Barnard, op. cit.
4 See Stewart E. Fraser and William W. Brickman, *A History of International and Comparative Education,* Scott, Foresman, Chicago, 1968.
5 See Stewart E. Fraser, *American Education in Foreign Perspectives,* Wiley, New York, 1969, for details of visitors to the USA.
6 Hans, *Comparative Education,* op. cit., p. 2.
7 See Adolphe E. Meyer, *An American History of the American People,* McGraw-Hill, New York, 1967.
8 *Seventh Annual Report of the Board of Education: together with the Seventh Annual Report of the Secretary of the Board,* Dalton & Wentworth, Boston, Mass., 1844.
9 *Remarks on the Seventh Annual Report of the Hon. Horace Mann, Secretary of the Massachusetts Board of Education,* Little, Brown, Boston, Mass., 1844.
10 Victor Cousin, *Report on the State of Public Instruction in Prussia* (trans. Sarah Austin), Effingham Wilson, London, 1836. A digest of this report by J. Orville Taylor, professor of education in New York University, appeared in the report of the Superintendent of Common Schools in 1836 (Albany, 1836).
11 Taylor, op. cit., pp. iii–iv.
12 Mann, *Seventh Annual Report*, op. cit., p. 23.
13 H. Barnard, *Connecticut Common School Journal* (Hartford, Conn.), no. 11, 1 April 1839, in an issue devoted to 'An exposition of the Common School System of Prussia'.
14 Cousin, op. cit., p. 292.
15 V. Cousin, *On the State of Education in Holland as Regards Schools for the Working Classes and for the Poor* (trans. Leonard Horner), John Murray, London, 1838.
16 M. E. Sadler, 'The unrest in secondary education in Germany and elsewhere', in *Board of Education Special Reports on Education Subjects*, Vol. 9, *Education in Germany,* HMSO, London, 1902, p. 44.
17 Sadler, op. cit., p. 162.
18 W. T. Harris, in *Annual Report of the Commissioner of Education for the Year 1888—89,* Washington, DC, 1891, p. xxv.
19 Harris, op. cit., p. xxiii.
20 ibid.
21 A. I. Piskunov (ed.), *K. D. Ushinsky,* Progress Publishers, Moscow, 1975, p. 100.
22 Piskunov, op. cit., p. 102.
23 loc. cit.

24 ibid., p. 106.
25 I. L. Kandel, *Comparative Education,* Houghton Mifflin, Boston, Mass., 1933.
26 V. Mallinson, *An Introduction to Comparative Education,* Heinemann, London, 1957, p. 14, quoting Morris Ginsberg. Some modifications have been made in later editions.
27 André Siegfried, *The Character of Peoples*, Jonathan Cape, London, 1952.
28 G. Altbach and Gail P. Kelly, *Education and Colonialism,* Longman, New York, 1978.
29 S. Jayaweera, 'A comparative study of American and British colonial educational policy in Ceylon and the Philippines', unpublished PhD thesis, University of London, 1966.
30 Quoted and criticised in S. R. Dongerkery, *A History of the University of Bombay, 1857–1957,* University of Bombay, Bombay, 1957.
31 Martin McLean, 'A comparative study of assimilation and adaptationist educational policies in British colonial Africa, 1925–1953', unpublished PhD thesis, University of London, 1978.
32 Brian Holmes (ed.), *Educational Policy and the Mission Schools*, Routledge & Kegan Paul, London, 1967.
33 Unesco Constitution. See also Lionel Elvin, 'The philosophy of Unesco', in G. Z. F. Bereday and J. A. Lauwerys (eds), *The Year Book of Education,* Evans, London, 1957.
34 Unesco, *Fundamental Education,* Macmillan, New York, 1947.
35 See John Hall Stewart, *A Documentary Survey of the French Revolution,* Macmillan, New York, 1951, pp. 346–70.
36 R. H. Tawney (ed.), *Secondary Education for All – a Policy for Labour,* Education Advisory Committee of the Labour Party/Allen & Unwin, London, 1938.
37 Unesco, *Report of Meeting of Ministers of Education of Asian Member States Participating in the Karachi Plan, Tokyo, 2–11 April 1962,* Unesco, Bangkok, 1962.
38 Unesco, International Commission on the Development of Education (chairman: Edgar Faure), *Learning To Be,* Unesco, Paris, 1972.
39 I. L. Kandel, *The New Era in Education,* Harrap, London, 1955.
40 See Robert King Hall, *Education for a New Japan,* Yale University, New Haven, Conn., 1949.
41 See Benjamin C. Duke, *Japan's Militant Teachers,* East–West Center, University of Hawaii, Honolulu, 1973.

Chapter 2

Comparative Education, Scientific Method and Educational Planning

The desire to improve education persists. Two arguments have been advanced in favour of reform. Over the years, in international declarations, national constitutions and legislation, conference recommendations and the manifestos of political parties, the belief has been expressed that education is a basic human right and that governments should provide it in response to the wishes and expectations of parents, children and young adults. This aim undoubtedly inspired reformers after 1945. Other arguments have supported educational expansion. Everywhere statesmen have been persuaded that the schools are important agents of economic growth, social justice and political modernisation. Over the last quarter of a century an industry of educational planners has grown up. Members of it constantly advise governments on how to achieve their aims. They claim that planning techniques are now so good that decisions are not ideological but the fruits of social scientific research. In response to both arguments school populations have expanded dramatically since 1945.

These claims should be viewed with caution. Dubious attempts have been made to show that the two rather different aims of policy are compatible by suggesting that the expansion of education in response to consumer demand and assertions that it is a human right automatically confers economic and political benefits on society. The validity of such expectations depends, I suggest, on national circumstances and in particular on a host of policy decisions made at all kinds of level of government and by pressure groups throughout society. Too many decisions, prepared by planners and adopted by those who employ them, are presented as valid panaceas. In reality policy choices exist and the alternatives are usually loosely related to the aims of provision. Thus policies and practices designed to provide education as a human right may be (but are not necessarily) quite different from those whose purpose is to promote economic growth. Planners frequently disguise or ignore the fact that decisions are politicised and ideology informs most of them.

In practice expansionist policies in the industrialised nations have shown certain common characteristics and unique national features. In the previously dependent nations committed to expansion, whether wealthy or poor, a choice of policies and practices has been open to governments. They have been pressed by advisers to accept either Western European (with several variants), communist, or American models. Bilateral technical assistance programmes have provoked competition rather than co-operation between donor nations who were not unmindful of the political rewards which might flow from their generosity.[1] Multilateral aid programmes have produced, as stated, policies derived from consensus international politics and the conventional wisdom of experts.

For many reasons, governments continue to ask organisations like Unesco to provide solutions to pressing educational problems. Government representatives come together in organisations like the OECD to discuss ways in which the economics of member states and the less fortunate nations can be improved.[2] At conferences of national representatives held by such organisations as the Council of Europe and the International Bureau of Education educational policies are debated and recommendations made which for the most part identify future goals.[3]

Under these circumstances what service functions can comparative education perform? The answer depends on whether its practitioners are members of an international organisation, a national research bureau, or a university department. Each type of organisation places constraints on its personnel. Officials and research workers in an international organisation cannot ignore the political pressures of members who represent sovereign states. National research agencies are usually invited to conduct ethnocentric research in the light of political decisions. Philanthropic foundations are less vulnerable to party political pressures although the choice of projects they fund is usually made in accordance with a stated philosophy and aims. Financial constraints restrict the range of social functions university academics can perform. Their traditional obligations should also influence their choice. My position is that without violence to academic freedom they can contribute to a theoretical understanding of education and to its practical improvement.[4] If there is to be genuine co-operation between administrator and scholar the practical concerns of the former and the theoretical interests of the latter should be complementary. Basic to worthwhile co-operation is the need for a science of comparative education which will, as Harris hoped, provide us with general theories with predictive power and will, as Sadler and Harris made plain, enable us to recognise what is peculiar and incidental to local needs and to understand the unique features of a nation's 'living spirit'.

JULLIEN'S PRINCIPLES OF METHOD OF COMPARATIVE EDUCATION

The evolution of comparative education as a generalising and as an applied science should be seen in the context of expressed aims and discussions about the characteristics of scientific method. By the middle of the nineteenth century principles of scientific method had been formulated. One model, induction, has a long history, as William Whewell demonstrated in *The Philosophy of the Inductive Sciences*.[5] Certainly these views can be traced back to Aristotle and much later on to Francis Bacon. Basically the theory of induction, as the scientific method developed after the revival of science during the Renaissance, incorporated the principles of a comparative method.

Several commentators, of course, suggest that the comparative method dates back at least to Plato. His role as a cultural borrower has been mentioned, and the method adopted by him and successors described as inappropriate in comparative education. Aristotle adopted a more inductive approach. He collected a great many travellers' tales about the animals they had seen. Inadequate though Aristotle's own practice was in the history of biology there is a persisting thread of belief in the value of observing and classifying data about plants and animals. It is not surprising, therefore, that Franz Hilker,[6] a historian of comparative education, has maintained that the comparative method was first systematically developed by natural scientists and refers particularly to the work of George-Louis Lecleric de Buffon[7] in France. Buffon was a biologist who rejected artificial classification systems and maintained that men ought to observe and describe nature, differentiating between animals, plants and stones before further refining the taxonomy and comparing phenomena so that ultimately they could be brought together under general laws. This undoubtedly resembles the method of induction advocated by Aristotle and Bacon.

Justification for induction as an appropriate method in the social sciences and in comparative education has been found by Hilker in the method used to induce general principles about laws by Charles Louis de Montesquieu in preparing his *L'Esprit des lois*. He travelled through Austria, Hungary, Italy and England observing men, things and constitutions before he returned to Paris. In his monumental work (thirty-one books) he classifies his observations into six parts: (1) law and forms of government; (2) military arrangements and taxation; (3) manners and customs and their dependence on climatic conditions; (4) economic matters; (5) religion; (6) Roman, French and feudal law. On these carefully classified observations Montesquieu based his views on legal and political matters.

In many respects the method of Marc Antoine Jullien de Paris, regarded by many historians as the father of theoretical comparative education[8], resembles Montesquieu's comparative method. In so far as it has influenced the subsequent development of comparative education it is important that his proposal should be placed in the context of debates about scientific method. The key to Jullien's method and to his working definition of the purposes of comparative education is found in a passage from *L'Esquisse et vue préliminaire d'un ouvrage sur l'education comparée* which has been quoted with approval by many authors. Pedro Rossello[9], Hans[10] and M. B. Lourenço-Filho,[11] for example, all quote the following passage:

> Education, as other sciences, is based on facts and observations, which should be ranged in analytical tables, easily compared, in order to deduce principles and definite rules. Education should become a positive science instead of being ruled by narrow and limited opinions, by whims and arbitrary decisions of administrators, to be turned away from the direct line which it should follow, either by prejudice of a blind routine or by the spirit of some system and innovation.[12]

In this definition of aims Jullien expressed hopes that have been entertained by positivists ever since and a method of research approved by inductionists. Many present-day comparative educationists share these hopes and use methods of research which have their origins in J. S. Mill's *System of Logic*. The essential features of this method are (1) the collection of data using objective observation, (2) the careful classification of data, (3) the search for explanation by ascribing to each event an antecedent cause or causes, (4) the formulation of tentative hypotheses, (5) the collection of further confirming evidence and finally (6) the statement of universal laws whose validity can be provided. Positive science and its application in the social sciences along these lines was discussed by, among others, Auguste Comte, Claude Henri de Saint-Simon[13] and some would say effectively applied in social science research by Karl Marx who induced general laws about society from a careful and thorough description and analysis of conditions in a capitalist society.

It should be noted that Jullien is not accepted without question as the originator of the methodological principles on which comparative education is founded. Rossello 'discovered' Jullien and was a staunch supporter of his claim to fame. Subsequently William Brickman[14] has suggested that *L'Esquisse,* published in 1817, was anticipated by C. A. Basset's *Essais sur l'organisation de quelques parties d'instruction publique* of 1808. To be sure, since Rossello brought Jullien's work to the attention of scholars[15] in *M. A. Jullien de Paris,*[16] *Les Précursors du BIE*[17] and *La Pédagogie comparée. Un précurseur: Marc Antoine*

Jullien de Paris,[18] H. Goetz[19] and Stewart Fraser[20] have examined Jullien's plan and concept of 'education comparée'. Subsequently few authors have failed to suggest that he used the term for the first time and that he offered a succinct definition of the purposes, methods and aims of comparative education which are accepted today. Moreover in his plan he envisaged an international commission for the collection of data, an institution in which exceptional teachers could be trained and a bulletin issued for the dissemination of information.

Jullien also worked out what facts should be collected and how they should be classified. In the second part of *L'Esquisse* he established six categories into which he proposed to classify information. They were (1) primary or elementary education, (2) secondary and classical education, (3) higher and scientific education, (4) teacher training, (5) the education of young women and (6) education and its relationship to legislation and social regulations. Specific questions associated with each of the categories were designed to provide factual data and statements of opinion or judgement about the quality or effectiveness of educational provision. He asked about the origins, numbers and administration of schools and the conditions associated with admission to them. He wanted to know how the needs of different religious communities were met, how industrial training was provided and how teachers were trained. In most cases an obvious attempt is made to discover the ways in which formal schooling is related to the other social agencies in which education is provided.

Among present-day authors George Bereday[21] is perhaps implicitly Jullien's most faithful interpreter. He spells out most fully the method of induction (which lies at the heart of Buffon's, Montesquieu's and Jullien's comparative methodology) in *Comparative Method in Education* (1964). I think his judgement on Jullien's method is, in part, mistaken. He has written: 'Its emphasis was on cataloguing descriptive educational data: comparison of the collected information was then undertaken in order to make available the best practices of one country for transplantation to others.'[22] This succinctly states the position adopted by the cultural borrowers. I do not think that it adequately describes Jullien's own position. He had a different purpose in mind when he advised comparative educationists first to collect facts – one that was linked to his broader vision of the purpose of comparative method. In practice he hoped, through the comparative study of education, to find a way of realising a universal commonwealth. Some present-day practitioners share that aim. He also hoped that some universal principles of policy could be induced from comparative research. This aim, too, serves to motivate the work of some comparative educationists today. In other words, the establishment of a universal model of educational provision and the discovery of some universal principles of educational policies are dreams which give substance to the efforts of practical men and academic comparative educationists respectively.

In so far as Jullien's proposed method reflected emerging theories about scientific method and anticipated confidence in positivism he was a man of his time. In so far as he worked explicitly to apply the methods of the natural sciences to 'éducation comparée' in order to create a positive science of education he legitimised the subsequent research of historian philosophers, psychometrists, economists and sociologists in the field of comparative education. Until positivism was questioned by sociologists the doubts about it raised by philosophers of the natural sciences and indeed by some comparative educationists were disregarded.[23] Since then comparative educationists have been more willing to enter into debates about the characteristics of scientific method. Before turning to the positivist debate in comparative education (Chapter 3) I propose to touch briefly on discussions in the philosophy of science and among pragmatists which influenced my approach to comparative education research and which have some bearing on the positivist dispute.

THE PARADIGM REVOLUTION IN THE NATURAL SCIENCES

Optimism among nineteenth-century social philosophers was no doubt influenced by the success of Newtonian physics. Confidence in the inevitable progress of mankind was associated with assumptions that the nature of the millennium and general laws predicting the evolution of societies towards it could be discovered using the methods of science. Hegel and Marx described their ideal state and ideal society. The latter not only prophesied that it would be realised but described the stages through which societies would pass before arriving there. Other social philosophers were less certain about the millennium's characteristics but were fascinated by social change and the prospects of discovering laws of social development that would give man the same power to control his social environment as the laws of physics, chemistry and biology had conferred on him to control his natural environment. A distinction should be drawn between theorists of social change who prophesied millennia and those who worked, more modestly, to analyse the characteristics of change and the problems to which it gives rise.[24]

Mill's view of society[25] differed from that of Marx although in many respects their methodological assumptions were similar. Saint-Simon (1760–1825), who influenced Mill, Comte and Marx, constantly referred to the importance physiology would assume in the study of mankind when it became a positive science. The aim of William Graham Sumner (1840–1910), too, was to develop a 'science of society'.[26] A series of articles by Herbert Spencer provided Sumner with a framework within which he subsequently worked. He was not able, however, to find in Charles Darwin's theory of evolution justification for believing that social progress was inevitable. Like Marx he anticipated conflict between workers and capitalists but his sympathies were with the middle classes. These and other issues debated by social scientists in the nineteenth century are mentioned simply to indicate that in retrospect agreement between the founders of positivism may appear greater than it was in fact. My concern is to refer to major issues in the light of which debates among comparative educationists can be examined.

The influence and rejection by Popper, of Mill's carefully worked out method of induction as the method of the physical sciences is one framework within which debates among Anglo-Saxon comparative educationists may be placed. The influence of Spencer's social Darwinism on American pragmatists and the acceptance of problem-solving techniques among American research workers is a second framework. The question is whether as comparative educationists induction and positivism or alternatives to them should determine the research techniques we use. My belief is that the optimism of many nineteenth-century social philosopher-scientists was misplaced and that post-relativity science offers a more useful paradigm within which to work.

By the end of the century belief in the inevitability of social progress had been tempered. Confidence in man's ability – if he were active – to control his destiny persisted. The view that rational man could improve society continued to receive support. As a representative of the school of thought that nature is the domain of law and man is a product of it, Lester F. Ward could write:

> Man is a product of that law, but he has reached a stage on which he can comprehend the law. Now, just because nature is a domain of rigid law, and just because man can comprehend that law, his destiny is in his own hands. Any law that he can comprehend he can control. He cannot increase or diminish the powers of nature, but he can direct them.[27]

And he could add:

> . . . To the developed intellect nature is as clay in the potter's hands. It is neither best nor worst. It is what man makes it, and rational man always seeks to make it better. The true doctrine, then, is to *meliorism* – the perpetual bettering of man's estate. This will be possible in precise proportion to man's knowledge of nature.[28]

Meliorism is not the same as historicism.

Meliorism need not imply that man can better his estate only in terms of a known future. It is in this sense that it is not the same as historicism. Both meliorism and historicism may justify the analysis of one or several causal factors – technology or the organisation of industry – to explain change in a particular social system.[29] Historicists would claim that such an analysis gives rise to laws which explain the transformation of one system of society to another and indeed why all societies will eventually arrive at the same millennium. Belief in the universality of natural and social laws justifies the assumption that all societies and systems of education are moving in the same direction towards the same universal models. Meliorism is, however, deterministic in another sense. The application of laws may be limited but if they are known men can control their destiny.

Evidently the early pioneers of comparative education were meliorists in the sense that they were more interested in the consequences of change within a national system than in the sweep of social transformation. They recognised, as sociologists did, that historical studies could contribute a great deal to any analysis of social interaction. Indeed, along with some sociologists who maintain that sociology is an extension of history, some concluded that comparative education was an extension of the history of education. Moreover they laid stress on the relationships between education and other aspects of society – law, economics, politics. This view gave rise, in effect, to the search for the causal factors that determine what goes on in education. Today the strong historical bias of the pioneers has given way to the analysis of contemporary factors by sociologists and economists. These kinds of study will be discussed more fully in Chapter 4.

Events in the natural sciences, however, overtook the social scientists. By the end of the century progress in the natural sciences had moved so quickly and far that the theories which had served scientists so well during the Newtonian epoch were proving inadequate. Electromagnetic phenomena, line spectra and the thermodynamics of radiation threw increasing strains upon Newtonian concepts and particularly on those of the ether. An attempt by Michelson and Morley to measure the motion of the earth through the ether was one of several important experiments which culminated in a new cosmology, a questioning of the logical validity of the traditional concepts of mass, force and the like, and new theories of measurement. Through this thorough transformation of theoretical physics came the branch of science known as 'relativity'. And, Herbert Dingle has written: 'It is not a trifling change, touching only the latest refinements of physics; it affects the very foundation, the primary definitions and concepts on which the whole science is built.'[30] Philosophers of science have been discussing these consequences ever since then, but in some ways this revolution has had little effect on the discussions of many social scientists. If comparative educationists still wish to follow methods similar to those used in the physical sciences, the changes in outlook brought about by relativity have fundamental implications for them.

Basically the whole positivistic and deterministic view of how science advanced was challenged. The concept of absolute measurement was questioned. This led to doubts about the absolute nature and unconditional validity of general laws and to a re-examination of the role given to the quantitative aspects of science as vital ingredients. Theories of causation and induction as *the* method of science were questioned and hence the search for causal factors became outmoded. New roles had to be given to observation, theory and hypothesis. Lester Ward's position that nature was 'the domain of rigid law' and man was a product of it is difficult to sustain if the implications of relativity are taken seriously. According to Dingle:

> The philosophical importance of relativity arises from the light it sheds on the character of physical thought . . . In pre-relativity days it was possible for a physicist to be a naif realist – as, in fact, more physicists, consciously or unconsciously, were. He could believe that he was discovering laws of a world of matter which was external to himself – laws which had nothing to do with his own thought and which simply described relationships between objective qualities of matter which he could discover but could not create or destroy. Today such an attitude is impossible. All such 'qualities' of matter are seen to be concepts which we define for ourselves, for the one which we have chosen as fundamental (namely, length), in terms of which to express all others, is itself a function of an arbitrary quantity 'v', which is at our disposal. Moreover, such so-called objective 'qualities' are not merely revealed as subjective concepts but are also seen to be detached from matter.[31]

This indeed raises the whole question of the objectivity of science.

From another angle, that of the American pragmatists, similar doubts were raised against the concepts of classical physics and *a priori* historicism. Drawing inspiration from Darwin the pragmatists gave significantly new turns to philosophic thought. The first is the idea of pluralistic empiricism which, Wiener has argued, 'is the piecemeal analysis of the diverse issues pertaining to physical, biological, psychological, linguistic, and social problems which resist resolution by a single metaphysical formula'. Secondly, again according to Wiener, there was a pragmatic temporalism which 'leads to a more empirical view of history and knowledge than that which finds eternal laws of development in social change and science'. In epistemology 'you have a contextualistic or relativistic theory of meaning: *the meaning of a statement varies with the spatio-temporal, linguistic, or socio-*

psychological conditions of its occurrence'. In ethics 'eternal and infallible rules are replaced by contextual, empirically tested generalisations as probable guides, subject to revision in the light of observable agreement or disagreement with predicted consequences'. There is also an 'abandonment of mechanical determinism in physical and social sciences by viewing laws as probable or contingent'. This means, in effect, 'the denial of any necessary or privileged status for the findings of "laws" of either physical or physical phenomena'.[32] It implies, with Protagoras, that 'man . . . is the measure of all things, of the existence of things that are, and of the non-existence of things that are not'.[33] The responsibility this places on the shoulders of men is infinitely greater than that implied by those who thought that the ample acquisition of knowledge would make it possible for the world to be improved.

Relativistic theories of science give to the scientist a crucial role. He selects the data, he formulates hypotheses and theories and he draws implications from them when applying theory to practice. According to these theories men and women do not behave in accordance with natural laws even though they may be able to comprehend them. Their actions may under certain circumstances be predictable. Sometimes they are not predictable. If the freedom of all men and women to accept or reject ideas and to act as they think fit is accepted then the long-term flow of events is uncertain and the determinism, or fatalism, of Marx and other historicists has to be radically modified by asking to what extent is man master of his destiny and by what methods can improvements in society be planned. The choice lies between Mannheim's total social planning, in democratic or non-democratic societies, and Popper's piecemeal social engineering.

Popper's theory of 'critical dualism' or 'critical conventionalism' implies that while man is free to accept or reject the values he finds in society his control of his social and physical environments depends on his ability to formulate hypotheses or generalisations and to manipulate relevant social and natural circumstances. His ability to control a sequence of events initiated by a man-made change is limited. For example, the consequences of starting a war cannot be predicted or controlled to any extent. If in the course of events he attempts to intervene when things go wrong he may set up another sequence of events. In Dewey's view he can only move from one partially solved problem to the next. In Popper's theory, having formulated a general proposition and made predictions from it, he can be sure of the outcomes only if he can identify and manipulate all aspects of his social environment – which is extremely unlikely.

In the post-relativity, pragmatic climate of philosophical opinion about the predictive sciences the need to specify the complete range of circumstances, that is, the context, is imperative. In Wiener's terms natural laws (and by analogy social laws) are no more, or less, than 'contextual, empirically tested generalisations'. Similarly the reservations made by Dingle (among others) about the objectivity of natural laws should be remembered. The criterion of usefulness rather than that of proximity to the 'truth' should be stressed when speaking of theories or laws with predictive power.

It is, therefore, within the constraints of this framework that possible refinements to comparative education as a social science should be considered. And we should agree with Otto Neurath that 'as social scientists, we have to expect gulfs and gaps everywhere, together with unpredictability, incompleteness, and one-sidedness of our arguing, wherever we may start'.[34] Consequently administrators should not expect planners to provide clear-cut scientific solutions to their problems on the basis of comparative studies. Understandably, governments and members of organisations like Unesco would like to know how to achieve certain aims if the success of any policy is to be judged by the degree to which aims are achieved. However well intentioned, attempts to use universal theories as the basis for successful policies should be treated with caution. They often show a quite dangerous lack of awareness of the methodological objections to social panaceas.

Certainly the growth of a predictive science depends on the ability of scientists to develop useful general hypotheses, theories and laws. The distinction between the three words should not be overemphasised. They are, let us say, statements from which a number of predictions about subsequent events can be made. Functionally, at least, they are similar. Nor are the processes of arriving at them dissimilar. But theoretically, and certainly in practice, no theory should be used to predict events unless it is accompanied by a careful analysis and statement of the initial conditions or circumstances associated with the prediction. This is of such fundamental importance that it cannot be overemphasised. It applies as much in the physical sciences as in the social sciences. Indeed, the failure of scientists to take into account significant conditions has often led to contradictions between predicted events and observed events and subsequent advances both in theory and in the analysis of influencing conditions. Instances of this are found in the Michelson–Morley experiment and in the effect of thoria on the release of electrons from a tungsten element.

This implies for comparative educators, as Harris and Sadler recognised, that it is necessary for them, before applying any theory for predictive purposes, to analyse the specific initial conditions or unique national circumstances in as much detail as possible. Some theory or problem should of course direct and guide the analysis itself. The one put forward by nineteenth-century pioneers, and widely accepted today, was that education influenced and was influenced by the whole cultural pattern. In practice each comparative educationist has accepted or created his own taxonomy to analyse national systems. Most agree on a division into the political, the economic and the social aspects of society. Of considerable methodological importance is the further subdivision of these categories into manageable components and the development of models for them.

From this perspective, the social sciences suffer at the moment from two disadvantages. The first is that it is difficult, if not impossible, either to specify all the conditions associated with a predicted event or to carry out experiments; that is, processes of testing predictions under rigorously controlled conditions. The second disadvantage lies in the absence of accepted standards of measurement in the social sciences: in other words, criteria of evaluation are difficult to agree upon. They are not acceptable to everyone (as criteria in the natural sciences tend to be) because they direct attention not to sense impressions (for example, meter readings in the physical sciences) but to evidence which may be connected with emotions, morals and ideology.

These difficulties throw upon the comparative educator responsibility for deciding what predictions are possible and how they can be confirmed or rejected. It is unwise to predict, for example, that the consequences of certain educational action will be 'happiness' or 'social maturity' or 'democracy' unless these terms are arbitrarily defined or defined in terms of accepted measuring procedures. For example, in many tribal societies the successful completion of an initiation ceremony confers on the individual the badge of 'social maturity'. In more complex societies equally arbitrary tests, for example, age, are used to determine, for instance, whether a person has the right to vote, but it is generally acknowledged that in these societies criteria of 'maturity' are not easily established and that age is an uncertain measure of 'maturity'.

An example of the need for caution before policy solutions are adopted may be mentioned in relation to proposals made by some comparative educationists. In multilingual countries they should, it seems to me, eschew panaceas designed to produce political harmony in terms of language teaching; they might identify, on the other hand, some educational and economic consequences of adopting one indigenous language for national purposes, for example, the cost of training teachers, providing textbooks, and so on. These implications might be weighed against the educational and economic consequences of adopting an international foreign language in an economy which requires, for growth, the expansion of technical education on a large scale. Ultimately, it is probably true to say that the social scientist can offer only a choice of solutions in the light of known outcomes and not *the* solution. Even then he cannot be sure his policy will succeed. Many conditions and considerations will help to influence the decision taken. Frequently these will be political or based on expediency.

A fundamental lesson to be learned from the new view of science is that the success of proposed solutions will depend upon the initial circumstances of the country under consideration. This means before any policy is adopted a thorough analysis and description of the nation (region or locality) in which it is to be implemented should be made.

To do this comparative educationists may have to call on many allied sciences – anthropology, sociology, political economy, social psychology, and so on. They will certainly have to initiate further research because, at the moment, the range and depth of available and appropriate case-studies are not adequate if the techniques of planning are to take account of modern theories of science. Predictions, if they are made at all, should be suitably tentative. More reliable ones wait on the availability of more detailed surveys of cultural areas and sovereign states and, in my view, on the more careful analysis of the problems to which education policies are offered as solutions.

Policy-oriented research in comparative education should start, not with the collection of data, but from a careful analysis of a limited problem. Innumerable problems are worth investigating. Many of them are suggested, usually in vague terms, by administrators. Others may arise in the context of debate in the investigator's own country.

Fundamentally the interests of the scholar and the administrator coincide when practical present-day problems are faced. Increasingly these are problems which are common to the world, or at least to large cultural or economic parts of it. In Europe much attention has been directed to the problem of providing equality of educational provision. A widely accepted solution has been the establishment of common secondary schools to which all adolescents from particular geographical areas would go irrespective of academic attainment. Details of policy differ, however. In the developing country the provision of elementary education has been seen as a problem. In Afro-Asian countries one solution to a similar problem has been to propose universal or mass primary schooling. As stated, a variant on this policy has been accepted, perhaps unwisely, on the assumption that 'fundamental education' or 'basic education' would suit the needs of all underdeveloped countries. At the same time policies relating to the organisation of technical education have tended to ignore the fact that some countries in the world are passing through their second industrial revolution while others are entering upon what is virtually their first. There has been, understandably, a great desire to re-educate the defeated nations. This has placed emphasis on solutions designed to use education to promote a democratic society. Indeed, since 1945 anxiety has been expressed in many forums about the chances of making democracy work, and of inculcating in man a love of peace. Of course all these issues, if our previous analysis is correct, are closely interrelated, but it is depressingly clear that very few of them even now seem to have been solved successfully.

It would be wrong to place all the blame on administrators and politicians. At the international, national and local levels they have had to take action in very complex circumstances. The results have not always been those intended. Thus the postwar decentralisation of administration in Japan tended to place the control of education in the hands of undemocratic forces. Fundamental education has been shown to be of limited value and applicability. The fault has been twofold. There has been a tendency to imagine that if certain institutions, like decentralised administration, and the community school, were transferred, certain objectives, like democracy, would be effectively promoted regardless of the context. The second mistake made has been to transform social experiments, or pilot projects, into universal panaceas, regardless of accumulated evidence.

What should now be clear is that administrators need a science of comparative education on which to draw. At the moment few people working in the field would suggest that there exists such a science. If it is to be developed satisfactorily attention should be paid to its theoretical bases, appropriate research models and techniques and to the social functions such a science of comparative education might serve. My analysis of what is needed is derived from Popper's hypothetico-deductive method. The functions comparative educationists can perform should be seen in the light of Popper's distinctions between explanation, prediction and testing, and more generally in terms of the distinction I have made between comparative education as a 'pure' (or generalising) social science and as an 'applied' social science. Broadly speaking the distinction lies in the extent to which as 'pure' scientists comparative educationists formulate policies, test them in order to eliminate those least likely to succeed and as 'applied' scientists they accept policies, advise governments how best to put them into practice and inform them what outcomes (good and bad) are likely to result when a particular policy is implemented.

COMPARATIVE EDUCATION AS A 'PURE' AND AS AN 'APPLIED' SCIENCE

Peter Medawar, a Nobel prize winner, has acknowledged Popper's pioneering role in describing the constituents of the hypothetico-deductive method of scientific inquiry. In *Induction and Intuition in Scientific Thought* Medawar has stated that the hypothetico-deductive method gives a reasonable account of how scientists work.[35] Its main constituents are the non-logical formulation of some hypothesis which is then exposed to criticism, usually through experimentation, which makes use of logic and empirical testing by comparing observations and experience with the logical consequences of belief. If events logically predicted from statements do in fact occur, confidence in the hypothesis is strengthened, otherwise it may have to be abandoned altogether.

In terms of our present discussion it is relevant to note that Mill outlined the hypothetico-deductive method of science as a poor alternative to induction, suitable for the social sciences until they had advanced to a point when inductive methods could be used.[36] Popper disagreed, but his main criticism of Mill's account of explanation is that it fails to take into consideration the specific initial conditions. For Popper 'to give a causal explanation of a certain *specific event* means deducing a statement describing this event from two kinds of premises; from some universal laws, and from some singular or specific statements which we may call the *specific initial conditions*'.[37] In practical terms failure to take into account these initial conditions (or the societal context) leads to unconditioned prophecies about the future of education as opposed to conditional scientific predictions. The party politician may like the former, the honest administrator needs the latter.

The difference has its implications. Testing that is designed to provide causal explanations in terms of antecedent causes or to show how the past has given rise to the present is valuable to planners on the assumptions that there are trends of development in education, that they are unconditional (or absolute) and that they are governed by universal or absolute laws (functional propositions which have been so thoroughly tested that they can be accorded the status of universal laws). Testing which attempts to deduce outcomes in a particular context and to compare them with the results of experience is based on the assumption that there are no absolute trends and that there are no absolute laws of development which govern them. It is based upon the belief that men can choose between alternative patterns of action and that they are responsible for the future because they make decisions and in trying to act in accordance with them may fail or succeed. Popper has also claimed that there is a unity of method in the natural and social sciences. However, he '*wished to distinguish between science and pseudo-science . . .*'[38] He concluded that '*the criterion of the scientific status of a theory is its falsifiability, or refutability, or testability*'.[39] He has often stated that the responsibility of a scientist lies not in the care with which he formulates his hypothesis but in the rigour with which he tests it with the intention of refuting it. Against his insistence that scientists should always seek to refute a general statement Thomas Kuhn[40] has argued that scientists, for the most part, work within a paradigm which they do not question and apply its constituent theories and hypotheses in a commonsense kind of way. Only occasionally do scientists question a major paradigm when it fails to meet a succession of experimental tests. Then they reject the paradigm or retain it as useful within a restricted context. The history of science is replete with examples of scientific revolutions and periods of commonsense scientific endeavour.

In parenthesis, I do not think the differences between Popper and Kuhn are as irreconcilable as some protagonists[41] in the argument claim but since Kuhn has been used by ethnomethodologists to support their case the differences are important. If the distinctions made by Popper between prediction, explanation and testing are used to classify scientific activities, 'commonsense' scientists and engineers accept general statements and statements about initial conditions in order to discover and apply new information. They expect to verify their conjectures in practice and do not set out to discover new generalisations (explanations) or challenge existing ones (testing). The fact that in the natural sciences experimental testing is morally acceptable, theoretically well defined and practically feasible while in the social sciences experiments are neither morally condonable nor practical places somewhat different obligations on the social scientists from those ascribed to natural scientists. In the natural sciences unsatisfactory hypotheses can be eliminated in the light of refuting experimental evidence and the ways in which natural scientists formulate their refutable hypotheses are not important. In the absence of decisive experimental tests the processes of formulating social science hypotheses are pertinent features of research.

The distinction between explanation, prediction and testing helps to place the claim that the scientist should always attempt to falsify or refute a general statement in perspective. Hypothetico-deductive procedures, whether for the purpose of explanation, prediction, or testing, are the same. Indeed the outcomes are not very different either. If a specific event is predicted it is also explained and a general statement has been tested. A theory or hypothesis is verified when predicted events are confirmed by actual observations; refuted when predicted and observed events differ.

The difference between the three activities lies in what the investigator is attempting to do. If he is seeking to discover a general statement and the initial conditions from which may be deduced a known outcome (prognosis) then he is looking for an *explanation*. If the general statements (laws) and initial conditions (context) are given and it is his intention to discover new information from deducing it from them then he is interested in *prediction*. If the law (general statement) and initial conditions are taken to be problematic and the investigator sets out to compare a deduced outcome (prognosis) with experience then the statement is being *tested*. In any case, and this is the crux of the difference between induction and hypothetico-deduction, the explanation of a specific event in the latter system requires that a statement describing this event is deduced from two kinds of premisses – a universal law and statements about specific initial conditions. In other words, general statements are contingent. Problems, solutions to them and predicted outcomes should be seen in context.

In general the requirements of the hypothetico-deductive method of inquiry satisfied the need in comparative education for general theories (hypotheses) with predictive power and for descriptions of national and local circumstances (specific initial conditions). The principles of educational provision and national policies may be regarded as hypothetical solutions which are to be exposed to criticism. Systematic descriptions of a nation's education and its infrastructure, that is, related political, economic and social aspects of society, correspond to Popper's specific initial conditions. The general aim of comparative educationists should be to subject proposed policies to critical examination either to eliminate those which are not likely to work in a particular country, to show what results will flow from the adoption of a policy, or to demonstrate how a policy may be made to succeed. The distinction made between explanation, prediction and testing thus enables the social functions of comparative educationists as 'pure' and as 'applied' scientists to be identified more precisely.

These research functions can usefully be examined in relation to planning procedures and policy processes. There is some debate about the range of activities which can be termed planning. Those definitions that stop short of acknowledging that all three policy processes – policy formulation, policy adoption and policy implementation – are involved in planning seem inadequate to me. For example, planning activities are sometimes restricted by definition to the process of preparing a set of decisions for action in the future.[42] I prefer to include in planning the role advisers may have in the adoption and execution of decisions. Thus I propose to assume that piecemeal social engineering or planning is future-directed, includes all three policy processes – formulation, adoption and implementation – and involves explanation, prediction and testing.

In so far as a comparative educationist hopes as a result of careful problem-analysis to discover novel policies (formulate new hypotheses) or to describe more adequately the national circumstances in which the problem arises and the solution is to be applied, he is involved in planning procedures designed to formulate decisions for future action. Such planning procedures correspond to *explanation* in the hypothetico-deductive method but involve additional features which are not relevant in the natural sciences because experimental testing eliminates useless hypotheses or policies. Policy formulation is a task for the 'pure' comparative educationist who is asked to propose decisions which will, when executed, achieve stated aims or goals. If these decisions or policies are to be scientific rather than pseudo-scientific they should be stated in a way that makes them testable and capable of refutation. This means they should be stated as functional propositions or sociological laws. The crucial importance of problem analysis as an additional part of these procedures has been overlooked by most planners. It is, of course, a central feature of my problem (-solving) approach.

In practice educational policies are formulated with scant regard to problem analysis. Nor can it be said that they have been induced, as Jullien wanted them to be, from carefully observed and classified data. International statements of intent (hopes, expectations) inform world policies. National policies frequently stem from party political manifestos. In some countries, consequently, policies may compete for acceptance. Processes of adoption are usually highly politicised and it matters little whether the policy has its origins in ideology or has been formulated as a consequence of planning procedures. Faced with a policy which has been adopted, the comparative educationist can undertake two functions. He can, given that the national circumstances are known, *predict* what is likely to happen when the policy is put into practice. Or, and this is what he is most likely to be asked to do, he can attempt to advise on the best ways of achieving the stated aims of policy. In either case the general statement and statements about initial conditions are given and he is acting as an 'applied' scientist by providing additional information that will, it is hoped, help the policy to succeed.

Rather rarely will a comparative educationist be invited overtly to discriminate between alternative policies advocated by political parties in a sovereign state or between alternatives produced by the same or by several international agencies. As a pure scientist this task of exposing policies to critical examination with the intention of discriminating between them so as to eliminate the least useful is the one comparative educationists should welcome most. In *testing* policies, for this is what is involved, the research worker must not assume that the national circumstances are sufficiently well known for him to predict with confidence the outcomes of alternative policies. He must describe the living spirit, institutions and natural environment of the nation as fully and accurately as possible. Then, if he can do so, to test the policies experimentally he should predict the outcomes of alternative policies and compare these with events so as to reject the policy that fails the test. This critical function is vital. It reflects Popper's claim that the scientist's responsibility lies in his willingness to devise tests that will refute scientific statements. It is a task that in education we are unable to operationalise either because we are unable to control conditions or because the consequences flowing from educational policies show through in observable events many years later. Nevertheless the stability of national characteristics, if we can find ways of describing them adequately, and the uniqueness of each nation's characteristics, give rise to the hope that the reactions of identifiable groups of people – politicians, teachers, parents, pupils and students – are to some extent predictable. If they are, then some of the outcomes of policy are predictable. In so far as common and different characteristics can be identified, the past experience of one nation may help the comparative educationist to throw light on the future turn of events in another nation which adopts (somewhat later) policies similar to the first. Outcomes in the two nations are, to be sure, likely to be different but there is a good deal of evidence to justify my confidence in the contribution comparative education research can make to the avoidance of disastrous policies and the elimination of those least likely to succeed. In short I am satisfied that a combination of the problem(-solving) approach and the hypothetico-deductive method could improve educational planning very considerably by introducing a critical element into planning procedures.

Of course, comparative educationists who accept that their social function is to criticise policy should not expect to be popular or to be asked for advice by national governments or international agencies. Governments are likely to regard as valid research that appears to support already agreed policies. International agencies can rarely abandon politically determined policies. Such considerations should not dissuade comparative educationists, who are free to do so, from taking a critical stance as 'pure' and 'applied' scientists. The distinction between these roles stems not from the kind of problem we study, nor from the position we hold, but the kind of interest we have in general policy statements and the uniqueness of the national circumstances in which policies are to be introduced. As 'pure' scientists we should attempt to formulate alternative policies to carefully analysed problems and eliminate those we think will be less successful in particular countries. As 'applied' scientists we should be prepared to see how far we can help those responsible for policy to implement adopted policies and to help them to anticipate the outcomes and problems which are likely to arise when a policy has been put into effect.

In our physical world the link between the speculations of 'pure' physicists, chemists and biologists and the common sense of engineers lies in experimental testing. In the social sciences the link between the ideological speculations of politicians and the day-to-day work of administrators may be in comparative research – in education, in comparative education. For this reason I turn next to debates among Anglo-Saxon comparative educationists.

NOTES AND REFERENCES: CHAPTER 2

This chapter appeared in somewhat different form in the *Journal of Higher Education*, Ohio State University, vol. XXIX, no. 5, May 1978, 'Comparative education and the administrator', when I was clarifying my views on scientific method and pragmatism.

1 See E. E. Ekuban, 'British and American policies in technical assistance in education in West Africa with special reference to higher education in Ghana, 1945–1968', unpublished PhD thesis, University of London, 1970.
2 See terms of reference of OECD; OECD, *Activities of OECD in 1970,* Report of the Secretary General, OECD, Paris, 1970, and subsequently annually; *OECD, History, Aims, Structure,* OECD, Paris, 1972; *OECD at a Glance,* OECD, Paris, 1975. See also OECD, *Centre for Educational Research and Innovation,* 1971, when it became fully established within the OECD framework. The studies initiated by CERI constitute an important change of emphasis in the methodology employed in comparative research by international organisations. As analytical documents they leave something to be desired but as contributions to policy-making in education they are very valuable.
3 IBE/Unesco, *Recommendations 1934–1960,* IBE, Geneva, 1962, represents the degree to which ministry representatives not only outlined distant aims but were able to agree on what they should be.
4 See Holmes, *Ivory Towers, the Glass Bead Game and Open Societies*, op. cit.
5 William Whewell, *The Philosophy of the Inductive Sciences*, 2nd edn, John W. Parker, London, 1847.
6 Franz Hilker, *Vergleichende Pädagogik. Eine Einführung in ihre Geschichte Theorie and Praxis,* Huebner, Munich, 1962.
7 George-Louis Leclerc de Buffon; *Histoire naturalle,* Paris, 1749; and *Oeuvres complètes,* Paris, 1778.
8 See *Esquisse d'un ouvrage sur l'éducation comparée*, no. 243, IBE, Geneva, 1962.
9 P. Rossello, *Les Précurseurs du Bureau International d'Education,* International Bureau of Education, Geneva, 1943.
10 Hans, *Comparative Education,* op. cit., p. 1.
11 M. B. Lourenco-Filho, *Educacão comparada*, Edições Melhoramentro, São Paulo, 1961, p. 16.
12 Taken from Hans, op. cit.
13 Stanislav Andreski, *The Essential Comte*, Croom Helm, London, 1974; F. Markham (ed.), *Saint Simon, Selected Writings,* Blackwell, Oxford, 1952. See also Alan Ryan, *The Philosophy of the Social Sciences,* Macmillan, London, 1970.
14 W. W. Brickman, 'A historical introduction to comparative education', *Comparative Education Review,* vol. 1, no. 3, 1960, and 'The theoretical foundations of comparative education', *Journal of Educational Sociology,* vol. 30, no. 3, 1956.
15 A recent book is Alessandro Leonarduzzi, *Marc-Antoine Jullien de Paris (1775–1848)*, 'La Nuova Base', Udine, 1977.
16 P. Rossello, *M. A. Jullien de Paris,* IBE, Geneva, 1943.
17 P. Rossello, *Les Précurseurs,* op. cit.
18 P. Rossello, *La Pédagogie comparée, Un précurseur: Marc-Antoine Jullien de Paris*, SEVPEN, Paris, 1950.
19 Helmut Goetz, *Marc-Antoine Jullien de Paris, 1775–1848,* (trans. into French), Institut Pédagogique National, Paris, 1962.
20 Stewart E. Fraser, *Jullien's Plan for Comparative Education, 1816–1817,* George Peabody College, Nashville, Tenn., 1962.
21 George Z. F. Bereday, *Comparative Method in Education,* Holt, Rinehart & Winston, New York, 1964.
22 ibid., p. 7.
23 The failure of Newton's paradigm towards the end of the nineteenth century to explain a number of phenomena gave rise to a paradigm revolution, of the kind

Thomas Kuhn describes, in the form of Einstein's theories of relativity. My acceptance of Popper's analysis represented a rejection of positivism. E. J. King, while not accepting my position, also advanced an anti-positivist appraisal. See Brian Holmes, 'The positivist debate in comparative education – an Anglo-Saxon perspective', *Comparative Education,* vol. 13, no. 2, June 1977, pp. 115–32.

24 Among the historicists Popper has identified Plato, Aristotle, Hegel, Mill, Marx and Mannheim.

25 See Mill, *System of Logic,* op. cit., and Popper's analysis in *The Open Society,* op. cit.

26 See William Graham Sumner, *Folkways,* Dover, 1906, and *Social Darwinism,* Prentice-Hall, Englewood Cliffs, NJ, 1963.

27 Lester F. Ward, *Outlines of Sociology,* Macmillan, New York, 1898, p. 25.

28 ibid., p. 26.

29 Most theorists of social change assume one kind of factor, e.g. the organisation of work, a new technology, inevitably initiates change. Marx represents a historicist; Ogburn a meliorist. For a survey of social change see Amitai and Eva Etzioni, *Social Change,* Basic Books, New York, 1964.

30 Herbert Dingle, *The Special Theory of Relativity,* Chemical Publishing Co., New York, 1941, p. 5.

31 ibid., p. 89.

32 Philip P. Wiener, *Evolution and the Founders of Pragmatism,* op. cit., pp. 191, 195, 198, 199, 200, 202.

33 'Theaetetus', *The Dialogues of Plato,* 3rd edn (trans. B. Jowett), Macmillan, New York, 1892, vol. IV, p. 205, 152A.

34 Otto Neurath, 'Foundations of the social sciences', *International Encyclopedia of Unified Sciences,* vol. 11, no. 1, p. 27.

35 Peter Medawar, *Induction and Intuition in Scientific Thought,* Methuen, London, 1969.

36 Mill, *System of Logic,* op. cit., bk VI, ch. X, s. 4.

37 K. R. Popper, *The Poverty of Historicism,* Routledge & Kegan Paul, London, 1957, p. 122.

38 K. R. Popper, *Conjectures and Refutations,* Routledge & Kegan Paul, London, 1963, p. 33.

39 ibid., p. 37.

40 Thomas Kuhn, *The Structure of Scientific Revolutions,* University of Chicago, Chicago, 1962.

41 See Paul Filmer, Michael Phillipson, David Silverman and David Walsh, *New Directions in Sociological Theory,* Collier-Macmillan, London, 1972.

42 See C. Arnold Anderson and Mary Jean Bowman, 'Theoretical considerations in educational planning', in *The World Year Book of Education, 1967: Educational Planning,* Evans, London, 1967.

Chapter 3

The Positivist Debate in Comparative Education – An Anglo-Saxon Perspective

Three books highlighted debates about and gave new impetus to the study of comparative education during the 1960s. My own *Problems in Education* was published in 1965, shortly after the appearance of Bereday's *Comparative Method in Education* (1964), and preceded by some four years *Toward a Science of Comparative Education* (1969)[1] by Harold Noah and Max Eckstein. Bereday, a product in part of the London School of Economics, applied the methods of induction explicitly and in my view accurately to the study of comparative education. Noah and Eckstein rejected some aspects of this approach but remained faithful to its main features in their hypothetico-inductive method. In *Comparative Studies and Educational Decision* (1968)[2] Edmund King criticised my position but paid no substantial attention to Bereday's inductionism and hypothetico-inductive and positivist developments in the literature in proposing his own rather eclectic methodology.

These initiatives should be evaluated in the light of methods developed by prewar scholars such as Isaac Kandel, Nicholas Hans and Friedrich Schneider.[3] All three men had a worldwide influence on the postwar development of comparative education. Hans worked with Joseph Lauwerys in London and inspired a new generation of comparativists. Kandel's influence was widely disseminated in the USA and elsewhere from Teachers College, Columbia.[4] Schneider's influence can be detected in the work of practically all German comparative educationists. Yet in spite of the national styles which developed under their influence, the methodological assumptions of Kandel, Hans and Schneider were sufficiently similar to give a measure of methodological unity to the field. They collected data and explained national systems and the differences between them in the light of cultural traditions. Data collection and explanatory studies are components in the historical development of comparative education.

THE CLASSIFICATION AND COLLECTION OF DATA

Carefully written though the early reports were, they did not add greatly to a 'science of comparative'. The categories proposed by Jullien were used to some extent but the problems associated with the observation and classification of educational facts did not receive very explicit attention although the collection of national information improved.

Some principles were established, however. For example, in his report on Prussian education Victor Cousin had stated what kind of data he collected. He 'invariably followed one course, first to procure the laws and regulations, and render myself perfect master of them, next to verify them by an accurate and detailed inspection'.[5] Cousin's observations touched on the responsibilities of parents and communities and the content and supervision of education and special education (schools for handicapped children). At the request of his government Cousin observed primary schools and teacher training in Prussia and Holland. Both reports were translated into English (by Sarah Austin and Leonard Horner respectively) and are among the more sophisticated of the early reports.

Horace Mann's principal interest was in the methods of teaching and the ways teachers maintained discipline in primary schools in twelve European countries. He placed them in rank order on his criteria of quality but Mann did not pursue systematically his interest in comparative education. As the first US Commissioner of Education Henry Barnard did. He collected in the *American Journal of Education*[6] historical accounts of developments in various countries by publishing details of legislation, extracts from foreign reports and periodical articles. From the start he hoped that the US Bureau of Education would be able to collect statistical data. This had already been attempted by several state boards of education but the US Office was to do it on a nationwide basis – in itself an interesting comparative task. He appreciated how difficult it would be to get complete returns from the states and cities of his own country but under his successors at the Bureau, John Eaton[7] and N. H. R. Dawson,[8] the size of the annual reports grew and the mass of statistical data reproduced became enormous. Salary schedules, teacher–pupil ratios, the proportion of female teachers, per capita costs, the total national expenditure on education and percentage attendance were among the statistical data collected. Eaton recognised that if international statistics were to be collected some agreement on nomenclature would be required but given that, educational statistics would promote the development of a positive science of education.

Implicit in the views expressed by Sadler and Harris is a rejection of positivism and the notion that a universal model for education could be induced from 'facts'. Nevertheless the period of cultural borrowing was followed by a stage during which some of the requirements laid down by Jullien were restated and further developed. Sadler, for example, is given credit for adding a clear sociological dimension to comparative education by asserting that school systems could be understood only in their relationships with other aspects of a social system. This view has subsequently been accepted by all comparative educationists. It has meant that classification systems have had to take account of the socioeconomic and political infrastructures of education and moreover that school systems *per se* have become only one aspect of careful comparative description.[9]

The rejection of 'cultural borrowing' by Sadler and Harris,[10] who met, resulted perhaps in more emphasis being placed on the formulation of general principles of policy from comparative studies. Sadler and Harris held that these generalisations should have predictive value. The search for 'principles', 'generalisations' and 'laws' with predictive power is implicit in the methods advocated by the philosophers of science during the nineteenth century. The successful predictions made during the eighteenth and nineteenth centuries from Newton's Laws of Motion had added greatly to the confidence of the natural scientists. The positivist social scientists hoped to emulate their colleagues and worked out methods of inquiry which they hoped would result in the formulation of some general laws of societal development. If laws of societal development, why not laws of educational development? Such an objective would fit logically into methods based on induction.

Bereday's book in particular located the desire of the pioneers of comparative education to describe and explain differences between educational systems and to discover general principles which inform all systems firmly in the context of the inductive method. It reflected the positivism of postwar social scientists and the canons of induction described by Mill. Basically Bereday proposed in *Comparative Method in Education* that data should first be collected and classified. In order to do this research workers must acquire language skills and be trained to observe aspects of school systems at first hand. Thus equipped they could collect and classify empirical data objectively. Parenthetically in his debate with King, Bereday suggested that enthnocentrism interferes more with the interpretation of data (about which more later) than with the objective collection of them. Colligation as the first and vital empirical stage in Mill's method of induction was accepted by Bereday, who proposed how to systematise the process and illustrated how it should be done.

This commitment to the colligation of information was perfectly in line with the proposals of Jullien, who recognised that it could be done on an international scale only if appropriate agencies were established. He recommended that an international commission should be set up to collect and arrange relevant data about schools. Pedro Rossello[11] saw in this suggestion a concept which influenced the growth of national bureaux such as the Musée Pédagogique in Paris, the US Bureau of Education in Washington and Sadler's London Office and international agencies such as the International Bureau of Education in Geneva and Unesco in Paris. Certainly, as mentioned, these bureaux have gathered in an impressive amount of information. It is doubtful, however, whether principles of policy have been induced from the 'facts' collected in this way. On the contrary, normative models of what a national system of education should look like have determined what 'facts' ought to be collected. Data collection is important but not, in my view, at the first stage of inquiry.

It has to be done on the basis of a clearly established classificatory system. During the 1960s a good deal of progress was made through the co-operation of individual scholars and officials working in international agencies. At a meeting at the Unesco Institute for Education in Hamburg in 1963 working groups proposed systems for classifying data about educational systems, about their infrastructures and about individual schools. Hilker played a prominent role in identifying stages and levels of educational provision which have subsequently been used to classify information on a comparative basis. A report, *Relevant Data in Comparative Education,*[12] was presented by myself and Saul Robinsohn which went some way towards establishing major categories for the classification of educational data but was less successful in building up categories for infrastructure information. According to Leo Fernig in a lecture delivered in London the report made a contribution to the descriptive accounts of national systems prepared by Unesco and the International Bureau of Education (IBE) in Geneva.

For many years both organisations have systematically collected information about national systems of education. Rossello's[13] efforts at the IBE should not be disregarded; they enabled him to discern trends of development and to classify for future reference emerging aims of educational development. The structure of the *World Survey of Education* improved as it went through its various editions. As director of the IBE in Geneva, Fernig promoted documentation services based upon carefully worked out classificatory systems. The Unesco/IBE publication *Education Thesaurus*[14] represents an extremely detailed breakdown of educational terms and therefore identifies in a systematic manner most aspects of education. An equally extensive taxonomy has been developed under the guidance of Lauwerys for Unesco.[15] Its International Standard Classification of Education (ISCED) identifies courses in each of several stages of education and in non-compulsory adult education. The courses are classified according to length and type, and so on, in a manner that would allow a very complete profile of information if it were required to be gathered about any national system of education. Finally, at the international level mention should be made of improvements in the collection of statistics.[16] Not all the difficulties of establishing indicators on the basis of which unambiguous data can be obtained from statistical offices have been solved, but many of those which faced Hans in the 1930s have been overcome by international agencies in recent years. Today reasonably trustworthy statistics are available.

In addition to descriptive studies prepared by international agencies the number of area-studies and case-studies grew during the 1960s. Most of them were case-studies rather than systematic area-studies based on a clear classificatory system.[17] Collectively these books add to our knowledge of foreign systems but cannot easily be used for comparative purposes in spite of the efforts made by some editors of some series to provide categories into which data should be placed by individual authors. Reports by national agencies on their own system of education or on foreign systems are frequently clearly structured but much less interpretive.[18] They provide an additional source of information about several major aspects of an educational system. The proliferation of area- and case-studies which do not provide a basis for comparisons suggests that there is little value in descriptive studies unless they are prepared either with some clear problem or problems in mind (case-studies) or in accordance with a well-defined ideal-typical model (area-studies). The further development of classificatory systems is necessary so that the systematic collection of educational data can be quickly done when the need arises. A good deal of progress has been made since Jullien established his categories for the classification of information.

EXPLANATORY STUDIES

The pioneers' second major aim, namely, the desire to understand systems of education and explain differences between them, received attention in Bereday's method. His views about explanation did not differ noticeably from those of Mill who explained events by inducing relationship hypotheses from objective data. For Mill an event or collection of events (or facts) is explained by relating it (or them) to an antecedent event (or events), so linking 'causes' and 'effects'. One question arising from this position is whether relationships expressed in hypotheses are reversible. Some, in physics and chemistry, are reversible and the simplest hypothesis can be mathematically stated as $y = mx + c$. It is unlikely that social relationships are reversible and thus causal explanations or hypotheses presuppose a cause–effect model or a historical sequence of events. Bereday proposed to interpret educational data by appealing to explanatory hypotheses drawn from established social sciences – economics, psychology, anthropology, political science, history and philosophy.

For Bereday the comparative approach begins when information about national systems of education is juxtaposed in order to highlight differences and similarities. This procedure clearly depends upon the classification of material and from it comparative hypotheses are derived. Such hypotheses state the purpose for which comparison is to be made. Bereday illustrated this procedure by hypothesising that strong executive powers do not guarantee progress in the reform of education and that, on the contrary, the conservatism of bureaucracies prevents or holds up rapid change. In the light of such an induced hypothesis Bereday maintained that the purpose of final comparative studies was to prove the hypothesis. Thus far, without providing quantifiable indicators, Bereday followed Mill and implied how the methods of agreement and difference might be used.

He went further. By naming Kandel, Schneider, Robert Ulich, Rossello and Lauwerys as proponents of total analysis Bereday seemed to accept Mill's final goal, the discovery of general, unconditional laws of social development. 'As in all social sciences', he wrote, 'this final stage of the discipline is concerned with the formulation of "laws" or "typologies" that permit an international understanding and a definition of the complex interrelations between the schools and the people they serve. The total analysis, as the term indicates, deals with the imminent (presumably immanent) general forces upon which all systems are built.'[19]

I do not think Kandel or Hans had in mind the possibility that from carefully classified comparative data general laws of historical and educational development might be induced. I am less certain about Schneider's hopes. Clearly Rossello was simply interested in identifying 'trends' of development from documentary and modest statistical evidence. With the possible exception of Schneider none of these pioneers was a historicist in the way in which Popper uses the term. This tradition is absent from Anglo-Saxon comparative education but finds expression in the methodological assumptions of Soviet scholars and in the writing of Naiden Tschakarov of Bulgaria.[20]

Hans and Kandel were, however, interested in middle-range explanatory hypotheses. They identified 'causes', 'factors', or 'determinants' within a Millsian framework and both, consequently, were satisfied to assume that the presence of one of several factors in any situation would give rise to the same or similar outcomes elsewhere. In the *New Era in Education*,[21] for example, Kandel was convinced that all centralised systems of education were undemocratic. One of Hans's most persistently held explanatory hypotheses was that the power of organised religion would inhibit the growth of universal schooling.

Each of these pioneers conceptualised the study of systems of education in terms of factors and both stressed nationalism. Hans, for example, enunciated 'five factors which make an ideal nation: (i) unity of race, (ii) unity of religion, (iii) unity of language, (iv) compact territory and (v) political sovereignty'.[22] Kandel was less specific. 'Nationalism, then, implies a common language, common customs and a common culture.'[23] Their conceptions of what constitutes a nation were similar and both Hans and Kandel chose to describe the infrastructures of national systems of education in terms of generalised factors. In this they anticipated a position adopted by Noah.

Noah and Eckstein remained in the tradition of Kandel and Hans and as positivists inherited the 'factors' approach. They acknowledged Bereday's influence but rejected his view that inquiry should start with objective observation and classification on the grounds that such procedures lead to indiscriminate amassing of data and the dominance of *a priori* assumptions.[24] Their discussion of travellers' tales did less than justice, at least by implication, to Bereday's more systematic acceptance of Mill's inductive method. In so far as they attempted to justify their methodology, they leaned heavily on M. R. Cohen and E. Nagel who in *An Introduction to Logic and Scientific Method* stated: 'It is an utterly superficial view, therefore, that the truth is to be found by "studying the facts".'[25] For these authors a problem demanding solutions is the occasion for inquiry. Cohen and Nagel then proceeded to discuss how universal propositions may be established by intuitive, perfect and incomplete induction by using sampling techniques. One of their main concerns was to show how a guiding hypothesis is tested. Having disposed of Mill's first requirement, objective observation, Cohen and Nagel described in some detail Mill's methods of experimental inquiry designed to establish invariable relationships of increasing generality by using his methods of agreement, difference, agreement and difference, concomitant variation and the method of residues. All were designed to discover the 'cause' of phenomena. Cohen and Nagel, however, regarded Mill's view that the universe is governed by general laws as unhelpful and thus were not historicists. They found the doctrine of plurality of causes 'plausible only if we analyse the causes into a larger number of distinct types than we do to the effects'.[26] Modern prescriptions identify 'causes' as independent variables and 'effects' as dependent variables; otherwise they are logically derived from the methods of inquiry advocated by Mill and such interpreters as Cohen and Nagel.

Noah and Eckstein applied these *hypothetico-inductive* methods of inquiry to comparative education research but carefully avoided emphasising 'cause(s)' or 'effect(s)' and in discussing causal explanation were at pains 'to emphasise that the close correlations between variables by no means imply causal relationships one way or another'.[27] Many of their reservations echoed those I had made about sociological laws in various articles. The authors, moreover, agreed with me in asserting that correlation studies may justify the contention that 'predictions may be ventured in one sector of a policy if something fairly definite is known about future levels in another sector'.[28] There are, however, major differences in our two positions. Part of their discussion about functional relationships which refer to co-variation was suitably cautious. It should, however, be placed in context. They implied, for example, that statements may incorporate 'a clear formulation of cause-and-effect relationships'[29] but stated that 'the precise mechanism by which *x* causes *y* may still remain unstated'.[30] The pessimism which informed these assertions is justified since many correlation studies are of little interest unless the direction of influence is known or unless the processes of change described in the functional statement are reversible. If predictions are to be made then the establishment of co-variations is of little practical value unless they make it possible 'to extrapolate from the past to the present, thus providing at the very least a way of explaining how the past has generated the present'.[31] Pessimism was tinged with hope because the manipulation and quantification of data 'may one day lead to statements of immense value about the causative factors of change'.[32]

Thus optimistically Noah and Eckstein proposed no more than Hans and Kandel by suggesting that names of systems (i.e. countries) should be replaced by the names of concepts (e.g. variables). In *Relevant Methods in Comparative Education,* for example, Noah claimed that: 'A comparative study is essentially an attempt as far as possible to replace the names of systems (countries) by the names of concepts (variables).'[33] Once this has been done, hypothetical correlations (between variables) can be tested not dynamically by changing one variable and observing consequent change in the other but statically by plotting the results of measuring two variables in as many systems (countries) as possible. How functional statements are formulated other than on initial browsing was not made clear by Noah. Perhaps the processes are similar to those which produced the intuitive, research insights of historian comparativists. If neither the pioneers nor their present-day followers include historicists, both groups include determinists. In short historian comparative educationists have been succeeded by social scientist comparative educationists some of whom share many assumptions of the early pioneers.

One major difference between these two generations of positivists lies not so much in their intentions but in the testing procedures they use. Both seek to find the residual 'cause' of the differences between national systems of schooling. The historians looked for the antecedent 'causes' of events by studying historical documents. The new generation quantifies procedures and, by plotting one variable against another, runs a regression analysis in the hope that a linear relationship between the variables will be established. Techniques developed by social scientists and found in any introductory text on social science research methods dominate this new positivistic approach to comparative education research.[34] Among these techniques the manipulation, selection and collection of data, sampling procedures, measurement, the empirical testing of hypotheses by methods proposed by Mill and the reporting of conclusions in the form of levels of co-variation loom large in comparative studies of this kind and have dominated, as stated earlier, the research of economists engaged by the OECD to undertake comparative studies in the economics of education and particularly IEA's studies of educational achievement.

A second major difference lies in the type of variable or factor regarded as important in attempts to explain differences between systems. The Hansian factors – language, race, religion, geographical territory and ideology – have their origins in the distant history of a nation. For Hans their influence was exercised through ideas passed on from one person to another. The new generation of comparative educationists use more immediate factors in order to explain differences. Social class position, familial background, the level of investment in education, methods of teaching, the way in which schools are organised, and so on, are the variables to which attention is paid. Choice of variable is in part determined by the ease with which it can be quantified. Variables that can be operationalised and measured appeal to comparative educationists who wish to make their research empirical. They also conceptualise them so that their influence can be examined without regard for the ideas individuals may express or hold. These immediate variables are regarded by those who use them as objective. The way in which they interact can be examined in correlation studies. So, for example, social class can be operationalised using census data, it can be quantified by the research worker and its relationship to access to education (which can be operationalised and quantified) can be examined in what is taken to be empirical research.

INDUCTION AND COMPARATIVE TESTING

One claim made to support the kind of testing advocated by Noah and Eckstein is that the comparative method in the social sciences is a satisfactory alternative to the kind of experimental testing that can be carried out in the natural sciences. To be sure the technical difficulties involved in social scientific experimentation are very great. The moral objections are, moreover, frequently decisive in preventing experiments on people or communities. Consequently the claims made about comparative tests based on Mill's canons of induction should be examined.

The strength and weaknesses of hypothetico-inductive comparative education tests can be illustrated, in a very simplified way, by showing how the contrived results of a possible research study can be represented graphically.

Let us suppose that we wish to test the view that the wealth of a nation is related to the amount of schooling it provides. Let us operationalise these variables, and assume that per capita income (y) and per capita years of schooling (x) are appropriate measures. Research makes it possible to ascribe numbers for x and y in seven nations A, B, C, D, E, F and G. Let us suppose that the figures in Table 3.1 are obtained.

Table 3.1

Nation	Per capita income (US $)	Per capita schooling (years)
A	500	4
B	1,900	6
C	1,250	8
D	1,050	10
E	750	12
F	1,800	14
G	2,000	16

These results can be represented graphically (Figure 3.1). The equation for the straight line which more or less passes through the majority of points is $y = mx + c$, where m is the tangent of the angle giving the line a slope and c is a constant which suggests that in a country in which there are no schools to provide education the people will have some income.

Figure 3.1

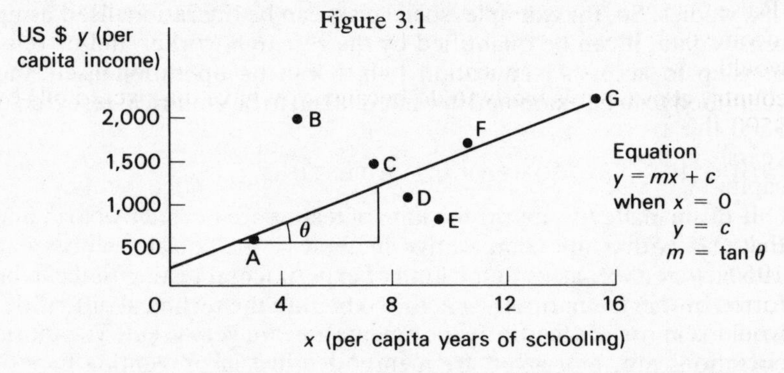

Figure 3.1 shows that (at least in the functional matrix) individuals in wealthier countries have attended school for more years than is the case in less wealthy countries. This fairly commonsense view is sup-

ported by the fact that points A, C, D, F and G fall more or less on a straight line, the equation for which is (in words) per capita income is equal to some constant multiplied by per capita years of schooling plus a constant amount of income which is provided under circumstances where per capita education is zero. In other words, the evidence (five countries out of seven fall on the line) confirms, as Bereday would hope, the initial hypothesis.

The nations B and E are interesting because they do not conform to the general pattern. Wealthy nation B provides less education in schools than would be expected. On the other hand, in poor country E individuals attend schools for more years than we might expect from our general proposition. Further regression analysis is necessary according to this method to find the residual cause of these non-typical cases. Very sophisticated techniques have been developed to explain how it is that some nations are not typical. In economic terms one of the most important residual causes of wealth was thought to be education. Our contrived test is in a sense designed to confirm this proposition.

Let us examine, however, the typical cases and see what assumptions are sometimes made in the light of this confirming evidence. A major claim would be that if nation A increased its per capita years of schooling by four years (from four to eight) its per capita income would rise from $500 to more than $1,000. On the other hand, what can nation E do to raise its per capita income? And what can nation B do to increase the amount of schooling it provides? Our general proposition does not tell us.

Education planners would like to think that on the basis of this comparative test they can advise governments to invest in education. They would like to say with certainty to the government of nation A: 'Raise the age of compulsory attendance by one year and the per capita income of your country will rise by $25.' It is less certain that planners would say to the government of nation D: 'If the per capita of your country rises (as it is likely to do because you have discovered oil) by $500 the average period of schooling will subsequently rise by two years.' They are more likely to say: 'We hope when and if your per capita income rises you will increase the provision of schooling.'

If this argument seems foolishly oversimplified it should be noted that many governments towards the end of the 1950s and during the 1960s were persuaded to pour money into schooling or were comforted by the claims made by economists that investment in education would reap its economic benefits. It might, I concede, under certain circumstances, but not inevitably and under all circumstances as indeed we now know only too well.

There is no logical justification for asserting from a general proposition (in the form of a relationship statement) which has been confirmed by this kind of comparative research that an increment of change in one variable in any of the countries tested (and by extension to any other country) will result in an increment of change in the other variable unless, and this is the crux of the matter, we assume that these general propositions have universal validity (i.e. hold good regardless of circumstances), and that social events are determined by factors such as those operationalised by many social scientists. To use such testing to justify policy decisions a planner must be, in my view, a positivist and a determinist. I am neither.

Consequently I consider the efforts of Noah and Eckstein and like-minded research workers who have used methods worked out by Mill laudable but mistaken. Elsewhere I argue that 'there is room in comparative education research for studies which are now regarded as anti-thetical rather than complementary. Indeed progress will depend on variety in research.' The use made of the results of research is important. Static pictures in the form of regression analysis lines drawn from comparative data at best confirm that a particular policy proposal (with certain goals in mind) is not completely nonsensical. Many policies are legitimised by ideology. Others do not need sophisticated, expensive empirical research to convince administrators that proposed policies make some kind of sense. A danger, exemplified by events in the 1960s, is that comparative tests, regardless of logic, might persuade those responsible for the formulation and adoption of policy that the general propositions have been thoroughly and scientifically tested. They have not, because the techniques are based on the assumption that general propositions are valid regardless of the context in which they are to be applied as policy. In other words, positivism assumes that universal general laws can be induced from classified data. Such examples are not contingent, that is, dependent on circumstances. This is quite contrary to the view taken by Popper in describing the hypothetico-deductive method of scientific inquiry to which I shall turn in another chapter.

The techniques are far more sophisticated than this simple account suggests. But I have serious reservations about the use made of this comparative regression-analysis testing. My first criticism is that too little attention is usually paid to conceptual analysis prior to operationalising variables. The assumption that internationally valid measures can be used depends on the possibility that, on the basis of cross-national philosophical analysis, unambiguous and meaningful indicators can be identified and operationalised. This assumption is barely tenable. Consider the meaning of social class, for example. To accept a Marxian interpretation of the term depends on our willingness to accept the notion that class conflict is inevitable under capitalism. We are under no such obligation when social class is defined in terms of the rank order of occupations on a Registrar General's scale. Implicit in the ranking is, of course, a scale of values. In other words ideologies, which differ, give specific meaning to terms which may seem perfectly unambiguous when viewed from only one ideological position.

My second criticism is that the 'initial browsing' proposed by Noah and Eckstein does not satisfy my requirement that useful research should start with the identification and analysis of a technical problem. Social scientific hypotheses, to be sure, may be dreamed up. They cannot, however, be tested experimentally and therefore more care should be taken to examine the ways in which hypotheses are formulated and the grounds on which they are adopted.

My third criticism is that the *hypothetico-inductive* method of Noah and Eckstein pays too little attention to the 'living spirit' of a nation's educational system. This is not given overtly a distinctive place among the variables that replace discussion of systems of countries. The omission of any account of the specific initial conditions in assessing the outcome of policy stems directly from this approach to the scientific study of education.

In practice, planners have advised governments to adopt panaceas as universal solutions to macro-problems. They have tried to find the residual 'causes' of failure, underachievement, slow economic growth, political instability, and get rid of them. At the same time they have tried to promote the 'causes' of success. Had they succeeded, a world-wide educational millennium might indeed have arrived. It is not yet on the horizon. We have had many educational panaceas offered to us – local control of schools, the democratisation of schooling, the expansion of higher education, investment in education, new science syllabuses, better curricula – and few outstanding successes in the past thirty years. Most of these policies, far from being induced as Jullien hoped they would be from facts and observations, have been derived from ideologies, hopes, expectations, that is, from models of education conceived in terms of what a few men and women think 'ought to be the case'. The current universal model of education is a normative one. Data throughout the world are collected in the light of it. At enormous expense social scientists have found universal explanations of why nations have not succeeded in realising this model in practice and why within schools children continue to fail or are low-achievers.

ETHNOMETHODOLOGY

Gouldner's criticism of traditional Western sociology was both of its methods and of the use to which its insights and findings were put. I believe that in *The Open Society* Popper anticipated by many years the kind of criticism Gouldner made. In the USA and Britain sociologists quickly turned to members of the Frankfurt school for inspiration and created a vogue for phenomenology and ethnomethodology.[35]

In this debate my anti-positivist position ought to be well known. My points of departure in the study of comparative education are found in the assumptions that inform post-relativity philosophies of the natural sciences and in pragmatism. These assumptions will be discussed in a subsequent chapter.

Unfortunately my position has been misunderstood. In *Problems in Education* I stated, in retrospect too briefly, that 'within any society there are causal situations whose operation can be understood through the establishment of sociological laws'.[36] I added: 'It is the study of relevant sociological laws that constitutes the science of education, or if preferred the scientific study of education.'[37] I still believe this. Unfortunately, if I recall correctly a brief discussion with Max Eckstein, he and Noah took up this challenge in *Toward a Science of Comparative Education* but placed their discussion of functional propositions and correlationship statements (as I have tried to show) in a framework which I do not accept – namely, that exemplified in Cohen and Nagel's book.

King, in articles and in *Comparative Studies and Educational Decision,* took up the challenge in another fashion. In a number of articles he claimed Popper's approval for his interpretation of some aspects of the latter's position. I have no wish to question this. Indeed, in so far as King concentrated his attention on Popper's discussion of 'trends' and the 'logic of the situation', I agree with his interpretation. Moreover I welcome him as an ally in his anti-deterministic stand. He might have criticised somewhat earlier those positivists among comparative educationists who have failed to acknowledge the implications of post-relativity science and remain in a very real sense positivists and determinists. He is simply mistaken when he tries to make me a determinist by ascribing to me an interpretation of 'sociological laws' which I do not hold and could not possibly hold as a follower of Popper.

King's own anti-deterministic position and the contribution he and his colleagues made to methodology in their research on post-compulsory education are of interest in view of the debates between positivists, ethnomethodologists and Popperians, and the shift of emphasis in sponsored research in comparative education.

The high point of correlation studies was reached during the first part of the 1960s under the influence of economists, psychologists and sociologists. Towards the end of the decade members of the Centre for Educational Research and Innovation (CERI), set up in association with the OECD,[38] were giving new impetus to the kind of comparative studies promoted by *The World Year Book of Education,* the research on curriculum, teacher training and other aspects of education undertaken by Robinsohn and his colleagues at the Max Planck Institute in Berlin,[39] by Urban Dahloff in Gøteburg and at the Institute for International Education in Frankfurt[40] and in a number of other centres. The IBE in Geneva[41] launched a series of innovation studies on individual countries which supplemented CERI's international innovation research. Apart from these cross-national and case-studies, thousands of model-building articles and substantive accounts of innovation and development found their way into the literature.[42] Many of them restated in somewhat different ways the concerns traditionally shown by comparative educationists who were interested in the reform of education. The OECD itself undertook careful and critical studies of national policies in education which clearly were intended to take account of the particular circumstances of the nation whose policies were under review.

This welcome move away from correlation studies owed little to an overt reformulated philosophy of scientific inquiry. To be sure the problem(-solving) approach to comparative education research had been sufficiently well developed to offer an alternative to positivism and induction but it was overtly phenomenology and ethnomethodology which brought into question the assumptions of established social scientists. In so far as these critics were attacking positivism it is clear that by implication comparative educationists who accept positivism are required to defend themselves against the kind of criticism that had already had its effect on some sociologists. While some comparative educationists have shown an interest in and been impressed by the questions asked by E. Husserl, A. Schutz, H. Garfinkel, J. Habermas and P. Bourdieu, no comparative educationist has boldly followed through in his research the assumptions of this group of anti-positivists. King, in stressing ecology and the logic of a situation, seems to me to have come as near as anybody to embracing some of the views expressed, and in his research to putting them into practice. His account of how his research undertaken with Jennifer Mundy and Christine Moor for *Post Compulsory Education in Western Europe*[43] took shape as it progressed suggested that the involvement of the researchers with those who were being 'researched' became increasingly a feature of the work.

In some sense participatory research was always implied by a leading comparative educationist. Vernon Mallinson's[44] account of how knowledge of 'national character' should be acquired edged towards a participatory ethnomethodological approach. The doubts I have long held about the possibilities of knowing more than one or two countries in the way Mallinson suggested also apply to a methodology which implies that we should seek to understand society not by examining the stated ideas of a small elite but by participating with ordinary members of it in the construction of their social worlds. The suggestion that relationships between ideas and their social contexts can best be understood by looking at the structure of the commonsense world of everyday life has value. It may be contrasted with my proposal that constitutions, manifestos, legislation and philosophy should be studied to establish ideal-typical models. These latter may give little information about human motivation and behaviour whereas the value of participatory research lies in the insights into what people deeply believe and how they act.

The full implications of accepting participatory research as *the* research method in comparative education are, to me, not clear. At best it seems to offer some way of checking empirically the usefulness and validity of generalisations (and predictions made from them) derived from documentary evidence and test results. Clearly a research worker ought to see for himself what is going on by visiting foreign countries. Such visits should not be regarded as prerequisites, necessary in order first to collect data, as Bereday might have us believe, but as a way of testing assumptions. I question the feasibility in comparative research of using techniques developed by sociologists to collect data on the assumption that the participants are creating their own social world. I doubt the viability of phenomenology and ethnomethodology as satisfactory alternatives to positivism and psychometric and sociometric techniques and consider that a radical swing from positivism and induction (desirable though such a move is) to phenomenology and ethnomethodology is neither necessary nor useful. Nevertheless I hope committed ethnomethodologists will work out the implications of their method for comparative education research and attempt to apply it in practice.

By drawing attention to the positions exemplified by Bereday, Noah and Eckstein and King, I do not wish to imply that debates about methodology have been restricted to these authors. They are representative at least of discussions that have taken place in the USA and Britain. They have some bearing on the clearly defined approach of Soviet, DDR and Bulgarian comparative educationists and their books are frequently the foundations on which texts in comparative education in French, German and Spanish are built. My purpose in this chapter has been to highlight some of the differences in method which are found in comparative education before going on to clarify the assumptions on which my own approach is based.

NOTES AND REFERENCES: CHAPTER 3

This chapter is based on Brian Holmes, 'The positivist debate in comparative education – an Anglo-Saxon perspective', *Comparative Education,* vol. 13, no. 2, June 1977 (Carfax, Oxford), pp. 115–32.

1 Harold Noah and Max Eckstein, *Toward a Science of Comparative Education,* Collier Macmillan, London, 1969, and Bereday, *Comparative Method in Education,* op. cit.

2 Edmund J. King, *Comparative Studies and Educational Decision,* Bobbs-Merrill, New York, 1968.

3 Hans, *Comparative Education,* op. cit.
Kandel, *Comparative Education,* op. cit.
Friedrich Schneider, *Triebkräfte der Pädagogik der Völker,* Otto Muller, Salzburg, 1947, and *Vergleichende Erziehungswissenschaft,* Quelle & Meyer, Heidelberg, 1961.
See also Oskar Anweiler for a historical survey of the development of comparative education in Eastern Europe in 'Von der pädagogischen Auslandkunde zur vergleichenden Erziehungswissenschaft, Wie Entwicklung im Spiegel pädagogischer Zeitschriften von 1880 bis 1930', *Pädagogische Rundshau* (Ratingen), vol. 20, 1966.

4 Kandel edited the *International Year Book of Education* from 1924 to 1944. These volumes, prepared under the auspices of Teachers College, Columbia University, are of immense historical value providing, as they do, accounts of policies and practices in countries throughout the world.

5 Cousin, *The State of Education in Prussia,* op. cit., p. 3.

6 H. Barnard edited the *American Journal of Education* for many years. He kept his readers up to date with current issues by providing details of legislation and periodicals.

7 John Eaton was in charge of the US Bureau of Education and helped to add statistical information to the historical documentary data collected by Barnard for the Bureau. He hoped to make the data scientifically objective, based on agreed terminology.

8 Dawson was in charge of the Bureau for several years. Under his direction the volume of statistics on salary scales, enrolments, per capita and total costs, proportion of girls in school, and so on, grew enormously.

9 See the intention of the organisers of an expert meeting convened by the Unesco Institute for Education in Hamburg in 1963. The outcome was *Relevant Data in Comparative Education,* Unesco, Hamburg, 1963, presented by Brian Holmes and Saul B. Robinsohn.

10 See Sadler, *Education in Germany,* op. cit., and Harris, *Annual Report, 1891,* op. cit.

11 Rossello, *Les Précurseurs*, op. cit.

12 B. Holmes and S. B. Robinsohn, *Relevant Data in Comparative Education*, Unesco, Hamburg, 1963.

13 As deputy director of IBE and professor in the university of Geneva, Rossello had much to do with the collection of material which went into the IBE's *International Year Book of Education* which has recently been revived.

14 Unesco/IBE, *Education Thesaurus,* Unesco/IBE, Paris, 1973 – a faceted list of terms for indexing – owes much to the initiative and sustained interest of Leo Fernig in data collection.

15 Unesco's *International Standard Classification of Educational Data, ISCED Handbook,* Unesco, Paris, 1975, is based on years of work by J. A. Lauwerys with the help in the first instance of John Bowers and Brian Holmes. See also Unesco, *International Standardisation of Educational Statistics,* Unesco, Paris, 1958, final report of the director general.

16 See, for example, Unesco/IBE, *International Guide to Education Systems ibedata,* Unesco, 1979, prepared by Brian Holmes *et al.,* designed to provide national profiles, and the work carried out by the OECD. The latter has influenced the criteria on which statistics are collected, for example, OECD, *Statistics of the Occupational and Educational Structure of the Labour Force in 53 Countries,* OECD, Paris, 1969.

17 Several series of national studies were launched, for example, E. J. King (ed.), *Schools, Society and Progress,* published by Pergamon, and Brian Holmes (ed.), World Education series, published by Routledge & Kegan Paul and the World Education series published by David & Charles.

18 A series of national profiles has been prepared by the British Council and is to be

published by Wiley. These profiles are not intended to highlight problems. Accounts provided by the national ministries of education at the request of the IBE in Geneva are not controversial. Reports produced by foreign experts on selected national systems of education for the OECD have roused more controversy. Soviet comparative educationists such as Dr Zoya Malkova and Dr Vera Lapchinskaya tend to be area specialists; the former is an expert on US education, the latter on the English grammar school. Their students have taken special aspects of these systems as subjects for research.

19 Bereday, *Comparative Method in Education,* op. cit., p. 25.

20 Several articles on comparative education method are to be found in *Vergleichende Pädagogik,* published by Volk & Wissen Volkseigener Verlag in East Berlin. It reflects the research and comparative interests of members of the German Central Institute of Education. See N. Tschakarov, 'Methodologische Probleme der Vergleichenden Pädagogik', *Vergleichende Pädagogik,* vol. 1, no. 4, 1967.

21 Kandel, *New Era in Education,* op. cit., reflects Kandel's preoccupation with national systems of administration and the distinction he drew between centralised and decentralised systems.

22 Hans, *Comparative Education,* op. cit., p. 9.

23 Kandel, *Comparative Education,* op. cit., p. 8.

24 Noah and Eckstein, *Toward a Science of Comparative Education,* op. cit.

25 M. R. Cohen and E. Nagel, *An Introduction to Logic and Scientific Method,* abridged edn, Routledge, London, 1947, p. 89.

26 ibid., p. 160.

27 Noah and Eckstein, op. cit., p. 68.

28 ibid., p. 73.

29 ibid., p. 96.

30 loc. cit.

31 loc. cit.

32 ibid., p. 74.

33 Reginald Edwards, Brian Holmes and John van de Graaf (eds), *Relevant Methods in Comparative Education,* Unesco, Hamburg, 1974, p. 14.

34 C. Arnold Anderson and Mary Jean Bowman exemplify this approach. Harold J. Noah and Max A. Eckstein illustrated how the techniques can be used in (eds), *Scientific Investigation in Comparative Education,* Collier Macmillan, London, 1969.

35 See, for example, publications by A. Schutz, H. Garfinkel, P. Bourdieu, H. Passeron and P. L. Berger and T. Luckman.

36 Holmes, *Problems in Education,* op. cit., p. 53.

37 loc. cit.

38 Examples of studies prepared for CERI include *Alternative Educational Futures in the United States and in Europe,* OECD, Paris, 1972; *Recurrent Education: A Strategy for Lifelong Learning,* OECD, Paris, 1973; *The Nature of the Curriculum for the Eighties and Onwards,* OECD, Paris, 1972; *Creativity of the School,* OECD, Paris, 1973.

39 The Max Planck Institut für Bildungsforschung publishes *Studien and Berichte,* a list of research monographs included in each of the volumes. Among those of interest to comparative educationists, studies by Klaus Huhse, Werner Kalb, Peter Müller, Doris Elbers and Gisela Kahn illustrate the analytic research carried out. Saul B. Robinsohn *et al., Schulreform im Gesellschaftlichen Prozess* (3 vols), Klett Verlag, Stuttgart, 1970, represents an approach to the analysis of school reform.

40 The Deutschen Institut für Internationale Pädagogische Forschung has prepared a number of area and special studies of value to comparative educationists. See *Sonderdruck aus Mitterlungen and Nachrichten des Deutschen Instituts für Internationale Pädagogische Forschung,* Frankfurt am Main. Note should be taken of the publications from the Forschungsstelle für Vergleichende Erziehungswissenschaft

der Phillips-Universität, many of which deal with education in the Soviet Union and German Democratic Republic. Under Oskar Anweiler at Bochum in the Institut für Pädagogik the Centre for Comparative Educational Research publishes periodical papers and a *Bibliographische Mitteilungen*.

41 IBE innovation studies are by invited authors, for example, Unesco/IBE Experiments and Innovations in Education series, various titles from 1972 including *Innovations in Reading in Britain; Understanding change in Education*; and general national studies, e.g. Singapore.

42 Among many well-known authors may be cited H. G. Barnett, R. Chin, P. Dalen, E. G. Guba, R. G. Havelock, M. B. Miles and R. O. Carlson. A major study was undertaken by the OECD, *Case Studies of Educational Innovation,* OECD, Paris, 1972.

43 Edmund J. King, Christine H. Moor and Jennifer A. Mundy, *Post Compulsory Education,* Sage, London, 1974, and 2. *The Way Ahead,* Sage, London, 1975.

44 Mallinson, *An Introduction to Comparative Education,* 2nd edn, op. cit.

Chapter 4

A Framework for Analysis – 'Critical Dualism' (Conventionalism)

Constituents of the problem(-solving) approach in comparative education include:

(1) problem analysis or intellectualisation,
(2) hypothesis or policy solution formulation,
(3) the specification of initial conditions or the context,
(4) the logical prediction from adopted hypothesis of likely outcomes,
(5) the comparison of logical predicted outcomes with observable events.

My assumption is that 'problems' arise as a consequence of asynchronous social change and hence a theory of social change is needed if 'problem' analysis is to be successful and replicatable. Models are needed if the processes of policy (hypothesis) formulation, adoption and implementation are to be analysed and compared. Finally, a classificatory system is needed if relevant societal data are to be identified and if the outcomes of policy are to be anticipated. To meet all these needs I devised a classificatory system based on Popper's theory of 'critical dualism' or 'critical conventionalism'. It seemed to me to answer most of the dilemmas arising from the positivist-phenomenologist debate, allow problems to be analysed, specific initial conditions to be described and hypotheses to be formulated and used.

CRITICAL DUALISM (CONVENTIONALISM)

The 'critical dualism' or 'critical conventionalism' described in *The Open Society* seemed to me to take fully into account man's responsibility not only for the beliefs and values he is prepared to accept but for the institutions he sets up and operates. 'Critical dualism' made it possible for me, for the purposes of analysis, to draw a distinction between a social world of convention and a social world of institutions whose functioning can be understood in the light of law-like statements. Since this feature of my understanding of 'critical dualism' has been attacked and misunderstood it is necessary to spell out in some detail the principal assumptions on which it is based.

Popper describes critical dualism or critical conventionalism as the position reached when a conscious differentiation is made 'between the man-enforced normative laws or conventions, and the natural regularities which are beyond his power'.[1] He goes on to state that 'norms and normative laws can be made and changed by man'[2] by a decision or convention to observe them and consequently man is morally responsible for them. This is indeed a socially constructed world. But he goes on: 'this does not mean that all "social laws", i.e. all regularities of our social life, are normative and man imposed'.[3] There are 'important natural laws of social life also. For these, the term *sociological laws* seems appropriate.'[4] These laws, says Popper, are 'connected with the functioning of *social institutions*'[5] and play a role in our social life similar to natural laws in engineering. 'If we can formulate sociological laws and construct institutions on the basis of them we can build and supervise institutions which will increase our power for good or evil.'[6] I believe this assumption leads Popper to claim that, while total long-term social planning is theoretically indefensible and in practice leads to totalitarianism, piecemeal social engineering is within man's power. My claims for comparative education rest on this belief.

A little more should be said about normative statements and normative laws. They are man-made and can be accepted, rejected, or changed by man. Normative statements are commands – 'Thou shalt not kill' – and can usually be made into an 'ought' statement. Examples of normative statements are: 'All persons ought to be treated as equals.' 'All persons ought to be free.' 'All persons ought to have the right to work, to worship as they think fit and to enjoy the benefits of an education.' Noble declarations such as the USA Declaration of Independence or the United Nations Declaration of Human Rights omit the 'ought' but their intentions are plain. A careful study of national constitutions and major legislation reveals patterns of normative statements.

Normative laws connect normative statements. 'Thou shalt not kill. If you do you ought to be hanged' is one example of many normative laws which form the basis of national codes of behaviour and the intended consequences associated with acceptance or rejection of one side of the equation. It should be noted, however, that either side of a normative law may be rejected, thus changing it. 'Thou shalt not kill. If you do you ought not to be hanged' is a normative modification. Its new formulation may be: 'Thou shalt not kill. If you do you ought to be committed to gaol for life.'

Such normative statements and laws representing man's beliefs are part of the context in which schools are run. They must be known if we hope to understand how schools function. The establishment of an acceptable pattern of normative statements and normative laws for particular nations represents, for me, one of the most important of the many tasks a comparative educationist should tackle. For this reason I have spelled out in several articles ways in which I think normative patterns can be established and sources from which data for them can be drawn. They constitute important statements about the context or specific initial conditions under which a sociological or social law should be tested.

As for sociological laws, something needs to be said about their status and relevance in the study of education. They are neither normative nor prescriptive. Their function is to permit social regularities of a sequence of social events to be explained (predicted). They are the hypotheses on which the planned reform of education rests and consequently in terms of policy statements their status is different from that of normative laws. They correspond to the natural laws of physics, chemistry and biology from which, in engineering, predictions about the way machines and so on will behave can be made. Because my understanding of the characteristics of natural and sociological laws has been seriously misrepresented some common characteristics of both types of law within the framework of critical dualism should be restated.

First of all, the laws of physics and sociological laws are man-made statements remain, hypothetical, and if they are to be scientific should be refutable. They are, consequently, tentative and if we want to emphasise our uncertainty about their truth we refer to them as hypotheses. Careful and detailed observation about the data of our physical and social worlds need not, cf. Mill, and frequently does not, precede the formulation of physical and sociological laws. Mill's laws offer causal explanations by pointing to the antecedent 'causes' of subsequent 'events'. Popper's natural and sociological laws are used to explain events by prediction statements. Traditional scientists look backward to 'causes', modern scientists look forward to possible outcomes.

The second point is that natural and sociological laws are not universally valid: they are contingent. Consequently, to give an explanation two types of statement are needed: (1) a universal or general statement in the form of a natural or sociological law and (2) specific statements about the conditions under which the law is to be applied; such statements may be termed the initial conditions. The contingent validity of the laws of physics and sociological laws is fundamental to my position and has been since my rejection of Mill's inductivism. In practical terms it means that to make predictions, for example, about the effects of introducing a comprehensive school into a national system two types of statement should be made. 'If comprehensive schools are introduced and become more widespread, social equality will increase' constitutes a possible general hypothetical statement. The particular socioeconomic conditions of the nation into which this type of school is to be introduced need to be described to predict from or test this statement. For example, initial conditions in the USA differ from those in England, or in France, or in Sweden. Hence somewhat different outcomes may be anticipated in each of these countries when a similar institution, some sort of comprehensive school, is introduced into the educational system.

The third point is that the apparent confidence with which scientific predictions are made is misleading. Frequently they are very crude. And they are never certain, only probable. Lauwerys tells me that Otto Neurath preferred the analogy of betting. What odds would you lay that if this book were thrown out of a third-floor window it would fall to the ground? £10 to £1? Probably. £1,000 to £1? Possibly. Your life? No. The conditions under which the book is thrown out of the window must be known and they can rarely be known with the certainty that would justify betting your life on the outcome. But men do fly to the moon – and risk their lives.

The fourth point is that some events can be predicted and we can do little or nothing to prevent them. Popper gives the example of a typhoon. But, in contrast, we may be able to predict, he says, the kind of shelter we need to protect us from the typhoon. We can say how it should be constructed, in which direction it should face, and from what kinds of material it should be made. This second kind of prediction he calls a 'technological prediction', and argues that there can be something like a social technology. The methodology of the social sciences should aim at a technological social science. Piecemeal social engineering would, thereby, be facilitated.

In the realm of human events certain predictions can be made. It is clear that the epidemiological evidence on smoking makes statements possible about the chances of premature death for heavy cigarette smokers. We can anticipate that some 2 million persons will travel by train into London between stated hours during the morning of a given day. Insurance premiums are based on actuarial evidence and the anticipated behaviour patterns of specific groups of persons. The norms of behaviour among university professors encourages me to say in March that it is probable that Professor Y (about whom we know a good deal) will deliver his public lectures at a particular university in June. These examples should be sufficient to show that we are constantly anticipating social events and human behaviour. The odds we are willing to offer that our predictions will be confirmed by events vary enormously, and we rule out long-term prophecies.

Sociological laws apply to the functioning of societal institutions and are statements we make about relationships between institutions. If they are to be used in comparative education some idea of the range of institutions with which we are concerned should be identified. Clearly the school system as a collection of interrelated institutions is of particular interest to us. The school may be regarded as an institution which functions in an educational system and in a given national (or local) context. In schools, institutions such as the administration, the curriculum, examinations, classrooms, agencies of discipline, and so on, can be described and can be connected by formulating sociological laws about them. Outside the school there are economic, political (government), religious and social class institutions which we may assume are functionally related, not only to one another, but to educational institutions. Statements about relationships between educational and other societal institutions constitute hypotheses or sociological laws from which, together with statements about national specific conditions, predictions about the outcomes of education policy can be made.

In other words, in Dewey's conceptual framework, sociological laws are hypothetical policy solutions to identified problems. They are the basis on which the planned development of education should be built and, of course, they are statements which can and should be tested in experience.

NORMATIVE PATTERNS

Critical dualism (conventionalism) also suggested to me a way of establishing a classificatory framework which would help research workers to identify relevant conditions and make statements about them. I assumed that two patterns were important in any national context. One of them, the normative pattern, should include statements about the norms and normative laws which we assume men and women in a named nation recognise and are prepared to accept or reject. Techniques and models are required if out of the enormous range of normative statements are to be selected those relevant to our purpose. I have suggested (Chapter 6) ways of establishing normative patterns by using theoretical or rational constructs (ideal-typical models of the kind proposed by Max Weber) using philosophical sources and techniques of analysis and colligation. Choice of philosophers is somewhat arbitrary and the resulting pattern may not be nation-specific. Nation-specific, or actual, ideal-typical normative models can be derived from constitutions and legislation. Confirmation that normative patterns correspond to the beliefs held by men and women can be obtained by many empirical techniques. The relationship between 'philosophical' and empirical techniques in this realm of comparative research is one that needs further investigation.

In drawing up a pattern of normative statements theories of knowledge (epistemology), individuality (psychology) and society (political science, sociology) serve as classificatory criteria. How ought knowledge to be acquired? What should be its status? Who should legitimise it? How should individuals be regarded? How should they be treated? Again, how should communities and societies be organised? How and by whom ought they to be run? The answers to these questions will depend upon a philosopher's viewpoint. The extent to which the answers reflect personal belief and commitment is important in placing educational policies and practices in context. The assumption made by a comparative educationist is that national patterns of belief will differ, and indeed within a nation-state different normative patterns may vary on the basis of religion, race, class, sex, and so on. Nevertheless it is useful to assume that national institutions and major legislation, though subjects of debate, are likely to represent a measure of normative concensus. Thus the US Declaration of Independence, the constitution and its amendments are sources of a useful normative pattern for the USA.

Normative laws should also be included in a national ideal-typical model. Such statements include those which assert what relationships ought to exist between knowledge and the way society ought to be organised; or between the way individuals ought to be treated and the knowledge they ought to possess; or between statements about the way individuals ought to behave and the way society ought to be run. Examples of such normative laws have already been given.

Constructs of this kind may well indicate any consensus that exists. Certainly they provide a framework within which sense can be made of current political debates, cultural pluralism and educational discussions about aims and objectives. For it should be remembered that normative statements can be accepted or rejected. They constitute a major part of man's socially constructed social world. For this reason they make up that part of the social context over which men have direct and immediate control. This man-made context can be changed by statement actions. In open societies debates about what ought to be the case will be considerable. It is the relationship between normative statements (beliefs, values) and the extent to which they motivate behaviour that make societal predictions so uncertain. Social psychological theories suggest that the link between overt normative statements and behaviour (on which the operation of institutions depends) need be neither close nor stable.

The tests of coherence in relation to normative patterns are logical. A change in allegiance to one set of values in a traditional pattern without corresponding changes in all aspects of the pattern would, on my assumptions, be one source of a normative 'problem'. Again, the rejection of one side of a normative law without changing the other side may give rise to 'problems'. Practically any new constitution or new piece of legislation is likely to disturb the coherence of an ideal-typical national normative pattern for reasons which should become clear when the characteristics of two other patterns – the institutional and mental states – are discussed.

INSTITUTIONAL PATTERNS

The second main pattern of statements relates to institutions. Into this pattern should be placed descriptions of agencies of government, economic organisations, churches, schools, and so on. Taxonomies and models are needed if these descriptions are to be replicated and compared. I depend very much on a modification of Parson's *formal organisation* model to describe the statutory and non-statutory bodies that bring people together in the running of society. At the same time I have spent a great deal of time developing techniques for identifying and describing school systems and their infrastructures. In particular I worked closely with Saul B. Robinsohn when he was director of the Unesco Institute for Education in Hamburg attempting to classify relevant data in comparative education.[7] More recently I have co-operated with the International Bureau of Education in Geneva in the preparation of national education profiles.[8]

Relationship statements are also needed if the institutional pattern is to be useful. The characteristics of these law-like statements or sociological laws have been discussed in terms of philosophies of science. They can, however, be regarded as societal policies. If they are to be realistic the latter should not simply express hopes and desires but should relate aims to instituional innovation, and the practical outcomes of such change. Institutions are invariably set up with certain norms or aims in mind. Policy statements are usually formulated in the form 'if comprehensive schools then greater equality of opportunity' or 'if continuous assessment then improved learning'. The planned construction of institutions which will achieve in practice stated aims requires some understanding of the regularities and circumstances that place constraints and limitations on what can be achieved by the way people run institutions. Thus we need to formulate policies in the form of sociological laws that can be tested. Such hypothetical statements either link in-system educational institutions (e.g. curriculum and structure; examinations and methods of teaching; administrative systems and finance) or link educational institutions with non-educational institutions (e.g. curriculum and manpower; structure and social class; educational provision and political leadership).

With this caveat clearly in mind, I consider that knowledge of a nation's pattern of educational, economic and welfare policies adds another dimension to the information we need about the context in which school systems function. This knowledge has to be contrasted with statements of aims and objectives because, while these may be changed rather freely, changes in policy are not bound to succeed. No-change elements have to be identified if problems arising from policy innovation are to be analysed.

PATTERN OF MENTAL STATES

Since *Problems in Education* was published in 1965 it has become apparent to me that if we are to use sociological laws to predict outcomes in known national systems we need to know more about the mental states, the 'residues', the 'lower valuations', the 'mores', which are not quite synonyms for the forces within individuals which motivate their behaviour. They constitute, if you will, Sadler's 'living spirit', or Mallinson's 'national character'. If we cannot discover what they are we cannot anticipate how individuals will react to a new proposal or run a new institution. We must assume that change can be introduced into any society only because not everybody in that society possesses the same 'internalised values'. Some people are innovators, others dislike and resist change. Some innovators are ideologues, others are practical men. Consequently, while asserting that ideal-typical normative models are useful, I have no confidence in national stereotypes in terms of behaviour.

My approach to this difficulty is to assume that the behaviour of individuals can be judged against ideal-typical normative patterns and that (given most theories of social change) the consistency of 'tradition' or 'conservative' mental states and behaviour can be judged and anticipated by reference to a historically earlier ideal-typical model. Thus I select Plato's *Republic* as a conservative model in Europe, not because I believe that the majority of Europeans act in accordance with its prescriptions, or that individuals behave consistently, but because it is a model to which implicit or overt reference is made and from this model it may be possible to anticipate the future reaction of identifiable individuals or groups of individuals. The encyclopaedic, pragmatic and communist ideal-typical models serve the same technical purposes. Together they permit cross-national comparisons to be made of the political and educational postures of a wide range of spokesmen and women and make it possible to analyse 'problems' by comparing the rhetoric of reform movements with the persistence (among teachers particularly) of traditional behaviour-motivating values and beliefs.

In fact most theorists of social change assert that the most difficult aspects of society to change are the mores, traditions, or internalised values of people. William Sumner writes about mores; William

Ogburn identifies the non-material, non-adaptive culture as the least likely to change; Vilfredo Pareto speaks of persisting residues; Marxists talk of 'false consciousness'; and Gunnar Myrdal makes a distinction between 'higher' and 'lower' valuations. While these notions of what changes most slowly differ, there is a measure of agreement among theorists that a distinction should be drawn between the rhetoric of change and the persistence of behaviour patterns which reflect deeply held sentiments or values.

THE NATURAL ENVIRONMENT OR PHYSICAL WORLD

A fourth main category of contextual statements which should be known about national conditions if sociological laws are to be used to predict 'outcomes' I have called the natural environment. As in the case of the other patterns, several aspects of it should be pointed out. Clearly the presence of economic resources, for instance, coal, iron ore, oil, and so on, is likely to influence the success or failure of social policies. While man cannot create these resources they can only be exploited through the institutions he creates and technological expertise he possesses.

What we need to know about man's physical world, or in comparative terms, his immediate natural environment, is taken from the natural sciences, and from geographical and demographic data. So are the techniques of inquiry. If we are to evaluate the importance of these natural resources and the technology which exploits them to policy decisions we need to know what they are. We also need to know the accumulation of natural scientific knowledge available in a nation and the extent to which it is disseminated throughout the nation.

For example the discovery and extraction of oil in countries such as Kuwait, Saudi Arabia, and so on, have had a profound influence on the success of policies of educational expansion. Equally important in the slower growth in universal provision in India is the absence of easily exploitable economic resources. At the same time it can hardly be denied that the depth and extent of the scientific knowledge and skills possessed by a high proportion of Americans are important features of the specific initial conditions in the USA. Thus, while it is not easy to draw sharp distinctions between purely environmental features and the skills with which they are developed, an attempt should be made to do so.

DESCRIPTION OF CONDITIONS AND PREDICTIONS

This classificatory framework is designed to help research workers to identify and make statements about relevant features of the total context in which educational institutions exist. It enables recognisable and repeatable selection to be made from among innumerable conditions, that is to say, the investigations of one researcher can be built on by others. I have indicated in my writings that in describing the context of education not only has selection to take place but varying weights have to be accorded to the factors regarded as likely to influence policy. Doubtless the selection and weighting of factors are somewhat arbitrary processes. The success of these may be measured by testing predictions from general statements and statements about these factors. Controlled social experiments are, it hardly needs to be said, extremely difficult to carry out. Consequently choices based on experimental verification are rare.

A further point should be made about the four patterns. The normative pattern is theoretically subject to the least predictable changes because man can freely accept or reject the norms for which he is responsible. Choices in this pattern are not forced on men by transcendent or immanent determinants. Freedom in this area is, according to Popper, a measure of the open society. Institutional changes are more predictable. Once introduced, a new institution sets up a sequence of events which, provided that general and specific statements can be made about it and its context, are predictable within the limits already discussed. Were the context to remain fixed or, if it was possible, the most important features in it were to stay under man's control, the probability that predicted outcomes would be confirmed by actual events would increase. The natural environment is the pattern least susceptible to man's immediate control. At the same time changes within it, such as the cycles of seasons, the recurrence of monsoon conditions, and so on, can be anticipated (but not prevented) to a considerable extent. These regularities constitute an important part of the initial circumstances. Other changes in the natural environment may be by chance or as the result of scientific research.

The very high degree of uncertainty in predicting the outcomes of social policy is the result of man's freedom to change his mind. Innovations arise from decisions taken by men. Policy is formulated by individuals, it is adopted by others, and may well be implemented by yet another group of persons. At each stage the beliefs of members of these various groups will influence the decisions they take and, at each stage, their behaviour will influence the subsequent flow of events. If norms change radically or are widely accepted there will be a reorientation in this flow. Of course men are often highly motivated to reject norms. As stated, many social psychologists and sociologists have pointed to the persistence of deeply ingrained sentiments or values among members of social groups. Comparative educationists have referred to these more or less permanent, virtually subconsciously held sentiments as the constituents of national character. Consequently certain assumptions may be made about the continuance of a normative tradition. On the other hand men cannot at will reverse or avoid all the institutional outcomes of institutional innovation. A government cannot, simply by fiat, escape those consequences of deflationary policies that it does not like. The consequences of building large schools for 2,000 pupils cannot be dreamed away if they turn out to be unpleasant. Death from lung cancer cannot be avoided simply by saying that cigarette smoking ought not to be related to the development of cancerous cells. In this very limited sense some of the social consequences we experience are determined by previous action. Sound planning implies that the number of unexpected and unwanted consequences of social policy will be reduced and that appropriate means will be found to achieve stated goals, that is, statements of what ought to be the case.

It is as an applied science that comparative education can assist planners. Too often in education we experiment on a vast scale with the lives of children by not distinguishing sufficiently sharply between the theoretical educational scientist and the applied scientist: the educational technologist. Research workers should perhaps be more aware of the need to test, by refutation, their general statements so that the flaws in proposed policy are made clear before thousands of schools are built, or innumerable courses are introduced into schools in the optimistic belief that opinions are more valid and reliable than the more cautious, but no less creative, hypotheses reached and tested by scientific procedures.

The classificatory framework proposed serves the theoretical and the applied scientist in a number of ways. I have already proposed that the problem approach involves the intellectualisation of a problem, making statements of the conditions under which it is found, the formulation of proposed solutions to the problem (hypothesis), the logical deduction from these hypotheses of the consequences of accepting them as solutions in known circumstances, and the testing of each hypothesis in turn by comparing predicted and actual events. Agreement implies that the confused or problematical situation has been resolved.

Changes for problem analysis may be selected from any of the four societal patterns. A new constitution, new legislation, or a new declaration of universal rights are almost bound to be problem-inducing changes if only because neither associated beliefs nor institutions change immediately. The introduction of a new institution induces problems if the mental states of those who have to run the new institution do not change. There is no need to do more than mention how the persistence of traditional beliefs has created problems of development in countries where economic resources have been dramatically exploited in recent years.

This classificatory system, as already discussed, enables a description to be made of the conditions in which a problem exists. It suggests a range of outcomes – economic, political, educational – which should be considered. The patterns throw light on the changes that have to be brought about if a new policy is to succeed. In short, they are designed to facilitate dynamic studies based on well-known theories of social change. A classificatory framework is necessarily static. Data placed within it also appear static. But in order to examine innovations and to anticipate subsequent changes the context in which the innovation is made should be assumed to be static – because change can only be measured against something that is fixed. Needed in comparative education are instruments that will enable change against relative no-change to be studied with rigour. I have suggested that theoretical or rational constructs offer one starting point. Again, the institutional pattern of a nation's educational system should be described at a selected point in history.

When studying contemporary changes and problems it is valuable to look at the educational system as it was immediately before the Second World War. Traumatic social changes during the war set in train sequences of events which have given rise in many countries to more or less serious educational problems. On the other hand the assumed starting point from which change and problems stem may be farther back in history. The purpose of the research and the kind of problem to be studied help to influence a choice that finally is rather arbitrary.

Subsequent chapters deal in more detail with models and techniques that can be used with the general taxonomy based on critical dualism or conventionalism.

NOTES AND REFERENCES: CHAPTER 4

This chapter is based on a series of articles published over a number of years. They include:

(a) 'The problem approach in comparative education: some methodological considerations', *Comparative Education Review,* vol. 2, no. 1, June 1958; pp. 3–8.
(b) 'Comparative education and the administrator', *The Journal of Higher Education,* Ohio State University, Vol. XXIX, no. 5, May 1958.
(c) *Problems in Education,* op. cit.
(d) 'The contribution of education to educational research', *Paideia* (Warsaw), vol. IV, 1975.
(e) 'Comparative education as a scientific study', *British Journal of Educational Studies,* vol. XX, no. 2, June 1972.
(f) 'Comparative education as a scientific study', in Hans-Joachim Krause, Ernst Neugebauer, Jack Heinz Sislian and Jörn Wittern (eds), *Orientierungspunkte internationaler Erziehung,* Fundament-Verlag Dr Sasse, Hamburg, 1973.
(g) 'Vergleichende Erziehungswissenschaft als wissenschaftliche Disziplin', in A. Busch *et al.* (eds), *Vergleichende Erziehungswissenschaft,* Verlag Dokumentation, Pullach bei München, 1974.

1 Karl R. Popper, *The Open Society and Its Enemies,* op. cit., p. 51.

2 loc. cit.
3 ibid., p. 56.
4 loc. cit.
5 loc. cit.
6 loc. cit.
7 Holmes and Robinsohn, *Relevant Data in Comparative Education,* op. cit.
8 Unesco/IBE, International Guide to Education Systems, op. cit., and *International Yearbook of Education,* Vol. XXXII, Unesco, Paris, 1980.

Chapter 5

The Collection and Classification of Data – National Profiles

Disputes about the nature of science and scientific method turn on the role data collection plays, whether explanations should be in terms of antecedent 'causes' or predicted events, and whether natural and social laws have universal validity or are contingent. Regardless of the position adopted, one component of scientific method involves the systematic collection and classification of information. Comparative educationists are unanimous that information about educational systems and the societal contexts in which they function is required if we are to understand and compare national systems.

Jullien established a classificatory scheme for school systems which has been retained with modifications ever since. Hans selected and classified information about societal infrastructures in terms of three major categories, namely, natural factors, religious factors and secular factors. Refinements by the addition of sub-categories have been introduced throughout the history of comparative education. Recent work by the Unesco Institute for Education, Unesco in Paris, the International Bureau of Education in Geneva and the Organisation for Economic Co-operation and Development in Paris has added to the sophistication of the available taxonomies.

A second question concerns the sources of information or types of evidence to which comparative educationists turn. One source is documentary, and of the many which throw light on education legal documents have always been regarded as important. Cousin, for example, wrote: 'I invariably followed one course, first, to procure the laws and regulations, and render myself perfect master of them; next to verify them by an accurate and detailed inspection.'[1] Matthew Arnold was not convinced either that legislation told him very much or that compulsory education laws were necessary. He discovered how easily in France manufacturers got round the child labour laws. Nevertheless Barnard brought the collection of details of legislation up to a high level of competence. His approach to comparative education was largely historical but in his *American Journal of Education* he kept his readers up to date with current issues by publishing extracts from foreign reports and debates, details of legislation and periodical articles. Most of the pioneering reports, in fact, carried details of decrees, circulars, laws, and so on.

Personal visits to foreign countries and observations about them were regarded as important checks on the extent to which laws are enforced or put into operation. Reports based on personal observation can be checked to a limited extent, but the visits and the unique experiences of the observer cannot be replicated. One way of recreating in part scenes that may have attracted the attention of an observer is to collect the artefacts of education in a museum. Books, chairs, writing slates, blackboards, measuring instruments, canes, textbooks and writing materials serve to remind us of the physical atmosphere of schools. In proposing that an educational bureau and museum should be set up in France, Jules Ferry used arguments already advanced by Ferdinand Buisson, who adopted Jullien's view of education as a positive science; he referred to the existence of institutions which displayed educational works and materials and the need for more of these collections. In 1879 the Musée Pédagogique was established.[2] Until recently there was at the IBE in Geneva a collection of the artefacts of education.

A third kind of data to which comparative educationists consistently refer is statistics. They have, over a long period of time, been viewed with suspicion. From the start the US Bureau of Education had collected statistics about systems of education throughout the country. Barnard appreciated that no two cities in his own country were alike but under his guidance and that of his successors at the Bureau the mass of statistical data grew enormously. One of them, John Eaton, Jnr, seemed convinced that a science of education could be built up on statistics. Arnold had made the point, however, that statistical data did not necessarily give precision to comparative judgements, pointing out that the machinery for collecting statistics existed in some but not in other countries. He recognised that if comparable statistics on illiteracy were to be collected, established and accepted criteria of illiteracy were necessary. Harris and Sadler shared his doubts. Harris wrote: 'It must be borne in mind that these comparative statistics are only approximately correct. There are many obstacles in the way besides inaccurate local records. The technical terms used by one nation do not have precisely the same import as words used by another nation to translate those terms.'[3] Sadler added a further important caveat. He saw how necessary it was to interpret statistical data in the light of each nation's value system. He wrote: 'One country may pay for something called "primary education" which is intended to produce results that in another would be regarded as reactionary and objectionable.'[4] In short, the validity of comparisons made in the light of statistics depends upon the degree to which the statistics from each country are a valid measure of comparable institutions, practice and ideals. Progress has been made but the confidence with which statistics are used – in comparative arguments or explanatory studies or as a measure of cross-national achievement – is not justified.

Since 1945 a great deal of work has been done to establish frameworks for the classification of documentary, observed and statistical data relevant to comparative education. The classification of data about educational institutions is placed in the general framework of critical dualism.

RELEVANT DATA ABOUT NATIONAL SCHOOL SYSTEMS

Certain requirements should be met if comparable data about national educational systems and schools as part of them are to be collected. One set of requirements relates to the choice and cross-national meaning of *indicators* for classifying data. A second set of requirements relates to the types of *sources* from which descriptive information is drawn. And a third set of requirements draws attention to *models* designed to organise data selected for inclusion in one or other of the major categories. Finally, methods of collecting data should meet certain criteria.

It was with these and other considerations in mind that a group of experts were invited to a meeting at the Unesco Institute for Education in Hamburg in 1963[5] to discuss the collection and classification of relevant data in comparative education. Sociologists, psychologists and political scientists were invited, along with comparative educationists, to discuss the theoretical issues associated with establishing methods of identifying and classifying contextual data and to consider how a taxonomy of classification could make policy studies in comparative education more rigorous.

Obviously a full analysis and description of all the elements within major societal patterns should be made in order to provide a complete picture of an educational system in its total social context. Evidently the subject-matter of concern to sociologists, political scientists, psychologists and economists provides the ingredients of such a description. The models social scientists use to collect information are relevant if such data are to be included in comparative education studies. In practice it is clearly impossible fully to describe all the institutions that form the infrastructure of an educational system. How, then, are data to be selected? One answer suggests that it may be possible to choose from among all the social science data those that are essential if the system is to be described satisfactorily. There is a sense in which certain institutions are relevant to the analysis of policy. To this assumption should be added another, namely, that the purpose of the investigation – in the case of the 'problem(-solving) approach' the 'problem' itself – will suggest which pieces of information are relevant and the relative importance of each of them.

Once the comparative educationist has identified his problem, social scientists are in a position to help him describe relevant features of a societal context. Sociologists have worked out models that enable them to describe social class and small group institutions. Political scientists have collected data relevant to an investigation of the mechanics of educational control. Economists have described in considerable detail business and industrial institutions, while psychologists have developed and described a variety of institutions associated with the well-being of individuals. Lawyers are familiar with legal and judicial systems. The mass of data available suggests that it should be relatively easy to collect information about aspects of an educational system's societal infrastructure.

Here some general questions about the constituents of a taxonomy for the collection of educational data are under consideration. For example, it is obviously desirable to select and group data realistically. Is it possible to draw up a scheme that can be used to classify descriptive data from every system of education in the world? This may be possible. But are the problems that direct attention to *this* rather than *that* kind of information sufficiently universal for comparative educationists to use the same classificatory scheme for all countries? Are the problems faced in some countries, for example, the industrialised, so different from those in other countries, for instance, the low-income, that different taxonomies should be developed for major regions of the world? An attempt is made here to establish a taxonomy that has universal applicability, is useful in collecting information about a particular country and meets the requirements of worldwide problem analysis. Nation-specific information is not difficult to obtain. It will be useful in comparative cross-national studies only if it fits into a general taxonomy that meets previously listed requirements.

UNIVERSAL INDICATORS

Major aspects of present-day school systems are not difficult to identify because European prototypes have for the most part been copied everywhere. It is not unreasonable to assume that all systems have to be administered and financed; that there are different levels of education and that within each of them there may be different types of schools; that the content of education is arranged to form a coherent curriculum; that certain methods of teaching are adopted; that learning is tested by some form of examination or evaluation system; that discipline has to be maintained; and that teachers have some form of training.

The choice is not arbitrary and each of the above-mentioned components finds its place in the system on the basis of prior conceptualisation. In turn a description of each aspect of the system depends on how the specific indicator, for example, administration, curriculum, examination, and so on, has been conceptualised. Models facilitate this process so that, for example, a curriculum can be described in terms of the aims, objectives, skills and knowledge and methods of evaluating associated with it. A system of administration can be assumed to consist of interacting formal organisations. Models are also available which makes it possible to conceptualise and hence describe other features of any system.

If these categories of data are to be comparable, the indicators used for selecting information must be based on terms which can be given unambiguous cross-cultural meaning. If key terms about educational systems like 'secondary school' or 'higher education' (or for that matter terms like 'social class' within its infrastructure) could be defined so that their meaning was clear when translated from one language into another and what was defined had exactly the same characteristics in the different countries, most of the difficulties of comparison would disappear. In fact few, if any, of the more complex key educational terms can be defined in this unambiguous manner at a purely terminological level.

The Hamburg report was in English. Even so it is not easy to give unambiguous cross-cultural meaning to the term 'high school' used in the USA to identify a particular type of school. The term *lycée* has a specific meaning in France which cannot easily be translated. The same is true of the terms, *Gymnasium, Hauptschule, Realschule, Fachschule,* and so on, though each of them describes a well-known institution in the German system of education. In the face of such difficulties care was taken to find and use terms in English that do not relate to nation-specific institutions.

The status of data depends upon the extent to which they are public and can be replicated. It is very important if information is to be compared that it should be accessible to anyone. Thus for the most part public documents offer the most reliable source of descriptive data. Constitutions, legislation, decrees, memoranda and the recommendations of advisory bodies constitute major sources from which information about educational systems can be drawn. Such documents usually provide normative statements (see Chapter 6) but may also describe in some detail the characteristics of school systems. Frequently they ascribe statutory powers and lay down relationships between institutions.

At present international documents lack authority, so that national constitutions and the like are more obvious sources of descriptive data about institutions. Because constitutions are either copied or based on well-established theory, some features of them can be compared. Most of them, for example, describe the roles of three constitutions of government – the legislature, the judiciary and the executive branch. They may also lay down relationships between these institutions. The amount of detail provided in constitutions varies considerably as a careful study of the constitutions of the USA and the Indian Union reveals.

National legislation also varies. Sometimes, as in English parliamentary Acts, considerable room is left in the statutes for political manoeuvre. In other cases, for example some Acts passed by Canadian provincial legislatures, details are spelled out. In spite of these differences legislation offers a reliable source of public information about national institutions and provides a basis for comparison.

Decrees and memoranda may enjoy the same status as legislation and confer on personnel responsible for the running of institutions certain statutory powers. They differ from legislation principally in the manner of their formulation and adoption. Governments differ in terms of the use they make of decrees.

By their nature the recommendations of national advisory committees do not have the status of legislation or decrees. They do not confer statutory power and while policies are normally formulated by such committees the governments to which they report are usually free to adopt, reject, or modify the advice given.

Similar types of data may be issued by provincial or local agencies which can pass legislation or issue decrees but the statutory powers they bestow on institutions or persons differs greatly from one country to another. In the USA, for example, each state is responsible for most of the legislation governing its school system. In France local authorities have no power to legislate and the central government's power to administer by decree and memorandum is considerable.

In drawing on these sources for comparable data the question of terminology is of paramount importance. It cannot be easily answered by introducing numbers. Only when an indicator has been given unambiguous cross-national meaning is it possible to collect comparable statistics. For example, unless 'secondary education' can be given a universally accepted definition the numbers of pupils enrolled in 'secondary schools' throughout the world cannot be counted. Over the years attempts to establish neutral terms have met with some success. Statistical data have been collected in the light of retention rates rather than absolute enrolments in various types of school. Ambiguity has been reduced by these efforts to improve the terminology for the purposes of comparative description and the indicators on which to establish statistical data.

NATIONAL PROFILES

The nineteenth-century pioneers of comparative education helped to set up national bureaux to collect information about education at home and abroad and to disseminate it. The International Bureau of Education in Geneva was probably the first international agency committed to gathering and disseminating data on an international scale. After their creation Unesco and the OECD added to the growing accumulation of educational data. Each of these agencies had its own, and rather different, purposes in mind. A major non-governmental agency, the International Educational Achievement Association, has also created an education data bank which includes information about related societal institutions.

Choice of descriptive data consequently depends on the intentions and interests of the collectors. If a complete and unambiguous description is impossible the criteria for selecting the most useful information about national educational systems have been debated by comparative educationists for a long time. The International Bureau of Education has participated in these discussions and with experts in the field of comparative education has evolved principles and models of classification. Unesco, with the assistance of Lauwerys, has established a complementary International System for Classifying Education (ISCED).[6] The IBE *International Guide to Education Systems*[7] is intended to make available in telegraphic form accurate information about school systems that will be useful to ministers of education, administrators and teachers. Its second objective is to make possible the analysis of processes of change within national systems. ISCED provides a classificatory framework within which all the types of courses offered in school systems in the world can be located for the purposes of comparison.

The national profiles, ISCED and the descriptive indicators established in Unesco/IBE's *Education Thesaurus*[8] under the influence of Leo Fernig represent major advances in the techniques of collecting comparable information about national systems of education.

PRINCIPLES OF CLASSIFICATION

One principle of classification is that information in each category should relate to a major criterion of selection. In sub-categories should be brought together data selected in the light of logically related indicators. Data in each category and sub-category should be mutually exclusive. (Relationships between data in different categories may be the subject of special study.) Evidently the generality of the data is determined by the indicator. The more general the latter, the greater the scope of the information collected. Sub-category material should be selected on the basis of logically related criteria.

A main category of data in IBE's national profiles includes statements of aims. The specificity with which educational aims and objectives are stated varies from one nation to another, and considerable research needs to be done into the ways in which educational aims find expression in constitutions, legislation and other national documents. It is, however, possible in the light of generally assumed aims to compare national aims by careful analyses of national documents and the philosophical theories that inspire and inform them. Techniques for comparing aims and theories are discussed later (Chapter 6).

Here the second main category of data, which brings together descriptions of institutions, is discussed. Aims find expression in national policies which are in turn translated into institutions. Formal organisations are set up in the expectation that in operating them people will realise in practice their hopes and aspirations. If statements of aims are normative, descriptive statements can be made about organisations, the personnel who work in them and the ways in which the organisations are operated and interact.

As an international agency the International Bureau of Education works principally, but not exclusively, through sovereign states. Consequently it is within the framework of national governments and systems of administration that the provision of education is described. The information should make possible an analysis and description of the processes involved in the formulation, adoption and implementation of policy. These processes mediate between aims and practice in all aspects of a school system. A comprehensive analysis of them requires that a description is provided of the major national, provincial and local organisations and the functions they perform.

The resources allocated to a school system obviously influence its success and represent an important outcome of policy debate. Some indication of the amount of money spent in education can be given by reference to the percentage of the national budget allocated to it. Much more detailed information about sources and methods of raising revenue and the distribution of resources is needed than is given in the IBE *Guide*.

Systems of administration and finance provide contexts in which schools operate. Brief descriptions of the formal organisations involved and the amounts of money allocated to the educational services are useful but should be taken as starting points from which analyses of policy processes can be made. Subsequent categories in the profiles draw together information about schools. The choice of data reflects the concerns shown over many years by ministers of education and their officials. The relative importance given to aspects of school practice has changed. The forums in which priorities have been debated have also changed with time. Nevertheless three aspects of school systems have continued to be regarded as useful in sketching in pictures of national systems and analysing problems.

The structure and organisation of a school system has an important bearing on the achievement of aims. When children start school, how long they must attend and the choices open to them before they leave to enter the world of work or an institution of higher education are important indicators of the success of a system of schooling. The universalisation of provision has informed national policies since the end of the Second World War. A major aim of reform movements has been to modify structures and organisations so as to realise new aims. As school systems were expanded, restructured and reorganised, more attention was paid to the content of education. Curricula constitute another main category into which data have been placed. From the profiles can be inferred some general patterns of curriculum provision.

Teacher education is another aspect of policy that has received considerable attention since 1945. Its importance lies in the contribution teachers make to the achievement of aims. Again, static pictures of the institutions in which teachers are trained, the content of their courses and certification procedures are needed if an analysis of procedures and problems is to be made.

Implicit in the classification of data in national profiles is the major distinction between stated aims and the ways in which they are realised in practice. A further distinction is drawn between the administration and finance of schools and those aspects of school life that are important if educational goals are to be achieved.

For each of the categories *administration, finance, structure and organisation, curricula* and *teacher education,* models that might be used to classify data and analyse processes are described and discussed.

Administration

The model used to select and organise information about systems of administration is derived from formal organisation theory. It assumes that in formal organisations three groups of persons will be involved. A public interest group is usually elected. National assemblies, parliaments, or congresses are examples of such public interest groups. They are supported by a group of administrators or bureaucrats with special responsibilities. In a formal organisation directors of education and school inspectors are members of this group. Finally, there are the producers of the services provided by the formal organisation. Teachers constitute this technical group of persons in those organisations responsible for educational services.

National education systems frequently are administered through formal organisations at national, provincial and local levels. Responsibility is shared by these agencies and only careful comparative research makes it possible to show how these relationships differ from one country to another. In summary, a general system of administration may be represented as shown in Figure 5.1 below.

ADMINISTRATION:

FORMAL ORGANISATIONS INVOLVED

National	**Provincial**	**Local**
Elected body	Elected body	Elected body
Appointed bureaucrats	Appointed bureaucrats	Appointed bureaucrats
Teachers	Teachers	Teachers

National and provincial formal organisations are frequently called ministries of education. Local organisations established by municipalities are termed 'local school boards' in the USA and 'local education authorities' in the UK.

Static national profiles should describe in simplified form the major formal organisations involved in the administration of education. Personnel and their duties should be identified and placed in an appropriate position in the relevant formal organisation. It should be appreciated, of course, that not all national formal organisations include teachers as civil servants and that provincial organisations are not always established to help administer education. The virtue of this simplified model is that it draws attention to possible organisations of administration and personnel without specifying too closely any of them. To do so would almost certainly prevent systematic comparisons.

It should also be reiterated that the involvement of personnel in formal organisations can be described and analysed only after the aspect of education under examination has been identified. Thus personnel inside national formal organisations may be responsible for major educational legislation. (In other countries provincial governments will be responsible for similar legislation.) The same organisations, however, may not hire or fire teachers which may be the task of a local formal organisation.

More valuable than comparisons that simply juxtapose organisations and a specific task, for example, the number of national governments that raise money to meet the costs of education, would be one in which processes are analysed. A useful classification of these is based on the assumption that the processes of

(1) policy formulation,
(2) policy adoption,
(3) policy implementation

are somewhat different and frequently involve rather different persons.

In using a formal organisation model to analyse these decision-making-and-taking procedures I assume that they are criteria on which to examine interactions between individuals working in their personal capacity or as members of either statutory or non-formal groups. To illustrate this point it is necessary to consider how national assemblies *receive, debate and adopt legislation* before delegating responsibility for its implementation to other formal organisations. The growth of research and planning units indicates the growing importance given now to *policy formulation*. Training schemes for teachers and administrators draw attention to aspects of *policy implementation*.

In summary, useful dynamic profiles of the ways administrative systems work would be drawn up by:

(1) using a simple formal organisation model to identify personnel statutorily involved in education;
(2) identifying individuals and groups (either statutory or non-statutory bodies) outside formal organisations who influence policy;
(3) specifying the aspect of education under consideration, e.g. the system of control, finance, school structure, curricula, teacher education, etc.;
(4) describing the arena in which these aspects of policy are
  (*a*) formulated,
  (*b*) adopted and
  (*c*) implemented.

Evidently the accumulation of relevant data on these aspects of administration will take time, but the results will make for more meaningful comparisons of the dynamics of change and hence will contribute to 'problem' analysis.

Finance

The resources placed at the disposal of those running educational institutions influence the achievement of aims. In national profiles it is not always possible to do more than indicate which organisation provides the funds and what percentage of the national budget is spent on education. Much more detailed information would make for useful comparisons.

It is likely that money is raised to meet the costs of education at national and local levels, and where they exist by provincial organisations. The percentage of money raised at each level is some indicator of where the balance of responsibility lies. Equally valuable is knowledge about the extent to which national resources are used to equalise local finance.

Methods of raising money include income, property and sales taxes which may be levied at national, provincial and local levels. Income taxes are frequently national; property taxes local. Comparison of the group on which the tax burden falls in various countries is possible only if a detailed analysis is made of the types of taxes and the organisations empowered to collect them.

A distinction should be drawn between funding when taxes are levied specifically for the schools and tax systems in which money is raised for general services and part of it is then allocated to education. Again, in some countries funds for recurrent expenses are raised separately and in a different way from the method used to raise money to meet capital costs. These differences influence the degree to which direct support for education (and aspects of it) has to be stimulated if the schools are to receive substantial support.

Levels of taxation, of course, depend upon estimates, and the ways in which budgets are drawn up have been the subject of comparative research. More information is needed, however, in view of the heavy call now made by educational systems on national resources.

Given taxes are for general services, the next stage in the process is allocation. The processes leading to the allocation of a percentage of national budget to education are part of national, provincial and local politics. The final stage is accounting for expenditure or auditing accounts.

Each stage – the preparation of a budget, raising of tax money, the allocation of funds from national and local budgets and auditing accounts – would provide comparative information whose value to policy-makers might be considerable.

These processes add a dynamic dimension to crude statistics such as the percentage of the national budget spent on education, per capita expenditure on education, the proportions of publicly raised and privately paid money, and so on. Because resources may come from many national sources the proportion of the GNP devoted to educational services is often regarded as a better comparative indication than percentage of the budget. Even this figure can mislead because GNP may be extremely high in a country with a tiny population, in which case per capita expenditure may be high in spite of the fact that a relatively small percentage of the GNP is devoted to education.

In summary, comparisons of the resources raised for and allocated to school systems are valuable indicators of the value placed on education. Comparisons between resources devoted to competing social services (like health) and defence add to the picture. The distribution of resources within the educational system – to poor neighbourhoods, to pre-school or university provision, in teachers' salaries, to administrative services – indicates the order of priorities accorded to aspects of education. Clearly the information provided in brief national profiles does not match the wealth of data required if careful comparative research into the costs of education are to be made and kept up to date.[9]

Structure and organisation

In pursuing the aim of providing education as a human right, governments, educationists and members of the public have tried to expand and reorganise traditional school systems. Private schools for the few pre-dated national selective school systems. Universal, free and compulsory education became policy issues. Details of provision differ but in general first-level schools as part of a compulsory system are made available to all while admission to second-level schools and universities is selective. Differentiation by school type characterises this period of development. Periods of compulsory attendance are increased. A later development includes the reorganisation of second-level schools along comprehensive lines. This is followed by an expansion of third-level education, either in universities or in alternative institutions, by the creation of a fourth level and the introduction of short-cycle higher education. The revision of curricula and examination systems has tended to follow the universalisation and reorganisation of free, compulsory and extended schooling.

Consequently a model is needed that takes account of historical developments, facilitates present-day comparisons and directs attention to on-going debates. The early comparative educationists were aware that stastical comparisons depended for success on the possibility of finding suitable and unambiguous terms for the kinds of schools in which pupils in different countries were enrolled. Elementary schools, primary schools, *écoles primaires* and *Volkschulen* are national-specific school types. Grammar school, high school, *lycée*, *Gymnasium, liceo, lyceum,* and so on, are terms that take on special meaning in different countries. Franz Hilker and other experts worked on a model designed to reduce some of these ambiguities. In *Relevant Data in Comparative Education* agreed models suggested that attention should be drawn to at least four levels of schooling. Within each level one or more stages could be identified. It was suggested that the levels should be termed *first, second, third* and *fourth* in order to facilitate international comparisons. Within each level it was appreciated that as well as stages there would be different school types and different curriculum patterns. Each level, stage, or course may be concluded by an examination or examinations. A complete profile would describe all these aspects of a national school system (see Tables 5.1 and 5.2).

A statistical picture would provide details of enrolment at each level and stage and in each type of school. In comparative terms absolute numbers are less meaningful than percentages. Two indicators can be used. The first draws attention to the proportion of the age cohort in any level, stage, or school type. The second statistic shows the percentage of pupils moving from one level or stage to the next. The proportion of pupils entering and leaving each level with or without a leaving certificate, diploma, or other award is an important indicator of the extent to which the school system provides universal education and retains pupils.

The model used to select information for these national profiles should be intentionally simple. The details included in each national profile should in the first instance be minimal. Evidently it would be possible to build up a substantial data bank on indicators derived from this model. Specific research problems should, however, determine what kind of data are required and the degree of sophistication with which they should be collected.

In general the way in which children enter, pass through and leave the school system is of comparative interest. Pre-school education may socialise children, offer some basic skills, or attempt to compensate those whose home circumstances place them at some disadvantage. The age at which children are obliged by law to attend school varies but the first day at school is bound to be an occasion in anyone's life. How pupils are initiated into the first school is of considerable interest.

The progress of children through first-level schools is usually monitored by class teachers. How this is done, whether by one or several teachers, using examinations, other forms of assessment and record cards, are features of the way in which these schools are organised.

Notes to Table 5.1

1 Pre-school provision may be made for children between 2 and 6, depending on the system.
2 First school – the age of compulsory attendance varies between 5 and 7.
3 Compulsory *schooling* may be defined in terms of the numbers of years, e.g. nine, or by age, e.g. 16 years of age.
4 Transfer from the first to the second level may involve change of school and frequently occurred between the ages of 10 and 12 with, or more recently without, selection.
5 Second-level schooling has been the object of much debate and reorganisation.
6 The upper stage of second-level schooling is usually post-compulsory. One school type or course is usually pre-university. A range of provision at this stage is now made.
7 The third level includes university undergraduate courses. Alternative types of third-level institutions and shorter courses have been established.
8 Fourth-level institutions and courses include professional, doctoral and research students.

Table 5.1 *Structure of Educational System*

AGE	YEARS AT SCHOOL	LEVEL	STAGE	DESCRIPTION	SCHOOL TYPE	COURSES	EXAMINATIONS
22–23 –24		IV	(7)	FOURTH LEVEL[8]	e.g. PROFESSIONAL	e.g. postgraduate	e.g. PhD
		III	(6)	THIRD LEVEL Second stage	e.g. UNIVERSITY		e.g. BA, BSc
			(5)	THIRD LEVEL[7] First stage	e.g. Short-cycle, higher	Degree, Diploma	
18–19 –20				TRANSFER			e.g. 'A' level (England and Wales)
			(4)	SECOND LEVEL[6] Upper stage	e.g. SIXTH FORM (England and Wales)	e.g. (1) Pre-university (2) Vocational	
14–15 –16		II		COMPULSORY SCHOOL ENDS			e.g. 'O' level (England and Wales)
			(3)	SECOND LEVEL[5] Lower stage	e.g. MIDDLE (England and Wales)	e.g. Common and Options	
10–11 12				TRANSFER			
			(2)	FIRST LEVEL[4] Upper stage	e.g. JUNIOR (England and Wales)		
		I	(1)	FIRST LEVEL Lower stage	e.g. INFANT (England and Wales)	Common	
5–6 –7				COMPULSORY SCHOOL BEGINS[2 3]			
				PRE-SCHOOL EDUCATION[1]	e.g. Nursery, kindergarten		

Nation-Specific Terminology (England and Wales)

Table 5.2 *Structure of Educational System (Example)*

AGE	2	3	4	5	6	7	8	9	10	11	12	13	14	15	16	17	18	19	20	21	22	23	24
LEVEL							I				II							III					IV
STAGE					1		2				3				4			5			6		7
	Pre-compulsory						Compulsory schooling								General post-compulsory								
SCHOOL TYPE													Vocational		Technical								
													General academic					University first degree					
													Secondary school for teacher					Teacher training college					
																					Medical school		
																					Law school		
																					Theological College		
																					Postgraduate studies		

Notes
Compulsory examinations at end of 3, 4, 5, 6 stages.
Selection examinations at the end of levels/stages 2, 3 and 4.
School-leaving or professional examinations at the end of levels/stages 3, 4, 5 and 6.

Automatic promotion, retention in the same grade and drop-outs may characterise some systems but not others. The point of transition from the first to second level has important consequences for children in selective systems. The mechanisms of selection (and their disappearance) provide insights into the criteria on which children are selected and draw attention to the way in which second-level schools are organised.

Similar information about the progress of pupils through second-level schools to the point at which they leave school or continue to attend post-compulsory institutions is needed if the dynamics of school systems are to be compared. Again, some knowledge of the types of examinations that qualify pupils for the next state or level of education or that enable them to move out of the school system into the world of work is needed if the educational chances of children in different countries are to be compared.

The expansion of third-level institutions is a fairly recent development in most countries. Debate turns on whether the expansion should be designed to meet the desires of students to participate in third-level education or to meet estimated manpower needs. In either case the expansion of third-level institutions has been accompanied by some reorganisation of universities, professional schools, technological institutions and teacher training.

At the second and third level information is needed about the choice of school type open to pupils and students entering these levels and the stages within them. Opportunities to transfer from one school type to another should be known and the conditions under which transfer is possible the subject of official information. As the number of school types at the first stage of the second level declines, curricula choice becomes important if the progress of pupils is to be monitored. Indeed, as each stage becomes less differentiated in terms of types of school differentiation, in terms of content, homogeneous or mixed-ability groupings, methods of teaching, and so on, become practices on which information is needed if comparative descriptions are to be made.

Analysis is also required. The speed and success with which children move through school systems and their length of stay in them depend on many factors. Traditionally the race, language and religious background have influenced the educational chances of children in multicultural societies. Today the social class position of parents and the home background of children contribute to the success and failure of children in many school systems.

Curricula

In *Curriculum Innovation at the Second Level of Education*[10] I suggested that four general curriculum theories inform national systems. Three of them – essentialism, encyclopaedism and pragmatism – indicate criteria of selecting content. The fourth theory – polytechnicalisation – proposes how, once selected, the content of education should be treated. An essentialist curriculum is in response to the question: what subjects are essential in the general or liberal education of individuals? Encyclopaedism implies that all knowledge should as far as possible find a place in the curriculum. French interpretations of this theory gave priority to mathematics and natural sciences and among literary subjects to modern rather than classical languages. Drawing and other manual skills were to be included in this broadly conceived curriculum. The criteria of selection derived from pragmatic theory are social and personal. The content of education is determined by asking what knowledge young people will need (and therefore should have) to meet the problems of living – occupational, civic, family, leisure, health and moral – when they leave school. Polytechnical theory suggests that the social implications and the practical applications to productive life of all instructional content should be made clear.

A distinction can therefore be made between knowledge-centred and society-centred curricula; and between epistemologies that restrict the range of worthwhile knowledge and those that do not; and between social-psychological theories that emphasise the needs of individuals and those that stress the importance of economic life. On these distinctions curricula can be described and compared.

Knowledge-based curricula can be further placed into high-status and low-status categories. Academic, general, or liberalising knowledge usually has high status. Knowledge associated with skills and vocational and technical activities is often classified as low-status knowledge. The school types in which these different kinds of knowledge are provided are placed in a status hierarchy which reflects the esteem in which the knowledge is held. Hierarchies of knowledge persist among carefully selected subjects for inclusion in school and university curricula as well as in systems where a wide range of subjects finds a place.

In many systems extra-curriculum activities allow the content of education to be extended beyond the confines of worthwhile knowledge. Some information should be given about these activities because their importance in the achievement of school objectives may be high. In some systems, of course, they are regarded as an integral part of the regular school curriculum.

The explosion of knowledge has thrown strain on traditional approaches to the selection of knowledge for the purpose of education. Attitudes towards equality of provision have made the selection of content in the light of individual abilities to benefit from it untenable. National profiles should show how content differentiation has replaced differentiation by school type. Along with this practice has come the notion of a core curriculum and options. In general, core curricula occupy a majority-time position in first-level schools and first-stage, second-level schools. As pupils move up through the system the core occupies less and less time and options increase. Brief though profiles may be, they point to differences between curricula and illustrate some of the principles here enunciated. The selection of more detailed data will depend on the research problem in mind.

The processes of curriculum development should be studied. In analysing the politics of curriculum formulation, adoption and implementation a broad distinction should be drawn between the producers of knowledge – the teachers – and the way they structure, select and disseminate knowledge, and the consumers of education, namely, pupils and, vicariously, parents, industrialists and educationists themselves. What teachers offer as worthwhile knowledge is not always regarded by pupils, students and industrialists as such. Undoubtedly the status of knowledge is related to the power and position it can confer on those who possess it. Consequently a comparative analysis of the way knowledge is organised, and by whom, for the purpose of education leads us back to the kind of analysis of policy formulation, adoption and implementation which previously (under *Administration*) I maintained would give a dynamic dimension to static profiles.

All too frequently the assumption is, and finds expression in official statements, that the minister of education lays down the curriculum in national schools. On the other hand official statements may suggest that curricula are the responsibility of individual teachers. In brief profiles oversimplification is inevitable and neither of these polar statements does justice to the dynamics of curriculum development. Comparative studies of the curriculum innovation and the constraints that surround it are needed. As the traditional distinction between the various types of school and the two (or three) types of teacher becomes blurred the issue of curriculum control becomes a matter of considerable debate.

Teacher education

The public service teachers perform, their special knowledge and skills and control of entry to teaching are indicators which allow information about teacher education to be classified for comparative purposes. Within countries differences between types of teacher are as great as between countries. In some nations teachers for first-level schools are still trained in second-level schools while all second-level school teachers are trained in third-level institutions. A worldwide trend is to require all teachers to have trained in third-level institutions. What is not yet clear in some countries is who should control this kind of education and training.

An organising principle for this category of information might turn on the entry into, progress through, and qualifications received at the end of their studies by students wishing to become teachers. Comparisons may be made of the age and prerequisites for entry into different teacher training institutions. How selection is made and by whom have importance if the supply of teachers is to be related to future demand. The balance of studies should be compared. Subject-matter (general and specialist), social science foundation studies, professional subjects and practical teaching are usual components in teacher education programmes. The sequences in which these elements are offered and the proportion of each over the full period of training should be known if comparisons are to be made. Forms of assessment and the procedures leading to the issue of a qualification to teach are also matters of interest. In-service training requirements and their relation to promotion and salary levels differ widely, as do methods of appointment and salary scales.

It is easy to see how information about the training of teachers is related to data in the other categories. The *Aims of Education* influence the tasks teachers are expected to perform. The *Structure and Organisation* of a school system influence decisions about the types of training teachers should be given. *Curricula* determine what teachers should know and the skills of presenting information they should possess. *Administration* and *Finance* constitute national frameworks in which teachers are selected, trained, certificated and paid. The delicate balance between professional autonomy and national needs as governments see them has to be maintained. The salaries of teachers constitute such a high proportion of the costs of education that they cannot be ignored in judging the support given to the schools.

CONCLUSION

A distinction has been drawn between information that could well go into national profiles and the dynamic processes that might serve to make a selection of data for each category meaningful. Research studies will increase the data we have on education and thus contribute to the quality of national profiles. Basically they are designed to present in simplified form a comprehensive picture of a national system of education. Data making up the many national profiles should be comparable; hence the need for carefully constructed indicators, models and techniques of collection. Profiles based on documentary evidence may be complemented by statistical evidence but the criteria of selection should be the same.

There is a place in comparative education for more extensive area-studies. It would be helpful if authors adopted an internationally approved taxonomy into which to place selected information. If for each general category of data additional criteria were established much more sophisticated, but comparable, national profiles could be built up, adding to the accumulation of information we now possess.

I have also said that these taxonomies are useful in the preparation of national case-studies. These should be prepared with the intention of drawing out the unique features of an educational system while placing them in a context that is universal. Most authors who have prepared national studies on education have emphasised the unique features of the systems described without classifying their material in a way designed to facilitate comparisons.

Finally, I suggest that the attention of a research worker is drawn to data of a certain kind by the 'problem' he has in mind. The systematic presentation of basic data along agreed lines over a period of time would help research workers to identify changes in one or several of the categories. Problem analysis is based on the assumption that asynchronous change takes place. The identification of change in any one of the aspects named – administration, finance, structure and organisation, curricula and examination and teacher education – may be useful when planning a research project.

In the chapters that follow I pay particular attention to techniques designed to facilitate the comparison of national aims and theories and the analysis of problems arising from changes in aims or from the persistence of certain mental states.

NOTES AND REFERENCES: CHAPTER 5

This chapter relies heavily on Brian Holmes and Saul B. Robinsohn, *Relevant Data in Comparative Education,* op. cit., Unesco/IBE, *International Guide to Education Systems,* op. cit., and Unesco/IBE, *Bulletin, Educational Documentation and Information, Curriculum Innovation at the Second Level of Education*, 48th year, no. 190, 1st quarter, 1974, which includes Brian Holmes, 'Some general issues and proposed solutions in curriculum development', pp. 21–35.

1 Cousin, *Report on the State of Education in Prussia,* op. cit., p. 3.
2 *Le Musée pédagogique, son origine, son organisation, son objet, d'après les documents officiels,* Ministre de l'Instruction Publique et des Beux-Arts, Paris Imprimerie Nationale, 15 May 1884, p. 15. Jules Ferry, in advocating the establishment of a national education bureau and museum, used arguments already advanced by F. Buisson.
3 W. T. Harris, in *Annual Report of the Commissioner of Education for the Year 1888–89,* Washington, DC, 1891, Vol. I, p. xix. Under Harris the US Bureau of Education continued to provide an impressive number of statistical tables.
4 Sadler, 'The unrest in secondary education in Germany and elsewhere', op. cit.
5 While much work has been done on techniques of classifying education since 1963 the expert meeting brought together scholars like Franz Hilker and Pedro Rossello, who had done much to systematise data collection and establish a broad framework on which much subsequent development has taken place.
6 The International System for Classifying Education should be seen as complementing the *International Guide*. Courses within educational systems are classified in terms of level, stage, length and function to provide a basis for comparison. The compilers experienced particular difficulty in their attempts to classify adult, post-compulsory and further education.

7 The IBE *International Guide to Education Systems* was intended to test the desirability of republishing IBE's *International Year Book of Education*. It makes use of the model devised at the Hamburg expert meeting of 1963 and takes account of the more detailed system of classification used in the ISCED.

8 Unesco/IBE, *Education Thesaurus,* Unesco, Paris, 1973, itemises aspects of education for the purposes of computer and documentary research. In the Faceted Array of Descriptors and Identifiers there are eight series or fields within each of which there are subsections. Considerable attention has been paid to terminology to facilitate cross-national searches.

9 Several studies have been made of the proportion of GNP and the proportion of national budgets allocated to education. In some of these studies it has not been possible to take into account the private resources, e.g. tuition fees, endowments, and so on, which should be added to public spending if assessments of the total resources made available to education are to be made. Several useful considerations of fiscal procedures were included in *The Year Book of Education, 1956, Education and Economics*, Evans, London, 1956. See also H. J. Noah, *Financing Soviet Schools*, Teachers College, Columbia, New York, 1964.

10 Unesco/IBE, *Bulletin,* op. cit.

Chapter 6

Ideal-Typical Normative Models

The importance of aims and theories in the evolution of policy has been widely recognised. Statesmen and politicians frequently appeal to stated aims to justify their proposals. Philosophers of education discuss the nature and status of aims. Unfortunately, in the UK and in the USA techniques of conceptual analysis have not been used to show how far educational aims are nation-specific and the extent to which some of them have been internationalised. Comparative educationists have been inhibited by the danger that discussion of what philosophers have said 'ought to be the purpose of education' might degenerate into a defence or criticism of stated aims and objectives. Certainly at the expert meeting held in Hamburg in 1963 no attempt was made to identify and classify educational aims and theories. In 1975 Unesco, recognising their importance, convened seminars to discuss in an international forum philosophies and aims of education. In the first of them much of the time was, in fact, devoted to advocating one or other notion of what education ought to be and the purpose for which it ought to be used.[1] The IBE in Geneva, for similar reasons, invites governments to formulate the aims that inform their educational systems. By juxtaposing these statements it is apparent that at the highest level of generality considerable consensus exists on a worldwide scale.[2] Nevertheless, at another level the differences between nationally stated aims and theories are very obvious.

It is with the techniques of comparing the aims that inform educational policies that this chapter is concerned. In so far as internalised aims (beliefs, hopes, values) as the constituents of national character are related to mental states and have some bearing on human action, these techniques also serve as tools of analysis for each stage of the problem(-solving) approach. In particular, methods of constructing ideal-typical models are discussed and some reference is made to their value in analysing problems, comparing policy solutions and anticipating the outcomes of policy innovations.

IDEAL TYPES

The use of ideal types has been criticised by phenomenologists such as

Husserl, Schutz and their present-day followers.[3] Yet it is not easy to see how the technical difficulties faced by Max Weber and modern comparative educationists can be met without resorting to ideal-typical models. According to Weber[4] any view of the world must be limited, partial and conditioned by the observer's point of view. To reduce this kind of subjectivity and to make sense of many and complex data Weber proposed that ideal types should be established. If they are to be useful it must be possible to replicate them. That is, the sources on which they are based must be known and open to inspection. Weber proposed that logical, rational, or 'ideal-typical' constructs could be employed to examine structures and social relationships.

I do not propose to enter into the debate about 'ideal types'. Perhaps the most serious objections levelled against them relate to the use made of them. There is a danger that they may be used to stereotype individuals and ascribe to all of them the same personality traits and behavioural characteristics. Indeed, in practice pejorative statements about Jews, 'blacks' and other minority groups – symptoms of anti-Semitism and racism – stem from stereotyping. A second criticism of ideal types made by phenomenologists is that they reify reality, that is, reduce it to unacceptably simple abstract principles. These criticisms carry weight if it is assumed that ideal types correspond to reality and that from them can be accurately deduced the personality traits and behaviour of members of a group. I do not propose to use ideal-typical models in this way. Nor do I assume that in themselves they correspond to the complex reality of individual and group behaviour. I am not convinced that ideal types, used with circumspection, have no role to play in the analysis and understanding of a particular society. On the other hand, I firmly believe that ideal-typical models are necessary if we are to compare extremely complex situations, analyse certain problems and in particular if we are to compare the aims, hopes, expectations and attitudes of individuals and organised groups in different societies. It may be assumed that they simplify some constituents of national character but they should not be used to stereotype the behaviour of citizens of a nation-state.

The grounds on which this reservation is made should be clear. The relationship between expressed beliefs (normative statements) and human action is complex and rarely logical.[5] It cannot therefore be assumed that individuals will consistently behave in accordance with the constituents of an ideal-typical normative pattern or model. Many social scientists have indeed drawn distinctions between what individuals assert ought to be done, their mental states and their social actions.[6] Each of these aspects of personality is relevant to the analyses made by comparative educationists. In so far as they wish to anticipate the behaviour of individuals, comparative educationists are also interested in relationships between stated beliefs, mental states and action. The relationship between mental states and action is usually regarded as closer than the relationship between normative statements and either mental states or social actions. Only to the extent that individuals act entirely rationally (or, in Pareto's term, 'scientifically') can ideal-typical normative models tell us with certainty about human behaviour.

Ideal-typical normative models can, however, throw light on the norms people are likely to debate, accept, or reject. That is to say, they simplify complex patterns of normative statements. In so far as traditional normative statements are more likely to be internalised than more modern beliefs, ideal-typical normative models derived from traditional sources may tell us something about complex patterns of mental states. Mallinson, as stated, has pointed to the persistence of deeply held sentiments and their influence on behaviour in his analysis of 'national character' and educational thought and practice.[7]

It should not be assumed that all the normative statements in an ideal-typical normative model are accepted by all numbers of the group to which it refers, for example, Christians, British, Yorkshiremen. By the same token there is no reason to suppose that all members of an identifiable group share the same mental states or will behave in the same way. Indeed, central to my problem(-solving) approach is the assumption that in most communities, societies and nations there will be diversity of opinion and belief and that men and women will question the norms they recognise. Some of them will reject such norms, introducing an element of change into their socially created world. Other members of the group will continue to accept existing norms. The same assumptions may be made about changes in and the persistence of mental states among members of the group. These changes, given the persistence of other norms and mental states, are the source of certain kinds of societal problems. Against rational constructs or ideal-typical normative patterns analyses of change and no-change can be made, major national differences of belief and opinion can be identified and compared, and irrational, conformist and deviant behaviour within a nation can be judged. In other ways diversity within a socially constructed world of norms can be analysed.

In summary, ideal-typical normative models help to make sense of immensely multifarious subject-matter of a certain kind. They offer a pattern of logically related normative statements and give coherence to the multiplicity of beliefs that may exist in the society or nation to which they refer. Conceptual clarity and simplicity, in the form of general statements relatively lacking in content, are gained, to be sure, at the expense of accuracy and comprehensiveness. The more sharply and clearly constructed the abstractions made in the model are, the more unrealistic it is likely to be. At the same time the more useful it is likely to be to the comparative education research worker.

I suggest that an ideal-typical normative pattern should be derived from a selection of data about educational, political, religious and economic aims and theories accepted (or debated) by members of an organised community of individuals. I now propose to identify the criteria or indicators on which a selection of data should be made for the purposes of comparative education research and the public sources from which the data should be taken. Finally, while recognising that ideal-typical patterns simplify complex situations, I shall suggest how useful models can be constructed and applied to the analysis of problems in some major nation-states and cultural regions of the world. For it should be noted that an ideal-typical model may be associated with an identifiable culture, region of the world, nation-state, or community and that these classificatory categories are not mutually exclusive.

SOME CONSIDERATION OF AIMS IN EDUCATION

Educational aims can be stated in very general terms. In this form they are likely to receive international approval. For example, the all-round development of individuals, the satisfactory evolution of society and the acquisition of knowledge and skills are aims that commend themselves to most governments and educationists. Interpretations of all-round individual development, societal well-being and what constitutes knowledge are the source of cross-cultural and cross-national comparisons.

In so far as aims are statements of what 'ought to be the case' and represent man's hopes and aspirations not only for himself but for future generations, they are part of our socially constructed world and can be accepted or rejected according to taste. The normative components in statements of aims is not always explicit. Philosophers are inclined to describe education

(1) as something in itself, e.g. with intrinsic value.
(2) as a process, e.g. initiation into specified activities.
(3) in terms of its outcomes, e.g. the all-round development of individuals.

Thus education may be described as equivalent to the acquisition of knowledge or skills, or as a process of initiating individuals into worthwhile activities, or as a way of actualising the potential of individuals. In comparative perspective, however, these descriptive statements, which cannot adequately represent the aims of education everywhere, should be transformed into 'ought' statements to show that they are matters of choice and commitment and not susceptible to objective factual description.

Within a particular cultural or national context educational aims cannot easily be understood without reference to associated normative statements. These two are frequently couched in purely descriptive terms. Thus 'All men are created equal' is an assertion of fact (which may be disputed). Usually the intention lying behind this assertion is the normative claim that 'All men ought to be treated as equals'. Little sense can be made of the educational aim that 'All children ought to receive an education from which they can benefit' without reference to statements about the equality (or inequality) of all individuals. In the same way educational aims should be studied in the context of statements about how society ought to be organised. Similarly there is little point in asserting that all children should acquire knowledge and skills unless the kind of knowledge and skills worthy of acquisition is spelled out. Unless these features of the normative context are formulated it will not be clear about what section of a population we are talking and about what kinds of educational systems and curriculum we are talking when we identify educational aims.

To accommodate these features of the context in which aims are stated a distinction is sometimes made between aims and objectives that are *intrinsic* and those that are *instrumental*. The distinction is fine, normative, and in comparative terms difficult to sustain. Intrinsic aims imply that certain educational activities, moral, aesthetic, intellectual and physical, are worthwhile in themselves and need no further justification. The acquisition of knowledge for its own sake would represent such an intrinsic aim. The acquisition of certain skills without regard to the use to which they are put would be another. Frequently the justification of intrinsic aims depends on descriptive statements about the nature of education. My contention is that all educational aims acquire meaning only when seen in relation to normative statements about individuality, society and knowledge.

Instrumental aims can be described less ambiguously. They are identified by reference to observable outcomes. These outcomes are economic, political and educational. Thus the assertion that education ought to contribute to economic growth is an instrumental aim. The claim that political leaders ought to be selected (as an aristocracy of talent) on the basis of educational achievement represents another instrumental aim. As a final example it might be asserted that an instrumental aim of education is that it ought to prepare pupils for examinations. When these and other instrumental aims are examined they can be seen as linked with preparing good citizens, developing the good society, or inculcating worthwhile knowledge. Since I have suggested that intrinsic aims can be understood only by referring them to a wider range of aims I do not find the distinction drawn between intrinsic and instrumental aims useful. I prefer to draw a distinction between general aims which acquire meaning from a general normative context and more specific aims which can be understood by reference to the outcomes which are expected to flow from the practice of education.

The more general the statement of aims, the more likely they are to inform all aspects of education. Thus the administration and finance of schools, curricula and methods of teaching and teacher education should all contribute to the aim of all-round individual development and societal improvement. Less general aims – which may be called objectives – refer to specific aspects of an educational system. The acquisition of knowledge as an aim is closely related to the curriculum. Equality of provision may be achieved principally through systems of finance and administration. These limited aims or objectives are nevertheless logically derived from more general aims and consequently ideal-typical models derived from very general statements of aims are needed if nation-specific interpretations, which can be compared, are to be deduced from the specific theories associated with general philosophical aims.

CRITERIA FOR SELECTING DATA FOR NORMATIVE PATTERNS

Explicit in the problem(-solving) approach is the assumption that the 'problem' directs the attention of the research worker to data of a certain kind. I assume, however, that aims, theories and mental states usually have some bearing on the 'problem' to be investigated or are relevant constituents of the initial specific conditions associated with policy solutions. Consequently some discussion of the techniques I suggest should be employed to construct a normative pattern is necessary. The 'problem' taken as the starting point of any research and the contexts in which it is examined will influence the choice and amount of detail included in the pattern.

Enough has been said under consideration of aims and theories to suggest that normative statements (and hence attitudes, beliefs, aims, etc.) can be selected and classified in the light of three criteria or indicators. An ideal-typical normative pattern should usually include information about

(1) the nature of man,
(2) the nature of society,
(3) the nature of knowledge.

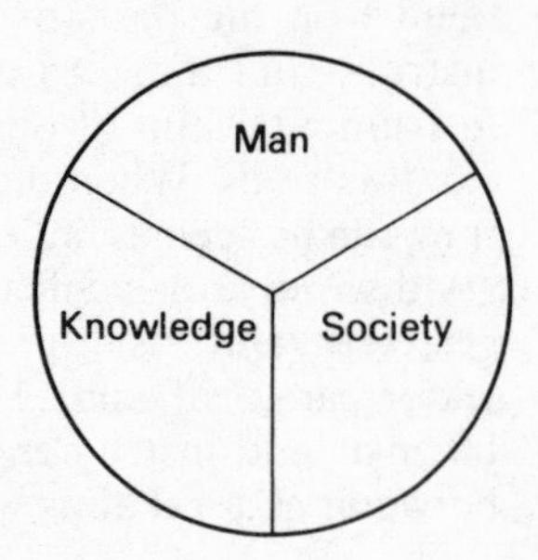

Ideal-typical normative model or construct

A distinction, as stated, should be drawn between statements that are explicitly normative (e.g. all men ought to be equal), and those that are descriptive (e.g. all men are born equal), and between aims and theories. This kind of construct is very general, it is relatively lacking in content but it should be comprehensive and coherent. The sources from which these types of data can be taken will be discussed later.

Statements of less generality can be inferred from the more general. It is possible, for example, to talk about the nature of 'political man' and the 'political society', about 'economic man' and the 'economic society' and about 'educated man' and the 'educated society'. Into political science, economics, sociology, psychology and education as social sciences are drawn data about specific aspects of man and society. The knowledge component in these subjects, in the form of theories and data, is substantial.

A more detailed ideal-typical normative model can be constructed in accordance with a classificatory scheme which would include categories into which the following would be placed (see Figure 6.1):

Figure 6.1 Normative Pattern

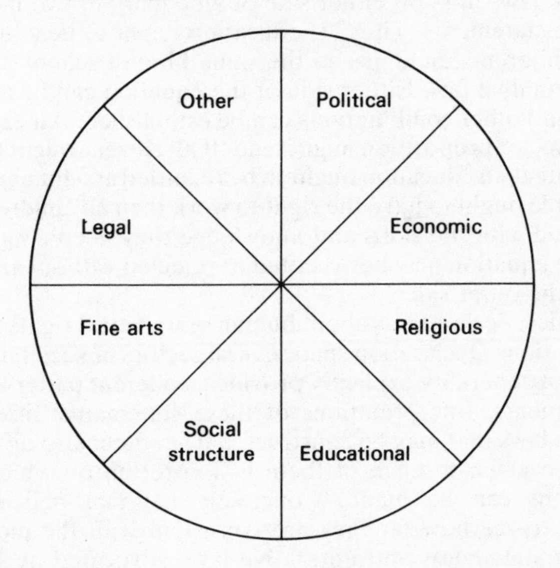

(1) political data,
(2) economic data,
(3) religious data,
(4) educational data,
(5) data about social structures,
(6) data about the fine arts.
(7) legal data.

The number of sub-categories within the general construct can be increased or reduced to meet the research worker's requirements but, theoretically, the information in each category should be exclusive of that selected for and placed in the other categories. The coherence of an ideal-typical pattern, however, depends upon the extent to which relationships within and between category data are logical and the extent to which all these statements are logically related to the more general ideal-typical construct.

A more detailed normative pattern would include statements derived from theories about the nature of man, society and knowledge under headings taken from an explicit societal taxonomy.

Two types of statement may be needed in research and a distinction should be drawn between them. Strictly, statements in the pattern should refer to one aspect of society and to one feature of a particular subsector of society. For example, take the notion of equality. It might be held that 'All individuals ought to be equal before the law'. Or that 'All individuals ought to enjoy the same political rights'. Neither statement makes reference to concepts of educational or economic equality. It is, however, possible and in some cases necessary to establish relationship statements which I have called 'normative laws'. Normative laws link, on either side of an equation, two independent normative statements. Thus, 'If education ought to be a human right then all children should attend the same kind of school' is a within-sector normative law. Either side of the equation can be accepted or rejected and other combinations can be established. An example of a between-sector proposition might read 'If all citizens ought to have the right to vote then education ought to be regarded as a human right'. Or 'If all people ought to have the right to work then all children ought to be provided with the skills and knowledge they need'. Again, either side of the equation may be accepted or rejected without affecting the status of the other side.

In practice, declarations about human or universal rights such as the United Nations Declaration span several sectors of societal life and at one level of generality explicitly provide a coherent pattern of normative statements. Interpretations of these statements differ and the normative laws that may be constructed from them also differ and the importance given to each of them is a criterion on which national comparisons can be made. Concretely national policies can be examined to see how far they are consistent with the most general normative statements and normative laws advocated by individuals and groups of individuals in the nations included in any comparative education study. Among these groups should be counted statesmen, politicians, the judiciary, educationists, teachers and parents. All of them are likely to hold views that can be studied within the context of a constructed normative pattern.

MIDDLE–RANGE (REGULATING) THEORIES

Social scientists, of course, cling to their own theories. Middle-range or regulating theories are usually derived from philosophical assertions and consequently a normative element is rarely absent from any social scientific theory. Theories are the constituents of working social science paradigms. Each group of social scientists works within an accepted paradigm. Political scientists, economists, sociologists, psychologists, theologians and lawyers have their own corpus of theories. Whether educationists have an identifiably distinct set of theories is at the moment in dispute but it is clear that political, psychological and sociological theories have a direct bearing on educational thought and practice. The fact that the same economic theories are not accepted by all economists, the same political theories by all political scientists, and the same theories about social structures by all sociologists accounts for pluralism among social scientists and debates about the provision of education. Theory mediates between general aims and educational thought. Politicians attempt to justify practice by appealing to aims; social scientists by appealing to theory.

The normative character of aims is frequently acknowledged. Social scientific theories are frequently held to explain features of our real social world and, therefore, are held to have a different status from normative statements in that they can be tested empirically. To date no empirical tests have persuaded social scientists conclusively to abandon one paradigm and to embrace an alternative paradigm. Parenthetically not everyone rejects astrology and competing theories continue to inform the work of physicists and biologists. The relatively high normative component in social scientific theories implies that decisive empirical testing of them is not practicable even if it is theoretically possible.

Testable hypotheses may be derived from theory. It is on this assumption that the empirical aspect of the problem(-solving) approach in comparative education depends. As stated, a hypothesis corresponds in practice to a policy solution. If we are to plan the development of education we should be able to test the effectiveness of policies and it was with this purpose in mind that I adopted Popper's hypothetico-deductive method and applied it in comparative education. The importance of testing hypotheses derived from theory lies in the fact that theories are used to legitimise educational practice. In so far as no appeal is made to observable data, the status of hypotheses, theories and normative laws is the same. Consider, for example, the extent to which

(1) *theories of knowledge* justify curricula, methods of teaching and examination systems;

(2) *theories of society* justify the kinds of provision made in terms of school types, e.g. general, technical vocational, within a school structure classified on the basis of level, e.g. first, second, and stage, e.g. lower and upper second-level schools;
(3) *theories of man* legitimise selection procedures and who should have access to various levels of schooling, how children should be grouped for the purposes of instruction, e.g. streaming and setting, how teaching is individualised and the appropriateness of curricula for different types of child.

The role of philosophers, sociologists, psychologists and economists in the study of education is determined by the extent to which the aims of education are regarded as intrinsic or instrumental. Philosophers and historians of ideas first made contributions to educational theory. Then psychologists entered the field, followed closely by comparative educationists. Sociologists began to contribute prior to the Second World War. Recognition that education provision could be regarded in economic terms and that it could be studied seriously by political scientists is a fairly recent phenomenon. Undoubtedly from their different perspectives social scientists can make a major contribution to our understanding of educational processes. These theories frequently mediate between general aims and practice. Because these theories include a substantial normative element I prefer to place them in constructed ideal-typical normative patterns, reserving testable hypotheses (sociological laws) for inclusion in constructed institutional patterns.

Theoretically, in unproblematic situations, aims, theories, mental states and policies (hypotheses) should form a logically coherent and consistent pattern. Within an identified context, for example, cultural community, nation-state, if everyone accepted and had internalised all the components of this ideal-typical pattern no 'problems' would arise. It is because consistency is theoretical and rarely found in practice and because some individuals accept traditional aims and theories while others advance radically different ones that 'problems' can be identified. In other words, certain kinds of 'problem' can be analysed by studying proposals to change educational aims and to adopt new social scientific theories on the assumption that neither mental states nor human behaviour are necessarily related to stated aims and theories.

SOURCES OF DATA FOR IDEAL-TYPICAL NORMATIVE PATTERNS

If ideal-typical normative models are to be useful the sources from which they are derived should be stated. Thus reliability depends upon the possibility that other research workers can independently check and replicate a construct, and verify its details. The validity of a construct depends upon the extent to which it is accepted as appropriate to the context for which it has been designed. Two types of choice have to be made, therefore, when selecting sources. One criterion turns on the reliability of the sources, in other words their 'public' character. The second criterion of validity is extended to ensure that the choice of 'public' documents is appropriate.

As for the construction of the most general ideal-typical models in terms of theories about man, society and knowledge, the obvious sources are the works of world-renowned philosophers. Their writings can be consulted and the extent to which they provide general conceptual frameworks and justify them logically can be assessed. Usually it is possible to establish, in the light of historical research, that the theories advanced by a particular philosopher have influenced legislation and institutions established in accordance with it. Historical evidence may show how philosophical theories have been disseminated and accepted by members of identifiable communities, for example, Christians, Muslims, Englishmen, French citizens, and so on. Such evidence makes choice of philosopher less arbitrary but historical justification is not the principal criterion on which such a choice should be made. A pragmatic decision to choose this rather than another philosopher will be justified by the extent to which the sources selected turn out usefully to illuminate the 'problems' under consideration. I shall suggest later that one test of usefulness lies in the relationships that can be established between the theories put forward by a philosopher or his followers and present-day documents that enjoy constitutional or legal status.

A distinction should be drawn between philosophers who provide a *Weltanschauung* and those whose discussions have been restricted to one or another aspect of social life. In the first category may be placed philosophers like Plato, Aristotle, Locke, Condorcet, Marx and Dewey. Some of them were educational theorists but their fame does not rest solely on this aspect of their contribution to aims and theories. On the other hand a list of educational thinkers whose general present-day philosophical importance is less springs to mind: Comenius, Pestalozzi, Froebel, Herbart and Montessori. Each philosopher and each educational thinker has his or her present-day followers. In short *schools of philosophy* can be identified and simplified general ideal-typical patterns constructed on data selected from their works in the light of our three criteria and from *schools of educational thought* can be selected information to fill out the educational sector of an ideal-typical pattern. In the same way the writings of philosophers who have directed their attention to economics, the law and social structures are potential sources of detailed information.

The choice of appropriate philosophical source or sources is bound to be somewhat arbitrary. In selecting from a wealth of sources the research worker should have in mind concepts of reliability and validity, his particular 'problem' and the context (or contexts) in which he intends to analyse it and the policy solutions offered to the 'problems'. Answers to the following questions should influence his choice.

(1) *Spatial context.* For what context is the construct intended? The world? A major continent? A nation-state? An area inside a nation?
(2) *Historical dimension.* Is the construct intended to simplify complex traditions and the deeply held sentiments of people sharing the same culture, living in a particular region, nation, or province?
(3) *Contemporary scene.* Is the construct intended as a way of bringing into focus present-day international and national debates about the aims of education? Or is its value limited to a culturally identifiable region?
(4) *Social change.* How far is the construct designed to enable hopes and expectations of some (or all) people (e.g. politicians, educationists, parents) to be analysed?
(5) *Policy aims.* Will the ideal-typical construct facilitate our understanding of the aims that inform educational policies?
(6) *Implementing policy.* Will the construct throw light on possible constraints against or positive influences favouring the successful implementation of educational reform?
(7) *Economic/Political considerations.* Are national (or regional) levels of economic and/or political developments important in choice of construct?

When spatial, historical and cultural considerations coincide the choice of philosopher, or school of philosophy, becomes fairly obvious. The following examples are offered as illustrating this point.

Among *European-North American* philosophers or schools of philosophy that provide statements about man, society and knowledge the following can be identified.

(1) *Classicism.* From among Greek philosophers Plato and Aristotle would be obvious choices from which to derive an ideal-typical normative pattern. Some scholars would wish to draw a sharp distinction between the two philosophers; while alternative philosophers such as the sophists may be preferred as a source of general normative theories.
(2) *Encyclopaedism.* A number of eighteenth-century philosophies provide concepts of man, society and knowledge as constituents of coherent constructs. Useful models can be derived from French and American thinkers.

(3) *Socialism and communism*. The choice of Marx as the spokesman of a particular form of society is obvious.
(4) *Pragmatism*. At the end of the nineteenth century a small group of American thinkers consciously worked out a range of new theories to meet, as they saw them, the needs of their time.

Cultural considerations suggest that to most, if not all, of these positions should be added data from Christian and Judaic sources.

Near East and *Oriental* sources would include world religions such as Buddhism, Judaism and Islam, and philosophies such as Confucianism, Hinduism and Shintoism which command the loyalty of many followers.

Tribal sources are important. Their value may be restricted to problems found in relatively small communities. In some cases documentary sources may be difficult (or impossible) to obtain but anthropological data are useful if an ideal normative pattern is required for research purposes.

The above list is simply illustrative. Over the centuries to 'pure' and easily identified sources such as Plato's *Republic,* the Bible and the Qur'an have been added elements from a great many different sources. Cross-fertilisation has also taken place so that the choice of a particular source will depend upon the 'problem' to be investigated. The many interpretations of and within these philosophic and religious traditions and the processes of disseminating them beyond the communities in which they had their origins are the sources of many 'problems' in comparative education perspective.

The illustrations imply that major religions are appropriate sources of normative patterns for cultural communities, for example, the Christian, Buddhist and Muslim worlds. These may or may not coincide with geographical regions. Such patterns are required when cross-cultural comparative education research is undertaken. The generality of the statements may be too great, however, to be useful in cross-national investigations within a region informed by one of these cultural traditions, for example, Europe. Since cross-national studies constitute the majority of comparative education research it is desirable that nation-specific patterns should be constructed.

Such patterns may be derived from major theoretical systems by reference to representative philosophers and interpreters of dominant religious beliefs. Choice of a representative national philosopher may well be a matter of debate and discussion. Similar considerations to those mentioned in choosing the source of a major abstract conceptual scheme are relevant. The following illustrations may stimulate discussion.

Several ideal-typical models can be constructed for use in the European context. All may be assumed to be variations by processes of acceptance and rejection on general Platonic or Aristotelian models. Information selected on the basis of the three major indicators – man, society and knowledge – from the philosophies of Descartes, Locke, Hegel, Spencer, Dewey and Lenin provide useful models for research into European and North American problems arising from the assumption that some aspects of classical Judaic-Christian traditions have been rejected while others are debated or have been retained.

For Europe and North America, nation-specific models identify present-day 'problems' and proposed solutions to them might be based on the following sources and combinations of them.

England Plato/Aristotle; the Bible; Locke (or J. S. Mill)
France Plato/Aristotle; the Bible; Descartes (or Condorcet)
USA Plato/Aristotle; the Bible; the sophists; Jefferson (or Dewey)
USSR Plato/Aristotle; the Bible; the encyclopaedists; Marx (or Lenin)

The common elements in these European–North American constructs are emphasised by the inclusion of the same religious and secular sources. Attention is drawn to nation-specific elements by including philosophies whose relevance to national educational systems is apparent when comparisons are made of these systems. In subsequent chapters more detailed but simplified accounts are given of the theories found in one or several of the major works of Plato, Marx and Dewey in the belief that they remain among the most useful paradigms within which international and national debates about education today take place. A brief summary of four models against which national policies can be compared is given here. The usefulness of each will depend upon the 'problem' under investigation and the contexts in which it is analysed.

Platonic Model (Context: Western Europe, traditional)
Nature of man. Men are unequal and for the most part inherit the qualities which make for inequality.

Nature of society. The just society is stable and unchanging; in it men have specific duties to perform, know their place and are content to occupy it and perform tasks appropriate to their abilities.

Nature of knowledge. Knowledge and wisdom inform the just society. Since knowledge is accessible to a limited number of persons it is they who should be the leaders of society – the philosopher-kings. Knowledge is of permanent 'ideas' and can be acquired intuitively.

Aristotelian Model (context: Western Europe, Roman Catholic)
Nature of man. Men are unequal. Some are destined to be free men,

others to be slaves. A major characteristic of free men is that they are rational animals.

Nature of society. The good society is one in which all free men participate democratically in the affairs of citizens. Rationality will ensure its success.

Nature of knowledge. Knowledge is of immanent ideas or essences. It is available to free men provided they use the correct methods of logic and inductive generalisation. Explanations are made in the light of final, formal, material and efficient causes.

Encyclopaedist Model (context: France, Western and Eastern Europe, traditional-contemporary)
Nature of man. Men are unequal but all are capable of reason which enables them to know their rights and to exercise their duties responsibly.

Nature of society. The just society is one in which all men are regarded as equal before the law. Its leaders are men who possess natural talents (an aristocracy not of wealth or of birth but of talent). It is democratic, informed by reason and progressively so. The rights of property are protected and the economy is based upon farming. Equality, liberty and brotherhood represent the aims of social life.

Nature of knowledge. All knowledge is worthwhile. Scientific subjects are more important than literary subjects: modern languages more important than the classics. Practical subjects have value. By this time different epistemologies had been proposed and induction as the method of science had been further developed.

Marxist Model (context: USSR, Eastern Europe, contemporary)
Nature of man. All men are equal. Differences in achievement are not wholly or principally due to inherited abilities.

Nature of society. The good society is based upon ownership of the means of production by the workers and upon the development of appropriate relationships between workers and between them and the modes of production. In such a classless society there can be no exploitation of one man by another. It is a technological society.

Nature of knowledge. Knowledge of the laws of social development depends upon an understanding of material conditions and the economic forces acting on society. Conflicts in history are sources of information, Dialectical materialism is the method of inquiry. In the nineteenth century a number of other positivistic epistemologies were proposed.

Pragmatic Model (context: USA, contemporary)
Nature of man. Men are unequal but as individuals possess intelligence which enables them collectively to solve their problems.

Nature of society. The good society is democratic and changing. It should provide equality before the law and freedom for individuals to compete without destroying the basis of brotherhood.

Nature of knowledge. Knowledge is relative, contingent and contextual. Methods of acquiring it are by problem-solving in which reference is made to empirical evidence.

These extremely brief and crude illustrations are intended to show how comparable data can be built up and classified in a meaningful way. They represent models derived from major indicators. In spite of the obvious limitations due to simplifications it should be noted that to increase the accuracy of ideal types by making them more complex may detract from their usefulness. Clearly a balance needs to be drawn between generality and simplicity and detail and complexity. In *Problems in Education* I called patterns drawn from philosophical sources 'pure ideal-typical models'. Their value extends to an analysis of problems in the Third World where European ideas have been disseminated.

CONSTITUTIONS AND LEGISLATION AS SOURCES OF 'ACTUAL' IDEAL–TYPICAL PATTERNS

The need for sources that are context-specific and whose validity is not in dispute has persuaded me since the appearance of *Problems in Education* that attempts should not be made to modify ideal-typical constructs in the light of historical evidence and judgements but that constitutions and legislation are useful sources of 'actual' or legitimised ideal-typical models. To be sure the processes by which international declarations and national legislation are legitimised can be examined by noting how policy is formulated and adopted and the individuals and groups who participate in these procedures. Procedures of adoption give some indication of the degree to which constitutions and legislation represent public opinion. This pragmatic justification for taking legal documents as the source of international and nation-specific constructs should not obscure the fact that they may stem from 'higher' rather than 'lower' valuations, that within any constitution or pattern of legislation logical inconsistencies may exist and that features of them will be the subject of considerable national debate.

Legal documents rarely spell out fully or justify the theories of man, society, or knowledge from which they have been derived. They legitimise theories which, while implicit, can be made explicit by analysis and reference to appropriate philosophical sources. It is unlikely that any one piece of legislation (or a constitution) will offer a complete construct. It will at best provide a partial picture of a major philosophical position or a previous formal document in some interpretation of one or the other. Furthermore, a constitution may include among its clauses proposals made by individuals holding different theoretical positions. These considerations imply that constructs derived from constitutions and legislation are likely to be less comprehensive and 'pure' than constructs based on the writings of philosophers. Their reliability and validity are less in question and frequently, as in the USA, they provide an overt framework within which educational policies are publicly debated

In the context of previous discussion some comments should be made about constitutions and legislation. First, each nation's legislation has unique characteristics. Naturally the content is national-specific but the style and amount of detail frequently differ from legislation in other countries. Examples of these differences can be found by comparing legislation in the USA and in the UK. Style is often determined by the amount of freedom for political manoeuvre legislators wish or are compelled to allow. Thus some types of legislation reflect 'higher valuations' and the substantive content is relatively small. Other types of legislation go into greater detail and confer a whole range of statutory powers on specified groups or agencies. A careful analysis should be made of legislative statements that express general aims or expectations and those that confer statutory powers. A distinction should also be drawn between statutory powers that can easily be enforced and those more difficult to implement. A final comment about legal documents is that for the purposes of research they may represent problem-creating changes or problem-solving solutions. The observer's perspective is bound to influence any judgement made along these lines.

Examples of statements intended to provide aims of policy for the whole world are found in the United Nations Declaration of Universal Rights and the charters and terms of reference of its special agencies such as Unesco. The United Nations Declaration states what rights – the right to freedom of speech, the right to work and the right to education – human beings should enjoy in an ideal world. In the real world they represent aims of policy. Because the agencies that make up the United Nations have few statutory powers over the policies and actions of sovereign states, the Declaration represents many 'higher valuations' that have not yet been realised in practice. Nevertheless, governments justify their educational policies by reference to the Declaration and demands for education have been made in accordance with its provisions. These, far from induced from practice, are normative and are so general that while receiving universal approval they are open to a range of policy interpretations. Neither the United Nations nor its special agencies have the power to insist that practices in line with the Declaration are implemented by national governments.

The same may be said about the status of education in another international document, the Treaty of Rome. As members of the European Economic Community, its signatories are under an obligation to accept the principles of co-operation laid down in the Treaty and to abide by the decisions reached by the Commission established under the Treaty with specific duties and powers. In the sphere of vocational training the Treaty commits its members to seek to harmonise policies and allow the free movement of labour within the Community. In the absence of specific powers it does not have the power to harmonise educational policy. In this respect the Treaty of Rome resembles in a more limited context the United Nations Declaration. The similarities and differences between the two documents should, however, be carefully studied if their usefulness in comparative education studies is to be assessed.

In many sovereign states social action is debated within the terms of written constitution. A major difference between national constitutions and international declarations lies in the powers conferred on the agencies established to realise aims and policies. The powers of three major branches of government – the legislature, the executive and the judiciary – are usually prescribed in a constitution. Over some aspects of policy one or other of these branches may have statutory powers which can be enforced. In some areas of policy a constitution may be very specific. In other societal sectors the power of the branches named in a constitution may be advisory rather than mandatory. Consequently, while using constitutions as the source of ideal-typical normative models, careful analyses and comparisons of the distribution of power are needed if they are to be useful in comparative education research. In particular it is necessary to note how far responsibility for education is laid down in a nation's constitution and what details of policy are made explicit.

In so far as constitutions represent traditional consensus they may be taken as no-change elements in a problematic situation. Challenges to established constitutions represent change and consequently may be regarded as a potential source of new 'problems'. Such 'problems' may be solved by amending a constitution or replacing it by a new one which may introduce new norms or reallocate power within the nation-state for which it has been designed. Numerous 'problems' are a result of introducing, in newly independent countries, constitutions that reflect the norms and power distribution of former imperial powers. The processes by which constitutions are formulated and adopted and the constraints they then place on legislation and judicial decisions are among the studies that are needed if this kind of ideal-typical normative model is to be useful in analysing and comparing educational 'problems' and if the political constraints on policy implementations are to be anticipated.

In nations possessing a constitution, legislation lays down detailed policies in accordance with principles enshrined in the constitution and creates or identifies institutions through which it is hoped that these aims and policies can be realised in practice. Agreement on aims and policies established in legislation and an overt willingness of individuals to work towards their achievement do not guarantee that appropriate institutions are established or that the psychological traits of individuals will ensure that whatever institution is set up will be run in a way that will ensure that the aims of policy are achieved. Gaps between legislation, the constitution and the running of institutions are common sources of problems that can be analysed in comparative education.

In the absence of a written constitution, legislation provides normative patterns for specific policies in a sovereign state. The general principles that inform the running of societal agencies and the treatment of individuals are likely to be implicit rather than explicit. Legislation nevertheless allocates statutory and advisory powers either in accordance with traditional norms or on the basis of novel principles. The fact that aims are vicariously or directly debated during processes of policy formulation, adoption and implementation means that in a restricted sense innovation can be brought about by legislative reform. Changes of this kind are basically normative. They may precede or follow institutional change. Generally speaking they precede the ability of the majority of individuals to internalise the values inherent in new legislation. In other words, the mental states of many people responsible for implementing new legislation will probably lag behind its intentions.

Constitutions and legislation provide ideal-typical constructs against which normative innovations can be judged. Since the date of the adoption of a constitution or legislation is known, the period in a nation's history when a measure of consensus on certain norms was achieved can be identified, that is, the period during which legislation remains on the statute book. Against this historical starting point changes in norms can be judged. The frequency with which constitutions and legislations are formally revoked or modified varies from country to country and from period to period. The extent to which these changes are associated with violence or take place within a legal framework also differs. Changes that take place in accordance with constitutional procedures create different problems from those changes brought about by revolutionary or extra-constitutional methods. In any case, constitutional and legislative changes may be regarded as problem-solving or as problem-creating. They are clearly important starting points for problem analysis in the approach I advocate.

EXAMPLES – CONSTITUTIONS AND LEGISLATION

The literature dealing with constitutions and constitutional theory is extensive.[8] Many sovereign states have constitutions. Some, like the US constitution, have a long history. In other cases, as in France, one constitution has been replaced by one or by several different ones. Most newly independent nations, such as the Indian Union, soon adopted constitutions; several of these were very similar to those of their former imperial power. Soon after the Second World War new constitutions were drawn up and adopted in Italy, the Federal German Republic and Japan. All these constitutions were designed to provide a political and judicial framework for action.

Of particular interest to comparative educationists are statements about education in the constitutions of major countries. These include the USSR (for which a new constitution was adopted in 1977), France (for which country de Gaulle helped to draw up a new constitution in 1959), Japan (whose constitution was adopted in 1947) and India (constitution of 1946). Education is not mentioned in the US constitution but judicial rulings on education under state and federal constitutions have an important influence on school systems. While there is no written British constitution the Westminster model has been widely copied. In the absence of a constitution, major legislation such as the 1944 Education Act must serve as an actual ideal-typical model for education in England and Wales.

In summary, criteria for comparing constitutions include the power ascribed to the legislative, executive and judicial branches of government; the relationships between these branches; the way in which individual rights are protected; and the rules given to the schools and the agencies controlling them. Broadly speaking, a distinction may be drawn between constitutions which confer considerable powers over aspects of education on agencies of the national (or federal) government and those constitutions which reserve most of these powers to local (provincial) authorities.

MAJOR CONSTITUTIONS AND LEGISLATION OF RELEVANCE IN COMPARATIVE EDUCATION

(1) *England and Wales*

In the absence of a written constitution and in the light of Parliament's sovereignty the 1944 Education Act is the most obvious source of an ideal-typical construct for education in England and Wales. Scottish and Northern Ireland Acts should be used as bases for appropriate constructs.

(2) *France*

Condorcet's report to the Convention in 1792 remains a classic in the field of educational legislation. Subsequently, constitutions of the five republics, including that associated with the accession to power of de Gaulle, are important sources of constructs. Major decrees on education were issued after 1959.

(3) *India*

The constitution of 1947 laid down in some detail the aims of educational policy and the respective powers of the federal and state governments.

(4) *Japan*

A new constitution was adopted during the Allied Occupation in 1947. It was associated with the Fundamental Law of Education 1947 which has been subsequently modified by decrees and other ministry directives. Of particular relevance is the 1966 Model of the Ideal Human Being which informs moral education in Japanese schools.

(5) *USSR*

The constitution adopted in 1935 allocated power to All-Union and republic ministries of education and laid down some rights in education. The 1977 constitution established principles of equal provision. The 1958 Khrushchev reforms in the *Act Bringing Education Nearer to Life* and subsequent modifications are important.

(6) *USA*

The constitution including the Bill of Rights and subsequent Amendments is the source of Supreme Court decisions on religion, race and academic freedom. Morrill (1862) and subsequent Acts provided federal funds for education under the Preamble to the Constitution – in particular the 1958 National Defense and Education Act and the 1965 Elementary and Secondary Education Act.

MAJOR MODELS – WESTERN EUROPE, USA AND USSR

Choice of model, we have said, should not be arbitrary. The value of a model relates to the extent to which it facilitates problem analysis, an examination of proposed solutions and some understanding of the national spirit associated with school systems. Pragmatically, and in the light of history, three major models compete today in the educational world. One, with its national variations, is derived from classical Greece. I consider it best exemplified in Plato's *Republic*. A second major model is derived from the pragmatists of the USA. I have taken Dewey as the source of my North American model. A third major construct is designed to throw light on assumptions and debates in the USSR. As a source of one pure ideal-typical model for the USSR I have selected the 'Communist Manifesto' by Marx and Engels.[9]

The amount of research which has gone into the preparation of these three models varies considerably. Having been educated in Europe and having visited the USA and USSR regularly over a period of more than twenty years, I am reasonably confident that present debates (and indeed some practices) in Western Europe, the USA and the USSR can usefully be located in the deliberately simplified national constructs that are presented in the next three chapters.

NOTES AND REFERENCES: CHAPTER 6

The ideas developed in this chapter were first presented in a lecture delivered at the second general meeting of the Comparative Education Society in Europe, held in Berlin in 1965; see 'Rational constructs in comparative education', in *General Education in a Changing World, Proceedings of the Comparative Education Society in Europe,* Berlin, 1965.

1 A panel of consultants met in Geneva in 1975 to discuss educational goals and theories. A report of this meeting was published by the International Bureau of Education, Geneva, 1975; see Brian Holmes, 'Aims and theories in education – a framework for comparative study', in this report.
2 Unesco/IBE, *Recommendations 1934–1960,* Publication No. 222, Unesco, Paris, 1962.
3 Alfred Schutz, *The Phenomenology of the Social World,* Heinemann, London, 1972; Peter L. Berger, *Invitation to Sociology,* Penguin, Harmondsworth, 1974; Roy Turner (ed.), *Ethnomethodology,* Penguin, Harmondsworth, 1974; Jürgen Habermas, *Theory and Practice,* Heinemann, London, 1974; Edmund Husserl, *Phenomenonogy and the Crisis of Philosophy,* Harper & Row, New York, 1965.
4 W. G. Runciman (ed.), *Weber Selections in Translation,* Cambridge University Press, Cambridge, 1978.
5 See V. Pareto's analysis of non-logical behaviour in Arthur Livingston (ed.), *Mind and Society* (trans. into English, 4 vols), Harcourt Brace, New York, 1935, on Marx's notion of 'false consciousness'.
6 See G. Myrdal, *An American Dilemma* (2 vols), McGraw-Hill, New York, 1964, and Pareto, *Mind and Society,* op. cit.
7 Mallinson, *Introduction to Comparative Education,* op. cit.
8 K. C. Wheare, *Modern Constitutions*, Oxford University Press, London, 1966.
9 K. Marx and F. Engels, *Manifesto of the Communist Party,* Foreign Languages Bureau, Moscow, 1959.

Chapter 7

Plato's Just Society

When I first visited the USA in 1955 'progressive' educationists were under attack. Academics held them responsible for lowered standards of achievement in the high schools and maintained that teacher training courses were repetitious, lacked content and were based on vague concepts of social relevance. Child-centred education and life adjustment courses were particularly severely criticised. Politicians, businessmen and an assorted collection of disillusioned members of the public attacked the social reconstructionist wing of the progressive education movement. In the 1930s, under the leadership of professors in the social foundation department at Teachers College, Columbia University, the social reconstructionists had argued that the quality of life in the USA during the traumatic economic depression could only be improved by the schools under the leadership of the professors of education who were training future and serving teachers. The social reconstructionists were influenced by Harold Laski, professor at the London School of Economics and Political Science and a leading member of the Labour Party, and Karl Mannheim who, deeply impressed by English tradition, was advocating total democratic planning. Later he was to persuade students at the University of London Institute of Education that they would be his troops in the reconstruction of postwar British society.

In the 1930s Robert Maynard Hutchins, then chancellor of the University of Chicago, was a leader of the academic opposition to proposals made by progressive educationists to make high school curricula relevant to the personal and social needs of millions of high school pupils. They claimed that such a reform would not in fact lower standards of achievement in colleges and universities and had carried out the *Eight-Year Study*[1] to make their point.

In *The Higher Learning in America* Hutchins advanced typically[2] European views about the purposes of university education and the subjects that should be taught to achieve these purposes. He asserted that the purpose of the university was to provide a sound liberal education for those few who had the potential to benefit from it. Basically the case Hutchins made was similar to the one made by Aristotle who argued that liberal education should develop the rationality of those individuals who were qualified to participate in the political life of a democracy and who would have time to develop leisure activities.

Aristotle proposed that a curriculum based on the seven liberal arts – the subjects of the trivium and the quadrivium – would help to achieve these aims. Hutchins, too, wanted the number of subjects taught at universities to be radically restructured. In the 1930s he favoured the inclusion of the classical languages but not modern foreign languages and the inclusion of the 'pure' natural sciences but not 'applied' subjects. Subjects had to satisfy two criteria. First, they should have logical coherence, and secondly, they should promote rationality.

Similar proposals were made in the 1950s by the opponents of 'socially relevant' and 'child-centred' curricula. A. E. Bestor, among others, in *Educational Wastelands* and *The Restoration of Learning,*[3] dismissed progressive curricula in favour of a curriculum restricted to the traditional disciplines. Hutchins had modified his position somewhat without in any real sense abandoning it. This subject-centred curriculum theory was very reminiscent of English theory and practices in the universities of continental Europe.

The political attack on progressive education was inflamed by the Cold War and the search made by the US Senate Committee on Un-American Activities under the chairmanship of Senator Joseph McCarthy for communist subversives. Earlier claims made by progressive educationists that society should be planned and that the schools should be the agents of social reconstruction made it possible for McCarthy to suggest that they were communists or fellow travellers and that practices based on their theories would undermine the security of the United States.

In this climate of debate, suspicion and, indeed, persecution I was invited in 1956 to deliver the Boyd H. Bode Memorial Lectures at Ohio State University. Bode had been a progressive educationist but in *Progressive Education at the Crossroads*[4] had made sympathetic criticism of some aspects of the movement. I took it upon myself in *American Criticism of American Education* to ask unsympathetic critics of progressive education how far in rejecting 'progressive' theories of education and in advocating European practices they were prepared to accept traditional theories of society, man and knowledge. And I made a first tentative attempt to draw up an ideal-typical model of normative theories which informed traditional school practices but which were increasingly debated by educationists in Europe. For various reasons I selected Plato's *Republic* as the most useful source of an European ideal-typical model which could be compared with an American model derived from the writings of John Dewey.

Plato's concern in the *Republic* was to describe the 'ideal society' and in the event he offered a coherent pattern of normative propositions about the characteristics a society ought to have, how people ought to be classified and treated, and how knowledge ought to be acquired and what status it ought to have. The arguments in favour of his proposals were logical rather than empirical and can be contrasted with the theories of the sophists, of whom Protagoras is a representative, and the materialists, of whom Democritus was an early spokesman. The arbitrary choice of author and document should, in short, be recognised. Justification of the choice lies in the usefulness of the model rather than in its correspondence to reality. From my point of view it was designed in the first instance to facilitate a comparison of those American and European assumptions about society, man and knowledge which have some bearing on school systems.

Take, for example, the notion of social change, and contrast the views of Plato and Dewey. Plato's assumption was that the perfect society was a just society and the just society was one that most closely corresponded to a transcendent ideal. Social change was a process of degeneration or social decay. Since Plato's main interest was in the political aspects of society, he considered that of the three forms of government – the rule of one man, of the few and of the many – a monarchy most nearly approached the ideal. Any change in it makes the society less perfect. Consequently any government by the many (a democracy) which replaces a government by one wise leader (a monarchy) is more corrupt. Plato describes the stages through which the process of degeneration takes place. In parenthesis it should be noted that a democracy may well degenerate into tyranny, that is, a government under the leadership of one unsuitable man. As we shall see, the perfect state depends on the qualities of its leader or leaders and the extent to which it is run according to established laws. Given this evaluation of change as decay it is necessary to examine in simplistic terms how Plato tried to construct an ideal-typical model of the perfect society.

First, to repeat what has just been said, the ideal society should be stable, preferably static, or at least one that changed as little as possible. The typically conservative reaction to politics is that governments ought to use their power to arrest all political change; that new tendencies are subversive and should be opposed; for only by maintaining the status quo can justice be ensured. In order to examine the logic of this position it is necessary to describe in some detail the characteristics of the 'just' society.

It ought to be functional. Since Plato's conception is principally political there should be in the just society rulers and ruled. From this point of view there ought to be two main classes in society: the ruling class, which can be subdivided into the true leaders (the guardians) and their armed auxiliaries or warriors; and the workers. This broad classification continues to inform European political analysis whether or not the distinction is acceptable. Plato's concern is, of course, with the education of leaders. Education for leadership remains an important aim for many European educationists.

In contrast, the training of workers is quite another thing. Its aims are different and its status is derived from the class of individuals for whom it is intended. Plato's interest in the workers was minimal and consequently he has nothing much to say on how they should be trained. There can be little doubt, however, that in his ideal-typical model education and training are functionally related to class structures in society: education for the leaders and their auxiliaries; training for workers who have specific economic tasks to perform.

In this kind of society the stability of the class structure is important. The rulers should rule; the workers should work. Leaders may be selected from the auxiliaries but only very exceptionally from among the workers. Social and political mobility is antithetical to good government. Indeed, the economic model is one in which each individual does only one, specialised, job. The carpenter should confine himself to making furniture; the shoemaker to making shoes. Each person should perform the job for which he is best suited. However, not much harm is done if workers change jobs. Great harm results from the promotion of unsuitable workers into the leadership class. In general, in the perfect society members of each class will mind their own business and will not meddle in the affairs of others. By extension members of the upper, middle and lower classes ought to recognise that they have different roles to perform and that society will benefit if they get on with the job suited to their abilities and class without interfering with the activities of members of another class.

This theory of society is based on notions of function. Not all the functions are equally important. How can a society in which some people occupy privileged positions and perform high-status tasks while others occupy lower positions and do menial jobs be regarded as just? Plato's answer is that social inequalities are the consequence of the natural differences between individuals. Men and women are different. And among men inequality is simply a fact. Some men are capable of being leaders, others are not. Unequals ought not be treated as though they were equal; this, according to Plato, can only result in injustice. The starkness of the assertion should not obscure present-day debates either about the wrongness of elitism and the rightness of 'positive' discrimination or about selective education for gifted children and special education for handicapped children. The point is that in this conservative ideal-typical model a theory of societal inequality is logically consistent with a psychological theory of individual differences.

In Plato's description of society these differences are inherited. Clever parents beget clever children. The sons of leaders are potential leaders. Indeed, so convinced is Plato of the innate character of ability that he suggests that in the ideal society, in order to avoid mixing the noble blood of leaders with the base blood of the workers, unions should be carefully arranged so as to keep the race of guardians pure. If this is regarded as too fanciful to be of present-day relevance I would remind readers of doctrines espoused in Hitler's Nazi Germany and the deep prejudices against miscegenation held by people throughout the world. Plato wishes to supervise breeding so as to prevent any degeneration or corruption of human beings. For such changes in human nature are bound to induce undesirable social change. The new generation of leaders will not be qualified to rule wisely and justly and presumably the workers will not be as suited by nature to perform their menial tasks.

Plato's theory of individual differences is expressed in an analogy. Just as there are noble metals, gold and silver, so there are people with these metals in their veins. Qualities of leadership are possessed by those who have (inherited) gold and silver in their veins. Bronze and iron flow in the veins of workers and endow them with the skills needed if they are to perform their natural occupation. In discussing the psychology of man's soul Plato divides it into three parts: reason, energy and animal instincts. Each part corresponds to the qualities that should be possessed by members of his three classes, guardians, warriors and workers, respectively. Here is a psychological theory that finds present-day expression in genetic theories of inherited ability and in Spearman's theory of general intelligence and its unequal distribution throughout any population, and indeed in the faculty psychology of such as E. L. Thorndike and his successors.

Social stability depends upon the willingness of members of the ruling classes to recognise that their internal unity should be preserved. In order that they should feel united they should regard themselves as members of one big family and should take care not to marry outside their class. Competition among them should be eliminated and property, women and children should be owned in common by the members of the ruling class. Education should be an instrument of class rule and, in so far as it prevents disunity among the rulers and hence inhibits change, is necessary if society is to remain stable.

The aims of education can be inferred from Plato's ideal-typical model. It should promote reason or rationality. It should develop class-consciousness and team spirit. Since the guardians and auxiliaries have to be fierce and gentle at the same time (shades of Machiavelli's *Prince*) their education should develop both these qualities of character: the games-playing Christian gentleman, no less. For Plato, gymnastics ought to promote fierceness; literary studies ought to promote gentleness. A balance should be found between these two aspects of education so that a proper balance of qualities is produced. Given this balance, rulers will be able to and indeed should treat the ruled neither too cruelly not too softly. In another context wisdom should be the virtue possessed by guardians and coinage the virtue proper to their auxiliaries or warriors. Education should make sure that these virtues are rewarded and the school system should be used to select future leaders and train them.

How should educationists fulfil these societal functions? To answer the question some further examination should be made of the virtues that should be possessed by leaders. Wisdom is essential; it is the source of goodness – and both should be informed by knowledge. Lack of knowledge, indeed, is the source of moral error. For this reason the leader should possess or seek truth. He should be learned. The philosopher fits this description and therefore the ruler of Plato's ideal state should be the 'philosopher-king'. Only such a person can acquire knowledge of the ideal state and the laws on the basis of which it should be governed. Moreover he alone is in a position to know something about the essential nature of man. Thus he can help to prevent undesirable change and realise in practice the perfect society. Collectively an aristocracy of talent should be the lawgivers and the founders of the just society.

As for knowledge, a major question for Plato and other Greek thinkers was: in a world of changing experiences, what is knowable? The answer philosophers of at least two schools of thought gave was similar. In the ceaseless flow of experiences only knowledge of what is permanent can be acquired. Atoms were permanent for the materialists. Ideas or essences were permanent for the idealists. For these philosophers knowledge is either of atoms and their movements or of permanent ideas. For Plato knowable ideas transcend but determine the nature of things, plants, animals, human beings and social institutions. In the event pure ideas are imperfectly realised in practice and as things change they become less perfect. Knowledge is of pure ideas that cannot change.

At the level of specific knowledge a philosopher should be trained among other things in pure mathematics, pure astronomy, pure harmonies and, most important of all, in the methods of acquiring knowledge, namely, dialectics. One segment of the true philosopher or king's world is 'all that the mere reasoning process apprehends by the force of dialectic'. And this knowledge is apprehended by the exercise of pure reason, to which intelligence and intuition make notable contributions. If the precise methods of acquiring knowledge are not made clear in Plato's *Republic* or even in his *Theaetetus*, there can be little doubt that for him sense impressions are unreliable and the knowledge that should inform human behaviour and social life is in some sense rational.

This very simplified account of Plato's major theories is designed to show the coherence of his thinking and to suggest that as constituents of an ideal-typical model they make tradition, change and debates about European systems of education understandable.

The limitations of this very simplified model and of ideal-typical models in general should be recognised. Some present-day sociologists suggest that they are not only invalid but their use is positively dangerous. In my judgement they are criticising an interpretation of the use of ideal-typical models that I too reject. Ideal-typical models should not be regarded as providing a comprehensive picture of reality, nor should they be used to stereotype the behaviour of any individual or group of individuals. An ideal-typical model should be compared with theoretical paradigms employed by natural sciences. It provides a framework of assumptions within which in a commonsense way research workers pursue their inquiries. Normative ideal-typical models of the kind sketched above for Europe are intended to focus attention on statements of what 'ought to be the case'. Clearly, if we accept Popper's opinion, normative statements will almost certainly be challenged. Even if they are expressed in formal constitutions or legislation they represent only a certain kind of limited consensus. Relationships between normative statements and human behaviour are logical but may be tested empirically.

Given these reservations about and restriction on their use, the fact that they are contrived and established on the basis of a selection from a range of normative statements should not be a ground for serious criticism. It is evident, for example, that my Platonic model for Europe is based on a selection of views, for the most part expressed in one of innumerable sources. It is also clear that objections may be made to my choice even if the criteria on which it is based, namely, theories about the nature of society, man and knowledge, are accepted. The enormous literature, both laudatory and critical, about Plato's meaning makes any assertion about his true intentions problematical. In drawing up an ideal-typical model I am not interested in the author's intention or indeed in the shades of meaning ascribed to its constituent parts and debated by philosophers through the ages. My intentions are specifically related to the requirements of the application of the problem approach in comparative education. A European ideal-typical normative model derived from Plato's *Republic* should help in (1) the analysis of problems, (2) the description and comparison of specific initial conditions, (3) the identification of conservative and alternative policy solutions and (4) the anticipation of articulated resistance to the implementation of one or other policy.

As stated, the purpose I had in mind when I undertook to examine and compare American and European assumptions was to see how far American critics of progressive education in the USA were prepared to go when confronted with a set of European theories. In Chapter 8 I shall present a model for the USA derived from the writings of Dewey. Readers might like to compare his views about change with those of

Plato. They might also compare Dewey's commitment to democracy and individualism with Plato's preference for a monarchy, and the stability of the state. Again, compare Dewey's view that individuals should work together to solve their problems with Plato's elitist intellectualism. Dewey concedes that individuals differ but is confident that everyone has enough intelligence to participate in the political life of a society. Plato's chosen few – the philosopher-kings – are the only ones in his society who can participate in politics. In each of these areas of debate Dewey's answers are very different from Plato's.

Of course, in looking for alternative solutions to major questions about society, man and knowledge it might be useful to compare and contrast features of my Platonic ideal-typical model with the views, for example, of Pericles, Socrates, Protagoras and Aristotle. Each offered rather different answers to the questions that intrigued most Greek thinkers. It should also be noted that Plato's own works have been variously interpreted through the ages. They have from time to time served as a stimulus to new thinking. My interest is in their value as representing a conservative ideal-typical model of normative statements against which present-day radicalism can be judged.

Historically attacks on Platonic assumptions have met with varied success. Not all of his political theories have been abandoned, although democracy is widely advocated. Absolute monarchs are not favoured, but leadership by an aristocracy of talent has not been entirely rejected as indefensible. The equality of all men and women before the law is accepted as a matter of principle; universal franchise is held up as an ideal; but psychological theories based upon differences in intelligence and abilities still find favour. In short, against Plato's model asynchronous normative changes can be analysed.

In making this kind of problem analysis care should be taken to identify the context in which changes have taken place or are taking place. Alternatives to traditional assumptions about society, man and knowledge represent formulated hypotheses. Some examination should be made of the extent to which such alternatives have been adopted and with what success they have been written into national constitutions or legislation; for the success of a normative challenge may be judged by reference to such documents.

The thrust and success of the challenges made in Europe to Platonic theories differ from one country to another. In Western Europe even among nations whose constitutions are democratic notions about democracy differ. In some countries still, and certainly until recently, belief in the value of informal leadership commands respect and support. Concepts about individual differences also vary and theories of knowledge may be said to be almost nation-specific. Some analysis should therefore be made of the ways in which the Platonic ideal-typical model ought to be modified if it is to be used to analyse problems and evaluate the future success of policy in different European countries. In Chapter 6 I have suggested how nation-specific ideal-typical models based on the writings of specific authors might be established. 'Actual' ideal-typical models can be prepared and compared by selecting from national constitutions and legislation relevant assumptions about man, society and knowledge.

NOTES AND REFERENCES: CHAPTER 7

I made an attempt in Brian Holmes, *American Criticism of American Education*, Ohio State University, Columbus, Ohio, 1957, at the height of the debate about American education, to identify two (alternative) ideal-typical models in an attempt to ask how far American critics of their own system of education really wished to return to European prototypes.

1 The first five volumes recording details of the Progressive Education Association's Eight-Year Study were published in 1942 and 1943 by Harper, New York, under the general title *Adventure in American Education*. See W. Aiken, *The Story of the Eight-Year Study,* Harper, New York, 1942.
2 Robert Maynard Hutchins, *The Higher Learning in America,* Yale University Press, New Haven, Conn., 1936.
3 A. E. Bestor, *Educational Wastelands,* University of Illinois Press, Urbana, Ill., 1953, and the *Restoration of Learning,* Knopf, New York, 1955.
4 Boyd H. Bode, *Progressive Education at the Crossroads,* Newsom, New York, 1938.

Chapter 8

Dewey's Reflective Man in a Changing Scientific Society

As a comparative educationist I consider that the writings of John Dewey constitute the source of an extremely useful ideal-typical model. They throw light on some aspects of educational theory in the USA. Again, any European reading Dewey will find debated many of the assumptions and theories on which traditional (including English) systems of education rest. Dewey's forthright attack on many sacred cows is refreshing. His views reflect progressive views everywhere and provide a set of assumptions against which it is possible to make sense of a highly complex system of American education. In particular *How We Think* seems to offer in a single volume as *useful* a picture of American educational assumptions as Plato's *Republic* provides for European education.

The theoretical key to Dewey's almost total dislike for Plato's theories of knowledge, society and the individual seems to lie in his attitude toward change. He observed: 'Plato took comparatively speaking a pessimistic view of change as mere lapse.'[1] Plato viewed the just society as the stable, static society in which each person finds personal happiness by knowing his place and being content to remain in it. As for individuals, he considered that each is born possessing innate immutable qualities of character and ability, a view that justifies a social class structure based upon the ability of individuals within each group to perform the functions appropriate to it. These tasks would be performed in the light of special knowledge, whether of the statesman or the carpenter, in Plato's ideal society. The belief held by most Greeks (other than the sophists of the Protagorean school) that behind the ceaseless flow of experiences there is something permanent, and that this and only this is knowable, was anathema to Dewey. No less harsh was Dewey's criticism of Aristotle, whose complacent view of change 'as tendency to realization' nevertheless left him as sure as Plato 'that the fully realized reality, the divine and the ultimate, is changeless'.[2] True knowledge is possible only of what does not change. Individual members of any species or class of objects show such variations and are so liable to change that nothing can be *known* about them except their essence or nature, which, embodied in each of them, is the distinguishing feature or characteristic of them all. Knowledge of essences was for Aristotle as important as knowledge of ideas was for Plato. Both distinguished between reason and experience and, in the last analysis, regarded reason, not experience, as a reliable approach to the acquisition of knowledge. With this dichotomy Aristotle associated two others. First, according to Dewey, there was the dichotomy between theory, which 'had to do with things which were supreme because divine and eternal', and practice, which 'had to do with things that were merely mundane, things at worst menial and at best earth-bound and transient'.[3] The second dichotomy, between manual work and intellectual activity, between the liberal arts and the useful arts, has helped to perpetuate sharp contrasts between what is considered to be liberal education and vocational training and inevitably between the cultured or educated man and the artisan. Dewey regarded these particular dualisms as among those most damaging to the progress of modern education. As for the American dream, to which Dewey in many ways was committed, Ralph Barton Perry wrote: 'Thomas Jefferson remains the most complete exponent of the Enlightenment – both in its general tone and its diverse doctrine.'[4] Quite central to this thesis was the idea of progress through the 'indefinite perfectibility of man'.[5] This justified belief in a theory of government in which an aristocracy by birth would be replaced by an aristocracy of talent. Even so, the best government would be one that simply protects the inalienable rights of individuals – life, liberty, property and the pursuit of happiness – and interferes least in their personal affairs. According to Jefferson, an ideal society would need no government, but he was driven to the conclusion that such an ideal was unattainable in the larger American society. Nevertheless, a modified form of agrarianism would give scope for self-government in communities smaller in size than a state or even a county. Dewey did not accept the view that Jefferson was merely the champion of state against federal government or that he thought of government simply as a necessary evil. On the contrary, Dewey's opinion was that 'the heart of his philosophy of politics is found in his efforts to institute these small administrative and legislative units as the keystone of the arch.'[6]

Political and economic theories of society depend for their successful implementation on the quality of individuals within it, according to Jefferson, who recognised that 'it is the manners and spirit of a people which preserve a republic in vigor'.[7] He regarded the masses with a certain suspicion. 'The mass of citizens may be divided into two classes – the labouring and the learned,' he said.[8] The learned citizens were to form the aristocracy of talent. As for the labouring classes, since conditions affected man's virtues, substantial virtue had been deposited in the agricultural workers – 'the chosen people of God'.[9] But the industrial workers – the class of artificers – were, to Jefferson, 'the panders of vice, and the instrument by which the liberties of a country are generally overturned . . .'[10] A nation could remain virtuous and the will of the majority prevail only 'as long as agriculture is our principal object'.

Under these conditions two principles should, according to Jefferson, govern the behaviour of individuals: reason and self-interest. Reason, argued Jefferson, would enable men to see that certain actions were in their own self-interest. A little education, for example, would ensure that the common people appreciated the need to 'preserve peace and order'. What remains somewhat obscure in Jefferson's writings is what exactly constitutes 'reason'. Undoubtedly he shared the faith of the encyclopaedists and Protagoras that all men possess an element of civic virtue, but not in equal amounts. Jefferson agreed with Rousseau, who wrote: 'I conceive that there are two kinds of inequality among the human species; one which I call natural or physical, because it is established by nature, and consists in a difference of age, health and bodily strength, and the qualities of mind or of the soul; and another which may be called moral or political inequality, because it depends on a kind of convention, and is established, or at least authorized by the consent of men.'[11] Moral and political inequalities were unjust and should be removed. Intellectual differences could not be removed, but each man through education could be improved.

Dewey disagreed with the *laissez-faire* liberals on two points. First, he found self-interest no longer an appropriate regulator of human affairs. He pointed out that in nineteenth-century America when the individuals were pioneering a wilderness 'the demands of the practical situation called for the initiative, enterprise and vigor of individuals in all immediate work that urgently asked for doing, and their operation furthered the national life'.[12] But this was no longer the case. Dewey's second serious point of disagreement concerned the characteristics of 'reason', and on this question Dewey was almost as much opposed to uncritical empiricism as he was to the rationalism of the Greeks and Descartes. The reservation is important because he approved Bacon's concept of knowledge as power and forgave him much on the grounds that he advocated a 'State organized for collective inquiry'.[13] These two points – individualism and reason – are so central to the whole of Dewey's theory of what constitutes an educated man that they need to be considered in greater detail. Preparing a description of the educated man would be tidy at least if offered in terms of the categories established by philosophers of the kind Dewey attacked. It would, for example, be useful to say what skills an educated man should possess, what knowledge he should acquire, what attitudes and qualities of character should distinguish him from the uneducated man. But the weight of Dewey's attack is, in fact, just upon dualisms that traditional philosophers have established. He rejected such dualisms as 'labour and leisure, practical and intellectual activity, man and nature, individuality and association, culture and vocation',[14] and 'mind (or spirit) and matter, body and mind, the mind and the world, the individual and his relationships to others'.[15] In proposing to synthesise what were previously antitheses, Dewey applied the principle of continuity to such an extent that Paul Crosser maintains it leads to complete nihilism.[16] Perhaps he states his case rather too strongly, but there is no doubt that any attempt to give precision to key terms used by Dewey involves some recognition of the constant and intimate interactions between ends and means, individuals and environments, thinking and behaviour, and so on.

In attempting to separate out from Dewey's writings his major concepts of the individual, society and knowledge as they bear upon his view of the educated man it is impossible to talk about the latter in isolation. In Dewey's thinking, the individual has no separate existence except in a limited physical sense, and even biologically he is to be seen as an organism continuously interacting with a natural environment. Individuality is neither originally given nor is it 'complete in itself, like a closet in a house or a secret drawer in a desk, filled with treasures that are waiting to be bestowed on the world'.[17] On the contrary, individuality 'in a social and moral sense is something to be wrought out',[18] or, in other words, 'created under the influences of associated life'.[19] The individual and the social should not be set against each other as separate entities, for without one the other has no existence. Therefore, under changing circumstances individuality takes on new forms and, in doing so, further modifies the circumstances. The antisocial concept of the individual, expounded particularly by Rousseau, linked him not with his immediate social environment but with nature. This was appropriate enough in the nineteenth century, but individualism in the twentieth century has to be given new meanings. 'Our problems', Dewey wrote, in an analysis of individualism, 'grow out of social conditions: they concern human relations rather than man's direct relationship to physical nature.'[20] His refusal to accept individuality as something in itself apart from these conditions is perfectly compatible with his warning against the dangers of a certain kind of child-centred education.[21]

Man must, therefore, be educated for a particular kind of society. The society in which Dewey found himself in the twentieth century was very different from that of the pioneering period of American history. The early pragmatists were, of course, products of the age of transition between two eras, the watershed of which was the last decade of the nineteenth century. Just as Dewey suggested that William James 'gave intellectual expression to the life of the pioneer who made the country . . .',[22] so Dewey himself has been described as an apologist of American commercialism and materialism. Bertrand Russell's claim that he found 'love of truth in America obscured by commercialism of which pragmatism is the philosophical expression; and love of our neighbour kept in fetters by Puritan morality'[23] was sharply challenged by Dewey, who seems to have been equally resentful when Lewis Mumford implied that he had willingly surrendered 'to industrial utilitarianism'.[24]

In this quite acrimonious debate it is important to distinguish between statements of what is and what ought to be. Except perhaps in his reply to Russell, Dewey neither accepted nor rejected the desirability of the kind of society envisaged by Jefferson, but he appreciated that it had largely disappeared under the forces of industrialisation and urbanisation. The changes, whether desired or not, had occurred and created a new type of society in which the old individual found himself submerged both economically and politically. Old techniques could not be used in this kind of society, and a new individuality, not just more of the same rugged self-interestedness, had to develop if the obnoxious features (the most dominating of which was 'corporateness') of commercial and industrial life were to be ameliorated. Because such conditions create problems for the individual and help to mould him, Dewey believed it important that he be aware of the forces of change around him, so that instead of being a helpless pawn he could, with his fellow men, control events.

Politically Dewey did not accept without question that American society should be based on a constitution drawn up over 150 years ago.[25] Moreover, he appreciated that fine Lockean ideals about government – such as that the best is the one that interferes least with the individual's everyday activities – do not prevent individual freedom from being seriously limited under modern conditions. Political liberalism in its extreme form, indeed, does not protect the freedom of individuals from 'further subjection to the owners of the agencies of material production and distribution'.[26] That is to say, the authority of economic forces has meant that 'economic freedom has been either non-existent or precarious for the large mass of the population'.[27]

Dewey, committed to a republican form of democracy, did not see democracy as a set of institutions, political forms and devices, nor yet as a 'final end and a final value'.[28] These are but means through which 'ends that lie in the wide domain of human relationships'[29] can be realised, and human personality developed. Democracy is a way of life made possible by the willingness of individuals to co-operate with one another. He declared: 'A democracy is more than a form of government; it is primarily a mode of associated living, of conjoint communicated experience',[30] and he was unable to accept the restrictions placed on individuality by authoritarian governments. Such attempts to maintain the status quo are bound to fail. Change is a fact of life. Since it is pointless to try to stop it, the object of education should be to help individuals cope with it. This represents a most revolutionary and generous view of society, for which Dewey gave James credit. He wrote that 'the fundamental idea of an open universe in which uncertainty, choice, hypotheses, novelties and possibilities are naturalized will remain associated with the name of James'.[31] Such a view does not perceive change as decay and loss, as Plato thought. On the other hand, progress is not assured as the encyclopaedists seemed to hold. Nor is change quite the mechanical process implied by social Darwinism. Certainly it offers tremendous opportunities. Dewey put it this way: 'Change becomes significant of new possibilities and ends to be attained; it becomes prophetic of a better future.'[32] But at the same time, change implies at least three closely related difficulties of adjustment. First, change inevitably brings with it more or less serious social problems that have to be faced and, if possible, solved. Secondly, the question of social control is raised when individuals seek to direct social change rather than allowing it to dominate them. Thirdly, in the process of problem-solving, individuals will change and should be prepared to do so.

In any society a number of forces are at work to bring about change. The directness and power of their impact are not distributed equally over all aspects of a society; thus asynchronous changes are set up within it. The most significant illustration of this phenomenon, to which Dewey constantly referred, is found by comparing the changes that scientific applications have wrought in man's material environment with the lack of adjustment in man's beliefs, attitudes, customs and social institutions – all instruments he needs to cope with this changed world.

Planning is an attempt to find a balance between stability and change and to adjust authority and freedom. Dewey believed that if social planning is to take place, it is important to ensure it the freest possible play of intelligence.[33] While not automatically rejecting planning, he was not prepared to accept 'social control by means of collective planned economy'.[34] And he realised that total planning is at best an uncertain operation. He wrote: 'Judging, planning, choice, no matter how thoroughly conducted, and action no matter how prudently executed, never are the sole determinants of any outcome. Alien and indifferent natural forces, unforeseeable conditions, enter in and have a decisive voice.'[35] The solution lies in changing the equipment of educated man. Too often habit determines man's course of action. Dewey explained: 'When tradition and social custom are incorporated in the working constitution of an individual, they have authority as a matter of course over his beliefs and his activities.'[36] In a changing society men have to change too; and 'the grip of the authority of custom and tradition as standards of belief'[37] must be relaxed. Associated with this emancipation should be a '*willingness to re-examine and if necessary to revise current convictions, even if that course entails the effort to change by concerted effort existing institutions and to direct existing tendencies to new ends*'.[38] Evidently men are not aware of change and its implications – a revolution would occur 'if we were to recognize that we live in a changing social order and proceed to act upon that recognition in our schools'.[39] Education should prepare individuals to meet and anticipate problems. Dewey advised: 'A nation habituated to *think* in terms of problems and of the struggle to remedy them before it is actually in the grip of the forces which create the problems, would have an equipment for public life such as has not characterized any people.'[40] The problem-solving, problem-anticipating individual cannot simply obey some external authority but must be able to make choices between one course of action and another. The component of individuality that enables men to make choices in problematic situations is 'organized intelligence'. As a measure of an educated man, intelligence helps individuals or a community to meet problems by effecting a 'working connection between old habits, customs, institutions, beliefs and new conditions'.[41]

As may be expected, intelligence is not something innate, in the accepted sense of the word, and possessed once and for all. Rather, declared Dewey, 'it is in constant process of framing, and its retention requires constant alertness in observing consequences and open-minded will to learn and courage in re-adjustment'.[42] Evidently it cannot be defined as the ability to perform any one operation unless it be to think reflectively. Intelligence includes intellectual ability and power to observe, but also certain attitudes of mind and qualities of character. Unless he possesses certain of the latter, an individual is unlikely to release his intelligence in action. And since no intelligent action can precede thought, intelligent behaviour is either a consequence of intelligent thinking or an integral part of it. The latter seems more likely. Certainly high intelligence reflects man's ability to perform all phases of reflective thinking and a willingness to act.

Dewey's view that intelligence can grow as an individual grows depends on certain conditions. He stated that 'the basic freedom is freedom of *mind* and of whatever degree of freedom of action and experience is necessary to produce freedom of intelligence'.[43] His attitude about differences in intelligence was, like Jefferson's, that equality was not a psychological fact but rather a legal, political and moral concept that is part of democratic ideology. Certainly his arguments in favour of equality of opportunity should not be taken to imply 'belief in equality of natural endowments'.[44] Dewey considered that equality is established by law to protect the less gifted from the competitive opposition of the more gifted. It is difficult to escape the conclusion that Dewey had a more traditional conception of intelligence than seems apparent from disclaimers.

One might compare his view of intelligence with what Protagoras called 'civic virtue' – the uniquely human characteristic that enables men to compete successfully with other animals and to live together in societies. All men possess 'civic virtue' but in unequal amounts. How, then, can democracy work? According to Dewey, through co-operation and the pooling of intelligence. He said that although 'intelligence may be distributed in unequal amounts, it is the democratic faith that it is sufficiently general so that each individual has something to contribute, and the value of each contribution can be assessed only as it enters into the final pooled intelligence constituted by the contributions of all'.[45] There is something like a 'collective organic intelligence'. And the development and release of individual and collective intelligence so that maximum reliance can be placed upon them is absolutely necessary to the successful working of a liberal democracy. On the other hand, were it possible to develop intelligence in societies other than democracies (and this seems to have happened in history) then the outcome would be the establishment of a democracy.

Looked at in another way, organised intelligence is synonymous with science – the initiator of change and at the same time the emancipator, offering above all, like intelligence, 'freedom from the limitations of habit'. Thus, through the applications of science, the conditions under which people associate with one another have been revolutionised. At the same time, science has successfully challenged the right of religion or theology to exercise social authority. The conflict, Dewey said, was not carried out simply at the theoretical level; rather it was between 'two alignments of forces'.[46] Institutional power remained in the hands of the theologians until the forces of science were able to gain recognition. These forces did so, not by stifling individual initiative and intelligence, but by fostering the spirit of free inquiry. The greatest advance in the authority of science has been in the physical field. Dewey wished to see the methods of science applied as widely as possible to human affairs.

Before science is accepted as the emancipator, Dewey wished to make it clear that only a certain view of what constitutes science can provide organised intelligence with appropriate tools of inquiry. Science, for example, should not mean that one kind of dogmatism is replaced by another. He quoted James as protesting rightly 'against science when it sets fixed bounds and restricts freedom'.[47] In *Reconstruction in Philosophy* he presented a critique of traditional science, and challenged the details of Bacon's method while agreeing with him that 'knowledge is power' that can be acquired only by an 'invasion of the unknown, rather than repetition in logical form of the already known'[48] and by co-operative inquiries in a 'State organized for collective inquiry'.[49] Dewey himself maintained that the authority of science 'issues from and is based upon collective activity, cooperatively organized'.[50] This statement, among many, illustrates why Dewey held that science as the method of organised intelligence is the kind of inquiry on which democracy should rest.

Evidently it was not science as an organised body of knowledge that was important to Dewey but the methods appropriate to its pursuit. If these are used correctly, they will lead to knowledge in its most characteristic and perfected form. In other words, knowledge is not of something fixed, immutable and outside human experience but is always the outcome of inquiry. Because a quite fundamental aspect of scientific inquiry is experimental testing, the knowledge to which it leads can never be certain or absolute, merely probable. If the predictions made from the propositions are confirmed by actual events, then the propositions can be said to have 'warranted assertability'. Dewey substituted 'warranted assertability' perhaps because the words 'knowledge' and 'truth' held so many philosophical implications that he rejected. One such was that scientific laws correspond to reality irrespective of the context. For Dewey, reference to the circumstances in which hypotheses are formulated and tested is essential if hypothetical statements are to be understood and their 'warranted assertability' established.

The so-called objectivity of the scientist arises not because of his personal insights (or intuition) or because his material consists of hard facts or 'things-in-themselves', but rather because his procedures of testing are public. Objectivity depends upon the possibility that individuals will agree with conclusions reached on the basis of tests and will accept the instruments of measurement used in these processes of verification and refutation. There are, of course, associated with this view a number of sociological and psychological assumptions and even, as Russell says,[51] prophecy. Because agreement has been reached so much more readily in the spheres of physics and chemistry (and to some extent in biology) than in the social sciences and morals, the argument has arisen that there are different ways of knowing and different kinds of knowledge. Scientific methods, according to this argument, are appropriate in some fields but not in others. This claim Dewey could not accept. 'The general adoption of the scientific attitude in human affairs', he wrote, 'would mean nothing less than a revolutionary change in morals, religion, politics and industry.'[52] This revolution depends for its success on the maximum use by all men of the method of organised intelligence and science, that is, reflective thinking. This view is, above all, basic to an understanding of Dewey's concept of an educated man.

While the theme of reflective thinking recurs often both in Dewey's articles and in his major writings, an orderly analysis of the process is presented in *How We Think*. According to William H. Kilpatrick, this analysis had a tonic effect on American teachers and enabled them to discover the 'problem approach' as a teaching device.[53] The process represents both an educational aim and a method, and the analysis is such that specific aspects of the complete act of thinking can be isolated (however improper Dewey may have considered such a procedure) and amplified. Reflective thinking can appropriately be used to identify a pattern of attitudes and the qualities of mind and character that should constitute the equipment of any educated man; it cannot, one must realise, be used to indicate what knowledge the educated man should possess or the hierarchy of values by which he should live.

What initiates reflective thinking? First of all, Dewey assumed, 'Thinking is not a case of spontaneous combustion; it does not occur just on general principles!' but originates in some 'perplexity, confusion, or doubt'[54] within the experience of the individual. Exhortations to think are bound to be ineffective unless this condition is fulfilled. If it is fulfilled, however, reflective thinking can proceed, with the intent '*to transform a situation in which there is experienced obscurity, doubt, conflict, disturbance of some sort, into a situation that is clear, coherent, settled, harmonious*'.[55] Between the pre-reflective and post-reflective situations occur the five states, or phases, of thinking. Dewey presented them in the following form:

> In between, as states of thinking, are (1) *suggestions* in which the mind leaps forward to a possible solution; (2) an intellectualization of the difficulty or perplexity that has been *felt* (directly experienced) into a *problem* to be solved, a question for which the answer must be sought; (3) the use of one suggestion after another as a leading idea, or hypothesis, to initiate and guide observation and other operations in collection of factual material; (4) the mental elaboration of the idea or supposition as an idea or supposition (*reasoning* in the sense in which reasoning is a part, not the whole, or inference); and (5) testing the hypothesis by overt or imaginative action.[56]

These phases do not necessarily follow each other in the stated order. In fact, there is likely to be fairly continuous interaction among the different aspects and any improvement in the quality of thinking in one phase does something for the others. Furthermore, in each of them judgements have to be made that 'are so related as to support one another in leading to a final judgement – the conclusion'.[57] Thus the quality of reflective thought depends upon the pertinence and discrimination of the thinker's judgement. Since scientific inquiry is collective, the greater the number of persons of sound judgement, the higher will be the quality of any inquiry and, therefore, of the operation of democracy. Very significantly, Dewey wrote: 'A man of sound judgement in any set of affairs is an *educated* man as respects those affairs, whatever his schooling or academic standing.'[58]

The qualities on which sound judgements are based are difficult to enumerate. Emotional awareness or sensitivity is necessary because without it the reaction of an individual to a total situation may be dulled. It is a sensitivity that perhaps precedes reflective thought but is essential to it by making the individual alert to the presence of an obscurity, doubt, conflict, or confusion. It is also something rather different from the first of Dewey's three levels of curiosity – 'a vital overflow, an expression of an abundant organic energy' or (and this comes nearer to sensitivity) 'a physiological uneasiness'. Even the next stage, developed under the influence of social stimuli, is only the 'germ of *intellectual* curiosity'.[59] Only on the basis of this curiosity, which education must above all keep alive and foster, is the process of intellectualisation possible.

Another important human quality is imagination, which enters into all phases of thinking particularly at the level of suggestions, hypotheses, or ideas. These are creative if knowledge, as defined by Dewey, is to issue from inquiry. For knowledge is not of 'things as they are' but the outcome of discovery, which always involves a 'leap beyond what is given and already established'.[60] The novel or imaginative idea often leads to radically new conclusions and implications and often runs counter to the hypotheses used in the past to seek solutions. There may, however, be a number of possible solutions, and each has to be tested before the most satisfactory one, that is, the one leading to the resolution of the confused situation, is found. The testing process takes place in a person's imagination, too, although the techniques of testing are often fairly clearly prescribed. Imagination, then, may be taken to imply a mental quality that makes possible the leap from sense experience or empirical data to ideas, and from ideas back to concrete, singular, experienced events.

The quality of imagination is supported by abilities traditionally regarded as belonging to man's rational capacity, independent of sense impressions. This view is not, of course, Dewey's, but it might be safe to say they enable an individual to intellectualise a confused situation. Analysis enables it to be broken down (though Dewey did not like this term)[61] into its constituent parts so that specific features of the problem can be emphasised. Synthesis places each such feature into its context, that is, into its relationship with other selected parts and with the whole. The processes of analysis and synthesis are complementary, one enriching the other. It should be noted that judgement takes place as a result of analysis, in so far as discrimination between the important and the trivial is involved. These processes are essential to selection and description of the circumstances or context in which the problem is located and in which the solution is proposed. An illustration carried to absurd lengths may serve to make the point. Any human problem occurs within the universe. Can the universe be described, and would the problem become more meaningful if it were? Evidently not. Similarly, an analysis of the solar system is not relevant to all problems, only to some. By the same token, there are world problems, but the context is so enormous that selection of relevant material has to be undertaken. This selection is a highly intellectual activity, demanding imagination and judgement.

Another important ability associated with intellectual activity is reasoning, in the limited sense of deductively inferring conclusions or consequences from given premises. In the physical sciences this type of reasoning is mathematical, but in all kinds of reasoning, the logical intention takes a similar form: 'if *p* then *q*'. Pragmatists place an important reservation on the application of this process. Judgement enters into it because the consequences deduced from any hypothesis may occur in a number of areas. If a social problem and its solution are considered, the hypothesis offered may lead to economic, political and educational consequences. Which of these sequences is selected for deductive elaboration will depend upon the investigator. In the physical sciences the predictions are usually reduced to the level of meter readings; in economics and commerce the predicted consequences are often quantifiable in terms of profit or loss; in politics the predictions may be expressed in terms of the retention or loss of power. Dewey wrote: 'It is folly rather than wisdom to include in the concept of success only tangible material goods and to exclude those of culture, art, science, sympathetic relations with others.'[62] The criteria of success should, however, be firmly based in experience so that the tests can be repeated by all and thus be public.

It is the public nature of testing that gives to the scientific method its objective character. Acceptance of this, the method of organised intelligence, depends upon the adoption by an individual of certain attitudes. First of all, there must be a desire to apply this method to problems. Then, and most important, there must be a willingness on the part of an individual to act. Dewey wrote:

> Even in moral and other practical matters, therefore, a thoughtful person treats his overt deeds as experimental so far as possible; that is to say while he cannot call them back and must stand by their consequences, he gives alert attention to what they teach him about his conduct as well as to the non-intellectual consequences.[63]

Two other qualities are essential to reflective thinking: open-mindedness and responsibility. Open-mindedness implies that the individual is free from prejudice and willing to entertain new ideas and examine them by the process of experimental testing. Responsibility means, not that an individual is cautious in proposing new ideas or novel solutions or that he avoids change and the problems it brings, but that he is prepared to put them to the test of experience and is prepared in the light of evidence to abandon such ideas as are unable to stand the tests applied to them. Out of these attitudes, which Dewey said are essentially moral in nature, there may grow a habit of reflective thinking. But moral attitudes, he insisted, are traits that have to be cultivated.[64]

Compared with social scientists, physical scientists have an important advantage. There is, nevertheless, Dewey maintained, a unity of method. He wrote:

> Every step forward in the social sciences – the studies termed history, economics, politics, sociology – shows that social questions are capable of being intelligently coped with only in the degree in which we employ the method of collecting data, forming hypotheses, and testing them in action which is characteristic of natural science, and in the degree in which we utilize on behalf of the promotion of social welfare the technical knowledge ascertained by physics and chemistry.[65]

He explained how methods of dealing with some of the many social problems – insanity, intemperance, poverty, city planning, the conservation of natural resources, and so on – depend upon the application of the methods and the results of the natural sciences.

Moral judgements, in his opinion, should be reached only after working out (predicting) the consequences of alternative (or several) moral injunctions. 'Thou shalt not kill', for example, should not be used as an absolute standard by which to make a judgement. First, it is necessary to consider the consequences of accepting this solution and the consequences of accepting the exact opposite. The alternative consequences should be deduced within a given context because no moral statement can, it seems, be valid under all circumstances. A choice of consequences now remains, and moral judgement is still required; it is still necessary to select and give additional weight to one consequence, or a pattern of consequences, rather than to another (or another pattern). Evidently it is necessary to have standards or a value system in accordance with which a moral judgement can be made even in the light of predicted consequences. Dewey pointed out: 'The development of inclusive and enduring aims is the necessary condition of the application of reflection in conduct; indeed, they are two names for the same fact.[66] Unfortunately, reflective thinking, or scientific method, cannot itself form the basis of a normative science. Historical traditions, of course, not only provide a pattern of norms or values but suggest by what authority they were established. These precedents are valuable in so far as they are used instrumentally, but there should always be a willingness on the part of an individual to re-examine and revise his value system if it seems necessary. Dewey implies that men have to use the accepted norms of their society as long as they find them applicable and appropriate.

The difficulty of finding values to which, under given circumstances, all men will subscribe is apparent. It would be reduced if a less sharp distinction than is usual were drawn between 'ideal' values and 'material' values. The answer seems to lie in consensus, a conclusion that must rest on an assumption that in the long run the majority of educated, intelligent individuals thinking reflectively will accept certain consequences as morally right and others as morally wrong. Thus a basis for moral judgement would be provided by the community itself.

A scientific assessment of the consequences that may flow from a proposed solution to a moral problem is difficult, because the psychological characteristics of the individual enter as important features of the context in which the elaboration of ideas is to take place. Successful prediction depends upon a knowledge of these, since a person's attitudes find expression in the very act of judging. Psychological knowledge and insight are required if another person's moral judgements are to be anticipated. Introspection will provide for any individual information that is necessary if he is to predict the nature of his own moral judgement. Controlled judgement requires, therefore, not only a sociological analysis of the social environment in which judgement is to be made but also a description of the associated attitudes and dispositions of the person who is to take the decision.

Two examples of the need for discrimination, as a result of the application of science in the modern world, may now be cited. Mass media of communication have placed in the hands of the demagogues a power previously unknown. Dewey was aware that the new media have transformed the means of influencing public opinion upon which political action depends.[67] In an address summarised in *School and Society*,[68] Dewey pointed out that while radio could tremendously improve the quality of a democracy and hasten its progress, it yet 'lends itself to propaganda on behalf of special interests'. He said: 'It can be used to distort and mislead the public mind.' The problem of educating the public to detect 'subtle propaganda and the motives which inspire it' is one of the most important in an age of mass media of communication.

Another aspect of modern life affected by the application of science is represented by automation, which has brought to many more people than previously a great deal more leisure. Mass media fill part of the gap with entertainment. How to solve the problem of more leisure and how to develop discrimination among people are questions education should attempt to answer. Stated simply, under conditions of unaccustomed leisure individuals must learn to discriminate between 'the enjoyments that enrich and enlarge their lives and those which degrade and dissipate'. As in the case of moral judgements, criteria of enrichment are difficult to establish without danger of contradiction. Since the links between leisure-time and aesthetic experiences are (or should be) close, it is of interest to note that S. C. Pepper in his essay on Dewey's aesthetics wondered whether Dewey, in *Art as Experience*,[69] had, in fact, abandoned his pragmatism. But Pepper's concluding remarks gave, perhaps, some indication of the main themes of Dewey's interest in aesthetics – his desire to see a breakdown in the artificial separation between art and life and his wish to encourage people to realise that 'there is beauty in the commonest and meanest things and on Tuesdays and Wednesdays as well as on Sundays'.[70] This opinion is perfectly consistent with Dewey's general aim to make the educated man appreciate that the old dichotomy between culture and the sordid materialism of everyday living is false, and that rather than reject the world he should attempt to improve it.

From all this we can derive a picture of an educated man who is able to make sound judgements, to discriminate, to make choices, to take decisions, and to act upon them, not on impulse, or from habit, custom, or tradition, but through controlled thinking. This method of problem-solving is appropriate to all aspects of his life – the economic, the political, the moral and the aesthetic. Nothing has yet been said about the body of knowledge with which he should be familiar. In fact information and data are relevant only to the degree to which they contribute to the process of inquiry. Dewey's proposals suggest, quite explicitly, the dissolution of traditional subject-matter as such. If subjects are to be retained, then ideally every one of them in the curriculum should be taught 'in connection with its bearing upon creation and growth of the kind of power of observation, inquiry, reflection, and testing that are the heart of scientific intelligence'.[71] But in fact history, geography, science, modern languages and other such subjects have no place in the store of knowledge that Dewey's educated man should possess, except to the extent that certain data from each of the disciplines might contribute to problem-solving or reflective thinking, for example, history should not be treated chronologically but used pragmatically. Dewey declared: 'The true starting point of history is always some present situation with its problems',[72] and for this reason economic, industrial, or intellectual history would be more appropriate than political history, because more likely to enlage young people's sense of the significance of direct personal experience.

In order to make any generalisations about what subject-matter an educated man should possess, it is necessary to ask not what traditional subjects he should study but what problems he should be trained in school to tackle, or, in fact, be given to tackle.

What is needed, said Dewey, is the development of 'new subject matter, as well organized as was the old . . . but having an intimate and developing relation to the experience of those in school'.[73]

Whatever they are, youth's problems largely reflect applications of scientific information to society. Young people will have to take up work in a technological age; many of them will need to become specialists or technologists in scientific fields. At the same time they will have to live in large conurbations whether they like it or not, with all the social and human complications associated with aggregate living. They will have to cope with complex machinery and devices – the products of science. In an observation typical of many he made on science and society, Dewey said: 'The stationary and traction steam engine, gasoline engine, automobile, telegraph and telephone, the electric motor enter directly into the lives of most individuals.'[74] Today we may add that H-bomb warfare threatens the lives of everyone. Few aspects of living are untouched by modern scientific development and judgements cannot be made on the basis of reflective thinking unless their physical and biological consequences in given situations can be predicted and weighed carefully. In short, the educated man's store of scientific information that through reflective thinking can be turned into real and human knowledge is today enormous. Any education designed to meet today's needs must take full account of this fact.

Dewey was always concerned about the false (as he thought) dichotomy between scientific and vocational studies and the humanising liberal arts. This dichotomy is part of the Aristotelian heritage, mentioned previously. It was related economically and socially to the distinctions drawn between the gentleman and the artisan or labourer. Brutish conditions of labour undoubtedly reinforced in a practical way the dislike an 'educated' man had for vocational courses designed to prepare their recipients for work. Conditions have changed. Automated factories reduce hard manual work to a bare minimum. At the same time, prejudices still need to be overcome. Dewey declared: 'We must surrender that superstitious tradition which identifies humanism with the interests of literary training, and which in our country, whatever it may have accomplished elsewhere, produces only a feebly pretentious snobbishness of culture.'[75]

Convinced as Dewey was that vocational studies and science should form the core of a general education, he had to face the question of how this would be done. First, he considered how it should not be done. Industrial education must not emphasise technical trade efficiency but rather should contribute to the efficiency of industrial intelligence.[76] Similarly, science should not be regarded as an organised body of knowledge, nor yet a technique or system of skills learned in the laboratory (however valuable these experiences may be). In the positive approach, he believed that vocational education, correctly used, would 'react upon intelligence and interest so as to modify, in connection with legislation and administration, the socially obnoxious features of the present industrial and commercial order'.[77] The object of teaching science, he said, is to encourage individuals to become acquainted with the scientific way of 'treating the familiar material of ordinary experience'.[78]

Science should be taught not only for the methods inherent in it. Most modern social problems have their scientific aspects, and to understand and help solve these problems data from the sciences must be selected. In short, science teaching should fundamentally concentrate on the social implications of science. A practical approach would be to organise courses around major social problems and select scientific data and theories in terms of the bearing they have on the solution to these problems. By the extent to which science education would help individuals to solve their problems alone or collectively, it would become truly liberal. But, if these are the main aims and methods of science education, less time will have to be spent on stuffing future specialists with hard facts and little understanding. Without some change in the quality of science education itself, the traditional approach may be justified. Moreover, at least two dangers of concentrating on the production of future specialists are apparent. In the first place, the division of the world into scientists and arts men, finding communication increasingly difficult, would be assured. Secondly, scientists would be turned out in increasing numbers who are apolitical, amoral, lacking in aesthetic sensibility and bereft of a sense of social responsibility. Dewey offered as a practical solution to this very real dilemma a reorientation of the liberal arts colleges. He counselled: '*The problem of securing to the liberal arts college its due function in democratic society is that of seeing to it that the technical subjects which are now socially necessary acquire humane direction*.'[79] Science is a human activity; Dewey envisioned making it a humane, liberating study.

Thus equipped with a method of inquiry and a desire to apply it to the problems of society, the educated man has a major task to perform. It is to study the changing world as he finds it and to improve it. He identifies the competing forces that are inducing change, creating problems and tending to give social development direction; one complex of forces is operating to make changes take one course, while another complex is moving it in another direction. The individual's responsibility is to decide which forces he will support. Since he is bound to make a choice, he should do so intelligently. The central question is the moral one: by what standards can this major decision be taken? Dewey said that his social objectives will be framed on the 'basis of knowing the forces and the causes which produce the evils from which we suffer'.[80] The social reconstructionist's lack of fixed ends towards which to work and the dangers of complete relativism are all too obvious. Perhaps, contrary to his intentions, Dewey presented an either/or choice that is too sharp: absolutism or complete relativism.

Yet, if this is in fact the choice that has to be made, then I have no hesitation in accepting the open society of Dewey and his faith in the authority of method of inquiry and in the ability of all men singly and collectively to use it and finally to reach agreement.

However serious the logical difficulties of Dewey's position and however uncertain the answer to the problem of conduct, his concept of the educated man is fully in accord with modern conditions. Increasingly, modern man is subjected to the pressures of industrialisation and urbanisation. More and more frequently he finds himself living in a society that offers wider opportunities of choice. This is the age of the common man and the industrial worker. Whether we like it or not, Dewey's assessment of the social situation is proving itself broadly correct. It seems fairly evident, too, that new forms of social authority are needed in a postwar world where changes brought about or accelerated by the war have been so traumatic that larger problems exist and touch more people than ever before. Acceptance of Dewey's solutions is a matter of personal judgement. His faith in our ability to educate individuals to recognise the problems around them and then to tackle them by the method of organised intelligence placed great trust in education. While his solutions were based upon faith, they are rich in possibilities and they are of the kind to which the peoples of most countries in the Western world are, in a sense, committed. Dewey offered no more than extremely illuminating clues to the way in which we may grapple with problems.

NOTES AND REFERENCES: CHAPTER 8

This is an edited version of Brian Holmes, 'The reflective man: Dewey', in Paul Nash *et al.* (eds), *The Educated Man*, Wiley, New York, 1965.

1 John Dewey, *Reconstruction in Philosophy,* Mentor Books, New York, 1925, p. 97.
2 ibid.
3 John Dewey, *Philosophy of Education,* Littlefield, New York, 1956, p. 162.
4 Ralph Barton Perry, *Puritanism and Democracy,* Vanguard Press, New York, 1944, p. 177.
5 John Dewey, *Democracy and Education,* Macmillan, New York, 1916, p. 106.
6 John Dewey, *The Living Thoughts of Thomas Jefferson,* Cassell, London, 1946, p. 22.
7 S. K. Padover, *The Complete Jefferson,* Tudor, New York, 1943, p. 679.
8 ibid., p. 1099.
9 ibid., p. 678.
10 S. K. Padover, *Thomas Jefferson on Democracy,* Mentor Books, New York, 1977, p. 69.
11 J. J. Rousseau, *Social Contract,* Everyman, London, p. 174.
12 John Dewey, 'Toward a new individualism (individualism, old and new III)', *New Republic,* vol. 62, 19 February 1930.

13 Dewey, *Reconstruction in Philosophy,* op. cit., p. 52.
14 Dewey, *Democracy and Education,* op. cit., p. 377.
15 loc. cit.
16 P. K. Crosser, *The Nihilism of John Dewey,* Philosophical Library, New York, 1955.
17 Joseph Ratner (ed.), *Intelligence in the Modern World,* Modern Library, New York, 1939, p. 415.
18 Dewey, *Reconstruction in Philosophy,* op. cit., p. 152.
19 ibid., p. 155.
20 Dewey, 'Toward a New Individualism', op. cit.
21 John Dewey, 'How much freedom in new schools?', *New Republic,* vol. 63, 9 July 1930.
22 John Dewey, 'William James in 1926', *New Republic,* vol. 47, 26 May, 30 June, 18 August 1926.
23 John Dewey, 'Pragmatic America', *New Republic,* vol. 30, 12 April 1922.
24 John Dewey, 'The pragmatic acquiescence', *New Republic*, vol. 49, 5 January 1927.
25 John Dewey, 'Education for a changing social order', *NEA Addresses and Proceedings,* 1934, pp. 744–52.
26 Ratner, op. cit., p. 354.
27 John Dewey, 'Can education share in social reconstruction?' *Social Frontier,* vol. I, October 1934.
28 Ratner, op. cit., p. 401.
29 ibid., p. 400.
30 Dewey, *Democracy and Education,* op. cit., p. 101.
31 Dewey, 'The pragmatic acquiescence', op. cit.
32 Dewey, *Reconstruction in Philosophy,* op. cit., p. 102.
33 Ratner, op. cit., p. 432.
34 John Dewey, 'Authority and resistance to social change', *School and Society,* vol. 44, 10 October 1936, p. 464.
35 John Dewey, *Quest for Certainty,* Minton, Balch, New York, 1929, p. 11.
36 Dewey, 'Authority and resistance to social change', op. cit., p. 459.
37 Dewey, *Democracy and Education,* op. cit., p. 356.
38 Ratner, op. cit., p. 777.
39 Dewey, 'Education for a changing social order', op. cit.
40 John Dewey, 'Schools and social preparedness', *New Republic,* vol. 7, 1 July 1916.
41 Ratner, op. cit., p. 452.
42 Dewey, *Reconstruction in Philosophy,* op. cit., p. 89.
43 ibid., p. 61.
44 Dewey, *Philosophy of Education,* op. cit., p. 60.
45 Ratner, op. cit., p. 403.
46 Dewey, *Philosophy of Education,* op. cit., p. 106.
47 John Dewey, 'William James', *Independent,* vol. 69, 8 September 1910.
48 Dewey, *Reconstruction in Philosophy,* op. cit., p. 49.
49 ibid., p. 52.
50 Dewey, *Philosophy of Education,* op. cit., p. 107.
51 P. A. Schlipp (ed.), *The Philosophy of John Dewey,* Northwestern University Press, Evanston, Ill., 1939, p. 145.
52 Ratner, op. cit., p. 459.
53 Schlipp, op. cit., p. 469.
54 John Dewey, *How We Think,* D. C. Heath, New York, 1933, p. 115.
55 ibid., pp. 100–1.
56 ibid., p. 107.
57 ibid., p. 119.
58 ibid., p. 120.
59 ibid., p. 38.
60 ibid., p. 96.

61 ibid., p. 248.
62 Ratner, op. cit., p. 772.
63 ibid., p. 856.
64 Dewey, *How We Think,* op. cit., p. 33.
65 Dewey, *Democracy and Education,* op. cit., p. 333.
66 Ratner, op. cit., p. 767. Also see John Dewey, *Human Nature and Conduct,* Holt, New York, 1935, and particularly pt 3, s. 6, 'The nature of aims'.
67 John Dewey, 'The relation of science and philosophy as the basis of Education', *School and Society,* vol. 47, no. 1215, 9 April 1938.
68 John Dewey, 'Radio's Influence on the mind, summary', *School and Society,* vol. 40, no. 1042, 15 December 1934.
69 Schlipp, op. cit., p. 384.
70 Pepper, in Schlipp, op. cit., p. 388.
71 Dewey, 'The relation of science and philosophy as the basis of education', op. cit.
72 Dewey, *Democracy and Education,* op. cit., p. 251.
73 Dewey, 'How much freedom in new schools?', op. cit.
74 Dewey, *Democracy and Education,* op. cit., p. 335.
75 John Dewey, 'Our educational ideal in wartime', *New Republic,* vol. 6, 15 April 1916.
76 John Dewey, 'A policy of industrial education', *New Republic,* vol. 1, 19 December 1914.
77 Dewey, *Democracy and Education,* op. cit., p. 374.
78 ibid., p. 257.
79 Dewey, *Philosophy of Education,* op. cit., p. 86.
80 John Dewey, 'Education and our present social problems', *School and Society,* vol. 37, 15 April 1933.

Chapter 9

The Ideal-Typical Soviet Man

The sources on which an ideal-typical Soviet model can be based are obvious and publicly recognised. Reference is constantly made by Soviet authors to Marx and Lenin as the founders of communism. The constitutions of the USSR of 1936 and 1977 reaffirm principles which have their origin in communist political theory. Major changes in policy are debated at Communist Party congresses and usually justified by reference back to fundamental assumptions about society and individuals.

Since 1917 a succession of interpreters have participated in the development of major theories. N. K. Krupskaya (1869–1939), A. S. Makarenko (1888–1939) and A. V. Lunacharsky (1875–1933), S. T. Shatsky (1878–1943), P. P. Blonsky (1884–1941) and L. S. Vygotsky (1896–1934) are among the notable writers on education who bridge the pre- and post-revolution periods. Not all of them have found favour in the Soviet Union. Krupskaya's work on the upbringing of children and Makarenko's analysis of the educative value of the collective have given direction to Soviet thinking since 1917. Krupskaya represents a child-centred approach, Makarenko a community-centred approach to education. In the ideal-typical Soviet model both can be accommodated without violence to logic. Nevertheless, central to any analysis of Soviet education is some understanding of the nature of capitalism and communism as forms of society.

CAPITALISM AND SOCIAL CHANGE

It is not easy to characterise a communist society without viewing it from the perspective of a capitalist society. Marx saw social change as inevitable and as a process leading to the millennium, in sharp contrast to Plato's view that change was necessarily a process of degeneration. It is also different from the position taken by Dewey who accepted that change was bound to occur but that its direction was uncertain. These three theories of change place major concepts of society in perspective. Marx himself placed the emergence of communist societies on a continuum. In the 'Communist Manifesto' he and Engels described features of capitalism as a stage in the development of society from feudalism to communism. They also described how through conflict and revolution change is brought about in society. Most commentators regard their analysis as deterministic in the sense that they assert that the sequence of events they describe is in accordance with discovered laws of social development. From our point of view it is necessary to select some key assertions about the characteristics of capitalism in order better to understand Soviet education.

In the 'Manifesto' Marx and Engels maintain that capitalist societies are made up of classes. However, the middle, lower-middle and 'dangerous' (social scum or *lumpenproletariat*) classes are in process of decay leaving the bourgeoisie and proletariat as the major contenders for political power.

Engels noted that the bourgeoisie, which in French means town-dwellers, is the 'class of modern capitalists, owners of the means of social production and employers of wage-labour'.[1] His gloss on proleteriat is that it is the 'class of modern wage-labourers who, having no means of production of their own, are reduced to selling their labour power in order to live'.[2] We can therefore describe the ideal-typical capitalist society as made up of capitalists (who own factories and machines and buy and sell labour) and workers (who can live only as long as they can find work).

In contrast to the view taken by Plato of a class society, a Marxian analysis suggests that under capitalism the major classes cannot exist in stable harmony because under certain conditions in order to accumulate wealth and power capitalists shamelessly and brutally exploit members of the other class – the workers. 'Naked self-interest'[3] determines relationships between man and man. The interests of the two classes are incompatible and the inevitable conflict, itself the result of internal contradictions within society, is the source of the downfall of capitalist societies.

The conditions under which exploitation and class conflict between the capitalists and workers reach a point when revolution is inevitable are briefly described in the 'Manifesto'. Capitalists are the product 'of a series of revolutions in the modes of production and of exchange'.[4] Modern capitalist industry is characterised by a world market for goods. Factories produce goods which are consumed 'not only at home, but in every quarter of the globe'.[5] Colonisation opens up new sources of raw material and markets for the sale of goods. Road, rail, sea and, in the twentieth century, air transportation give a cosmopolitan character to production and consumption in every country. In order to survive capitalists have constantly to improve methods of production by the introduction of new machinery. Nations have to enter into a world economic system in which free competition dominates the sale and purchase of consumer goods such as cars, clothing, radio and TV sets, and so on. In short, capitalism 'creates a world of its own image'.[6]

It is a world of large modern industries in which men and women, young and old, work. The extensive use of machinery means that most of the workers perform specialised, repetitive, unskilled or semi-skilled jobs. Monotonous, easily performed tasks by large numbers of workers in vast factories have to be organised according to the dictates of machines. The speed at which these produce goods and the length of time daily they operate determine work rates, hours of work, and so on. Few workers are any longer craftsmen who start and complete the manufacture of a single item. The individual character of work and the charm it may have cannot exist in factories where mass production is geared to the desire of capitalists to maximise profits. The introduction of machines, an extension of the hours worked, the payment of low wages and the hiring and firing of workers in accordance with fluctuations in the market make capitalist industry profitable and, since according to Marx workers do not receive their just rewards, result in the exploitation of workers by capitalists.

The capitalist world is also a world of enormous cities with a vast urban population compared with the number of people living in rural areas. Industrial cities allow the means of production and property to be concentrated in a few hands or large corporations. They also imply a centralisation of political power and the exercise of it in modern representative governments by committees representing the interests of capitalists. In short, economic conflicts of interest between capitalists and workers are the basis of the class struggle in capitalist societies but give rise to political struggles. Under capitalism, according to Marx, national and international struggles between the two major classes are inevitable.

The workers, for example, are more self-conscious and organise themselves not in craft guilds but as trade unionists. Education helps them to meet and fight successfully the owners of factories and machines. A small section of the ruling class is likely to dissociate itself from its own class interests and join the workers in their fight against economic exploitation and political subservience. The importance of this educated section of the bourgeoisie cannot be exaggerated because its members are capable of 'comprehending theoretically the historical movement as a whole'.[7] Education under capitalism therefore prepares the workers and a minority of bourgeois ideologists for the inevitable overthrow of capitalism.

THE IDEAL–TYPICAL COMMUNIST SOCIETY

Since the exploitation and alienation of workers are unacceptable features of capitalist societies they should be eliminated. Marx and

Engels outlined in the 'Manifesto' how the internal contradications in capitalism would promote the forces of revolution in the class struggle between the bourgeoisie and the proletariat. In establishing an ideal-typical model of society we are less concerned with the processes of change than with the constituents of the ideal society. It is however necessary to make clear that the elimination of private ownership – if necessary by revolution – is vital to the creation of a communist society. Marx and Engels wrote: 'The distinguishing feature of communism is not the abolition of property generally, but the abolition of bourgeois property'.[8] The absence of private property sums up the theory of communist society.

The absence of any private ownership of the means of production means that in the long run the institutions and ideas that flourished under capitalism will be very different. Class, nation, state and family as institutions should be given meanings appropriate to a communist society rather than to a capitalist society. Individuality, culture, freedom, law, brotherhood, and so on, have to be given new meaning in societies where in the absence of private ownership there are no capitalists.

In their absence only one class remains: the workers. In modern Soviet literature workers, farmers and intellectuals are identified but they are members of the same class. Since their interests are not in conflict, 'class' struggles are out of the question. In this sense the ideal communist society is classless or made up of only one class, the members of which are not in competition but are bound together by a common consciousness, common interests and an appreciation of the unity of working men and women all over the world. Internationalism takes on new meaning, therefore. It is dependent on the absence of classes within nations. 'In proportion as the antagonism, the hostility of one nation to another will come to an end.'[9] In short, communism presupposes a world classless society of workers as the ideal. It is no part of communist theory to develop internationalism in a capitalist world.

By the same token the communist family is not based upon the ownership of property which deprives those who do not own property from family life. In the communist family wives and daughters are not seen as instruments of production to be sold as commodities but as equal members in a community of women. Marriage is designed in a communist society openly to legalise this community. It is not sanctioned by the church and is designed to raise the status of women to that of equals in a classless society. Organised religion as an instrument of bourgeois power finds no place, although the religious sentiments of people are respected.

As for the state, it will enable the workers, as the only and ruling class, to centralise the instruments of production in their hands. This does not mean that individuals cannot acquire property by working hard; they simply cannot use it by virtue of ownership to profit from it at the expense of others. The social character of property is emphasised. Under the state wages and profits take on a social character too. The introduction of new machines and increases in consumer goods are for the common good rather than as ways of accumulating capital for the few. Competition in Soviet industry consequently takes on new meaning. It is designed to improve the quality of life for all.

Culture and intellectualism are components of this life. They should reflect, however, not the values of capitalism but the values of a communist society. Consequently all art forms are to be judged in relation to the extent to which they are part of, represent, and are the products of, bourgeois culture, or represent, and are the products of, communist culture. Morality in the same way should be judged in the light of the economic conditions that constrain or release it. Indeed, central to the analysis made by Marx and Engels is that within any society ideas exist that will help to revolutionise it and that 'the dissolution of the old ideas keeps even pace with the dissolution of the old conditions of existence'.[10]

In summarising constituents of the ideal-typical communist society in the 'Communist Manifesto', Marx and Engels end by identifying the following changes:

1. Abolition of property in land and application of all rents of land to public purposes.
2. A heavy progressive or graduated income tax.
3. Abolition of all rights of inheritance.
4. Confiscation of the property of all emigrants and rebels.
5. Centralisation of credit in the hands of the state, by means of a national bank with state capital and an exclusive monopoly.
6. Centralisation of the means of communication and transport in the hands of the state.
7. Extension of factories and instruments of production owned by the state; the bringing into cultivation of waste lands, and the improvement of the soil generally in accordance with a common plan.
8. Equal obligation of all to work. Establishment of industrial armies, especially for agriculture.
9. Combination of agriculture with manufacturing industries; gradual abolition of the distinction between town and country, by a more equable distribution of the population over the country.
10. Free education for all children in public schools. Abolition of child factory labour in its present form. Combination of education with industrial production, etc.[11]

Against this ideal-typical model can be judged the contents of, for example, Soviet law and that country's constitutions. It is also against these visions of the good society that Lenin's interpretations and policy directives should be analysed. In particular the evolution of Soviet educational policies bears a close relationship to the statements made about education in the 'Manifesto'. Finally, it is with the view of society that the models presented by Plato in the *Republic* and by Dewey in many of his books should be compared.

COMMUNIST 'MAN'

If Plato's 'Man' is constrained by the accident of birth, communist 'Man' is a product of his class. According to Plato account should be taken of exceptions to the rule that philosopher-kings would breed future philosopher-kings and the children of manual workers would become efficient manual workers. In the 'Manifesto' Marx and Engels make it clear that the class to which an individual belongs determines his attitudes and consciousness. Exceptions among the ruling class join forces with exceptions among the workers under capitalism to form a revolutionary group. Communists in every country are the most resolute section of the workers and offer leadership in the class struggle.

Communist objectives are to overthrow capitalism and destroy the capitalists so that a classless or one-class society can be established. In this new society individuals will acquire the attitudes and a morality of their class – the working class or proletariat. In the ideal-typical communist society all individuals will be members of the same class and consequently self-conscious social action will not be the result of minority movements but of the majority of individuals in the interests of the majority.

Individuality consequently has to be seen in the relations individuals have with each other on the basis of equality. The class, group, or collective has an important bearing on individuality. In capitalist societies the majority of individuals will be constrained by the false consciousness of the capitalist class or the false consciousness of exploited workers. Because man's consciousness is determined by his socio-historical experience, the destruction of capitalism by removing property from private ownership does not make it immediately possible to create a truly communist individual. This accounts, no doubt, for Lenin's appeal to the Young Communists to base their activities on deep knowledge rather than slogans.[12] With this kind of knowledge they were enjoined to educate and train their peers and re-educate older members of society who under the previous regime had become victims of the system.

In a communist society workers and farmers should have a profound understanding of their place and role in a society in which all men and women are equal. This awareness ensures that individuals do not behave in terms of what they conceive to be their own self-interest but in accordance with the needs of the group or collective of workers as a whole. In so far as communist ethics and morality are subordinate to the interests of the one class of workers, the criterion against which moral behaviour is judged is related to the welfare of the collective rather than to the self-interest of the individual.

There is of course no contradiction here because class struggle and conflict are not present in the ideal-typical communist society. What a man or woman does on his or her own behalf also benefits society as a whole. Members of the intelligentsia in such a society will through their efforts make an important contribution to the quality of life. The achievements of art, science and culture are made accessible to all members of society, whether they live in cities, towns, or villages. Thus under appropriate economic circumstances all individuals can succeed in a uniform educational system. The exceptions are those who suffer serious or permanent brain damage.

Equality of educational provision as a central principle of policy in Soviet education is justified on the assumption that inequalities of attainment are principally due to differences in environmental conditions. The all-round development – intellectual, physical, moral and aesthetic – of individuals in the educational system has to be seen in relation to this basic assertion derived from Marxist theory. The attention given to the upbringing of children in Soviet theory reflects the assumption that under appropriate conditions the education system can produce ideal-typical communist men and women.

The first characteristic of such persons is that they should be aware of their common tasks, material interests and purposes, and work for the common good. This consciousness is a product of a number of factors. Other animals respond according to biologically inherited instinct and environmental stimuli. The behaviour of men and women is also conditioned by biologically inherited factors and external stimuli but in addition they possess a consciousness based on an accumulation of experience transmitted from one generation to another which directs their behaviour in the real world. Thus individuals are not constrained either by innate ability, by their environment, or by education alone. These factors contribute to the full development of their consciousness and hence to their freedom from the constraints of the immediate situation.

Once the foundation of capitalism – private ownership of property – has been eliminated, human nature can be improved through education. The ideal-typical communist has consciously to work for the achievement of a truly communist society. He has to possess a thorough knowledge of the socio-historical experience of mankind which until the overthrow of capitalism has been a history of class conflict. This knowledge of accumulated experience is transmitted from one generation to another through language. The 'second signal system' of I. P. Pavlov's theory makes language, and man's use of words, a central feature of education. This, of course, is not the only environment in which children learn and develop. The distinction between learning and development in the upbringing of children is important in Soviet theory because the maturation of the organism is not, as stated, the sole factor in its ability to learn. L. S. Vygotsky (1896–1934) analysed the relationship between development and learning and took the view that the influence of learning was never specific and may be, for example, to create a zone of potential development.

In his report to the Twenty-Fifth Party Congress L. I. Brezhnev reiterated that

> Soviet Man is a man who, having won his freedom, has been able to defend it in the most trying battle. A man who has been building the future unsparing of his energy and making every sacrifice. A man who, having gone through all trials, has himself changed beyond recognition, combining ideological conviction and tremendous vital energy, culture, knowledge and the ability to use them. This is a man who, while an ardent patriot, has been and will always remain a consistent internationalist.[13]

Freedom, ideology, culture, patriotism and internationalism are all key terms in any description of the ideal-typical Soviet man. They should be interpreted in the light of the theory of society advocated by Marx and Engels in the 'Communist Manifesto'. For the same reason virtues such as honesty, truthfulness, kindness, sympathy, loyalty, and so on, which are commonly advocated as aims in communist systems of education, should be examined in the context of the socioeconomic theory that is central to communism. While not so contentious as the previously mentioned political terms, they should nevertheless be included in any ideal-typical description of the fully and all-round developed individual.

In the Soviet model individuality finds its true expression in the collective. Both terms should be seen in the context of a society in which the means of production and property are owned by workers. Class interests and self-interest in these circumstances can be reconciled; individualism and collectivism are not antithetical but in the event each individual member of the collective works for the collective and places its interests first. This view is, however, tenable only under the conditions described, namely, when 'social property' eliminates the possibility of exploitation. In these circumstances the interests of society and individuals are synonymous.

It should be noted that Plato advanced a similar point of view. His notion of his good society, however, differs from that advanced by Marx and consequently his account of how individual and societal interests can be reconciled differs in major respects. Equally Dewey's individualism should be interpreted in the light of his concept of the good society. In short, in each major model relationships between theories of man and society are logical and cohere. Comparative studies should be conducted with a view to illuminating internal inconsistencies rather than with the intention of demonstrating that one model is 'correct' while the others are wrong.

KNOWLEDGE

Of course philosophers frequently claim that their theories are not normative or matters of opinion but derived from objective knowledge. The substance of the communist ideal-typical model, it is claimed, is not based upon the opinions of Marx and the interpretations of them by Lenin but upon the scientific study made by Marx of the history of all societies. Objective laws of social development tell us how and under what circumstances societies everywhere will change. In the Soviet ideal-typical model, therefore, the main direction of social change and the adjustment in the attitude and morality of individuals to each new stage of development are not in dispute. Education and the knowledge it provides are, however, necessary if individuals are to become good communists.

The case is based upon the assertion that under capitalism only some workers and a few members of the working class are fully able to understand its internal contradictions and to work for its overthrow. Old attitudes live on even in societies in which the private ownership of property has been abolished. This is particularly so in socialist societies surrounded by capitalist societies. Education and knowledge of a certain kind are necessary to emancipate old and young workers from these persisting and, of course, no longer appropriate attitudes and ways of behaving.

In a speech to members attending the Third All-Russian Congress of the Russian Young Communist League in 1920, Lenin advised them that they would only become communists when they enriched their minds 'with a knowledge of all the treasures created by mankind'.[14] Students should make a profound study of capitalist society in order themselves to understand the socio-historical experiences that they inherit. This knowledge, as stated, is passed on through language and is essential to the development of individuals.

The basic assumption about the history of mankind as stated in the 'Manifesto' is that 'The history of all existing society is the history of class struggle'.[15] The laws derived from Marx's study of this history are as objective as the laws of physics, chemistry and biology. Scientific methods of inquiry guarantee this objectivity. The data of inquiry are material. The method of inquiry is the dialectic. Hence dialectical materialism constitutes the accepted form of scientific investigation in this ideal-typical model. It has to be contrasted with other forms of the dialectic and with the view, held by Plato, that the permanent and therefore real world was one of 'ideas'.

Knowledge in the ideal-typical Soviet model is encyclopaedic. The history of each and every subject determines its content. Physics includes statics, dynamics, properties of matter, heat, light, sound, electricity and nuclear physics. Its data are drawn from work published over centuries of endeavour – from classical Greece to the late twentieth century.

The application of knowledge is vital to the development of Soviet society. Lenin emphasised the need to modernise the new society by electrifying the country, establishing a system of communications and building up basic industries. Technological innovation is as necessary to the quality of life in a communist society as it is vital to the development of capitalism. The motives for seeking to improve industry, however, and the outcomes are different.

A major difference is that in a communist society technological innovation will not further alienate workers from the means of production. Nor will it increase competition based on self-interest. Because there is no rejection of industrial life by Soviet theorists, technological innovation under these conditions will benefit all members of society. Such benefits are dependent upon the relationships that exist between workers and these in turn depend upon the kind of knowledge workers possess.

Lenin and Krupskaya, his wife, criticised tsarist schools because they provided book knowledge, crammed pupils by using the methods of the old drill-sergeant and above all created a rift between books and practical life. The remedy is to ensure that all young people entering the productive life of a communist society should know something about it and acquire attitudes appropriate to it.

This kind of knowledge can be acquired through 'polytechnical' education. Krupskaya outlined its main features in an article, 'The difference between professional and polytechnical education'.[16] It was a central issue in the reforms designed to bring education nearer to life which found expression in the law of 1958 enacted during Krushchev's leadership. Polytechnical education is examined in its many aspects in S. G. Shapovalenko (ed.), *Polytechnical Education in the USSR.*[17] The central theme is that all knowledge should be used to illuminate the characteristics of productive life in an industrial society.

'Polytechnical' knowledge includes information about the entire cycle of production: where raw materials come from; how they are brought to factories; how machines are built and run. It also includes knowledge of how methods of production are organised, how factories are managed and how the products of industry are distributed. The roles played by factories and industry in general in the economy of the USSR are also ingredients of this knowledge. The history of each of these aspects should be included in the comprehensive knowledge of the young worker. In terms of emphasis, knowledge of chemical industries, agriculture and light and heavy engineering should receive priority but such an emphasis should not be taken as a denial of Lenin's dictum that all the accumulated knowledge of mankind is important.

The relationship between this kind of knowledge and the attitudes to which it gives rise is, of course, important in the model. These attitudes encapsulate the moral imperatives of a one-class society which should determine relationships between workers. They should also inform the relationship of workers to the means of production and thereby avoid alienation.

Knowledge of this kind is thus the cement that binds individuals and the collective together. It frees individuals and is the basis on which their true consciousness is built. It is thus the emancipator and mobiliser of all the people in a society of equals. In the appropriate circumstances of a society in which property is owned by the collective, this knowledge contributes to the development of individuals. For this reason knowledge is an essential and very important component in an ideal-typical model of a communist society.

CONCLUSION

Such a brief summary does less than justice to the vast volume of literature on Marxism. It is designed to serve as a useful model against which to study debates among Soviet educationists and their analysis of the stage reached in the evolution of society from an immediate post-capitalist one towards a truly communist one.[18]

NOTES AND REFERENCES: CHAPTER 9

1 K. Marx and F. Engels (ed. Samuel H. Beer), *The Communist Manifesto*, Appleton-Century-Crofts, New York, 1955, p. 9.
2 loc. cit.
3 ibid., p. 12.
4 ibid., p. 11.
5 ibid., p. 13.
6 ibid., p. 14.
7 ibid., p. 20.
8 ibid., p. 24.
9 ibid., p. 29.
10 ibid., p. 30.
11 ibid., p. 32.

12 *Lenin, Marx, Engels, Marxism,* Scientific Socialism series, Progress, Moscow, 1970, pp. 116–32.
13 *Soviet Union,* Progress, Moscow, 1977, p. 459.
14 Lenin, 'The tasks of the youth leagues', in *Lenin, Marx, Engels, Marxism,* op. cit., p. 132.
15 *The Manifesto,* op. cit., p. 9.
16 N. K. Krupskaya, 'The difference between professional and polytechnical education', in *On Education,* Foreign Languages Publishing House, Moscow, 1957.
17 S. G. Shapovalenko (ed.), *Polytechnical Education in the USSR,* Unesco, Paris, 1963.
18 *Select Bibliography (in English)*

A. M. Arsenyev, *The Soviet School of the Present and Future,* Pedagogica, Moscow, 1971, and *Soviet Education,* vol. XIX, November 1976, for a review of policies up to 1980.

E. A. Asratyan, *I. P. Pavlov: His Life and Work,* Foreign Languages Publishing House, Moscow, 1953. Much of the information in this book is drawn from Pavlov's own writings.

L. I. Bozhovich, 'The personality of school children and problems of education', in M. Cole and I. Haltzman (eds.), *A Handbook of Contemporary Soviet Psychology,* Basic Books, New York, 1969, pp. 224–5.

L. I. Brezhnev, *Following Lenin's Course,* Moscow, 1972, pp. 284–5; also *The 24th Congress of the CPSU and Its Contribution to Marxism-Leninism,* Novosti Press, Moscow, 1972.

See Urie Bronfenbrenner, *Two Worlds of Childhood, USA and USSR,* Allen & Unwin, London, 1971.

Michael Cole (ed.), *Soviet Developmental Psychology, An Anthology,* M. E. Sharpe, White Plains, New York, 1977.

Constitution (Fundamental Law) of the Union of Soviet Socialist Republics, Novosti Press, Moscow, 1977; *New Steps in Soviet Education, Materials of the Six Session of the USSR Supreme Soviet, July 17–19, 1973,* Novosti Press, Moscow, 1973.

N. DeWitt, *Soviet Professional Manpower: Its Education, Training and Supply,* National Science Foundation, Washington, DC, 1955.

Spartak Gazaryan, *Children in the USSR,* Novosti Press, Moscow, 1973.

Nicholas Hans, *The Principles of Educational Policy,* 2nd edn, King & Son, London, 1933.

Nicholas Hans, 'Recent trends in Soviet education', in *The Annals: The Soviet Union since World War II,* American Academy of Political and Social Science, vol. 263, Philadelphia, Pa, May 1949.

Nicholas Hans, *The Russian Tradition in Education,* Routledge & Kegan Paul, London, 1963.

Brian Holmes, 'Science education: cultural borrowing and comparative research', *Studies in Science Education,* Centre for Studies in Science Education, University of Leeds, Vol. 4, 1977, pp. 83–110.

M. I. Isayev, *National Languages in the USSR: Problems and Solutions,* Progress, Moscow, 1977.

Alexei Kalinin, *The Soviet System of Public Education, Its Organisation and Functioning,* Novosti Press, Moscow, 1973.

M. I. Kalinin, *On Communist Education,* Foreign Languages Publishing House, Moscow, 1950.

D. P. Korzh, 'Public education in the far north of the USSR', A. Rudakov, 'Public education in Komi Autonomous Soviet Socialist Republic' and S. J. Savvin, 'Education in the Yakut Autonomous Soviet Socialist Republic', all in R. K. Hall, N. Hans and J. A. Lauwerys (eds), *The Year Book of Education, 1954,* Evans, London, 1954.

N. K. Krupskaya, *On Education,* Foreign Languages Publishing House, Moscow, 1957.

N. P. Kuzin, 'The socialist revolution and education', in *Education in the USSR,* Progress, Moscow, 1972.
V. I. Lenin, *Articles on Tolstoi,* Moscow, 1953; S. A. Tostaya (ed.), *Tolstoi's Moscow Home,* Foreign Languages Publishing House, Moscow, 1957.
V. I. Lenin, 'The tasks of the youth league', in *Lenin, Marx, Engels, Marxism,* op. cit.
Ludwig Liegle, *The Family Role in Soviet Education* (trans. Susan Hecker), Springer, New York, 1975.
Frederic Lilge, *Anton Semyonovitch Makarenko: An Analysis of His Ideas in the Context of Soviet Society,* University of California, Publications in Education, Berkeley, Calif., 1958.
A. Markushevich, 'The problems of the content of school education in the USSR', in Brian Holmes and Raymond Ryba (eds), *Curriculum Development at the Second Level of Education,* Proceedings of the Comparative Education Society in Europe, Fourth General Meeting, London, 1969.
Karl Marx, *Capital,* Lawrence & Wishart, London, 1962.
Robert Maxwell (ed.), *Information USSR,* Macmillan, New York, 1962. This book lists Russian and Soviet scholars who have participated in various aspects of life.
John McLeish, *Soviet Psychology: History, Theory, Content,* Methuen, London, 1975, and particularly ch. 8, 'Half a decade of Pavlovian psychology'.
Y. N. Medinsky, in *Anton Makarenko, His Life and Work,* Foreign Languages Publishing House, Moscow (no date).
J. Pennar, 'Party control over Soviet schools', in G. Z. F. Bereday and J. Pennar (eds), *The Politics of Soviet Education*; Atlantic Books, Stevens, New York, 1960.
A. V. Petrovosky, 'Basic directions in the development and current states of educational psychology', *Soviet Education,* vol. XV, nos. 5–6, March–April 1973.
A. P. Pinkevitch, *The New Education in the Soviet Republic* (trans. Nucia Perlmutter, ed. George Counts), John Day, New York, 1929.
A. I. Piskunov (ed.), *K. D. Ushinsky – Selected Works,* Progress, Moscow, 1975.
G. V. Plekhanov, *Fundamental Problems of Marxism,* Foreign Languages Publishing House, Moscow (no date).
Mikhail Prokofyev, 'The right to education', in *The Rights and Freedoms of Soviet Citizens,* Novosti Press, Moscow, 1977.
M. Prokofyev, *Public Education, USSR, Yesterday, Today, Tomorrow,* Novosti Press, Moscow (no date).
Public Education in the USSR: in 1975–76, Moscow, 1977.
Seymour M. Rosen, *Education and Modernisation in the USSR, Addison-Wesley, Reading, Mass., 1971.*
Seymour M. Rosen, *Education in the USSR – Recent Legislation and Statistics,* US Department of Health, Education, and Welfare, Washington, DC, 1975.
Vassili Severtsev, *L'Enseignement secondaire spécialisé en URSS,* Novosti Press, Moscow, 1972.
S. G. Shapovalenko (ed.), *Polytechnical Education in the USSR,* Unesco, Paris, 1963.
Brian and Joan Simon (eds), *Educational Psychology in the USSR,* Routledge & Kegan Paul, London, 1963.
S. Soloveichik, *Soviet Children at School,* Novosti Press, Moscow, 1976.
Soviet Union, Progress, Moscow, 1977.
M. Souslov, *Le PCUS, Parti du Marxisme créateur,* Novosti Press, Moscow, 1972.
V. Strezikozin, 'The Soviet Union', in J. A. Lauwerys and D. Scanlon (eds), *Examinations: World Year Book of Education, 1969,* Evans, London, 1969, and also University of London, Institute of Education, *Education in the USSR,* 1976, 1977.
USSR Education, Novosti Press, Moscow, 1976.
S. Vygotsky, *Thought and Language* (trans. and ed. Eugenie Hanfmann and Gertrude Vakar), MIT Press, Cambridge, Mass., and New York, and Wiley, New York, 1962.

V. Yelyutin, *Higher Education in the USSR,* Soviet Booklet No. 51, London, 1959.
B. P. Yesipov and N. K. Goncharov, 'For Bolshevik character: the principles of moral education' and 'For the common good: education in collectivism', in *I Want To Be Like Stalin* (trans. G. S. Counts and N. P. Lodge), Gollancz, London, 1948.
L. V. Zankov *et al*., 'Teaching and development: a Soviet investigation', *Soviet Education,* vol. XIX, nos 4–5–6, February, March, April 1977, M. E. Sharpe, White Plains, New York.
M. Zinovyev and A. Pleshakova, *How Illiteracy Was Wiped Out in the USSR,* Foreign Languages Publishing House, Moscow (no date).
V. G. Zubov, 'Polytechnical education under present conditions', *Soviet Education,* vol. XVIII, no. 2, December 1975.

Select Bibliography

COMPARATIVE EDUCATION

D. Adams and I. N. Thut, *Patterns of Education in Contemporary Societies*, McGraw-Hill, New York, 1964.

C. A. Anderson, 'Methodology in comparative education', *International Review of Education,* vol. 7, no. 1, 1961, pp. 1–23.

C. A. Anderson, 'The University of Chicago programme in comparative education', *International Review of Education,* vol. 12, no. 1, 1966.

C. A. Anderson, *Designing Cross-Cultural Indicators of Education,* 1975.

C. A. Anderson and M. J. Bowman, 'Theoretical considerations in educational planning in *The World Year Book of Education, 1967*, Evans, London, 1967.

E. Ashby, *Universities: British, Indian, African*, Harvard University Press, Cambridge, Mass., 1966.

B. Barber, 'Science, salience and comparative education: some reflections in social scientific enquiry', in R. Edwards *et al., Relevant Methods in Comparative Education,* Unesco Institute for Education, Hamburg, 1973.

G. Z. F. Bereday, 'Some methods of teaching comparative education', *Comparative Education Review,* vol. 1, no. 3, February 1958, pp. 4–9.

G. Z. F. Bereday, 'Sir Michael Sadler's study of foreign systems of education', *Comparative Education Review,* vol. 7, no. 3, February 1964, pp. 307–14.

G. Z. F. Bereday, *Comparative Method in Education,* Holt, Rinehart & Winston, New York, 1966.

Walter Berger and K. H. Gruber, *Die Vergleichende Erziehungswissenschaft,* Jugend & Volk, Wien-Munchen, 1976.

M. J. Bowman and C. A. Anderson, 'Concerning the role of education in development', in M. J. Bowman, *Readings in the Economics of Education,* Unesco, Paris, 1968, pp. 113–31.

G. S. Browne and J. F. Cramer, *Contemporary Education: A Comparative Study of National Systems,* Harcourt Brace, New York, 1965.

Centre for International Research and Innovation, *Alternative Educational Futures in the United States and in Europe: Methods, Issues and Policy Relevance,* OECD, Paris, 1972.

Comparative Education, vol. 13, no. 2, June 1977; special issue on comparative education, its present state and future prospects.

Comparative Education Review, vol. 21, nos 2–3, June–October 1977; special issues on the state of the art.
Comparative Education Society in Europe Proceedings:
1963, *Comparative Education Research and the Determinants of Educational Policy,* CESE, London, 1963 (Amsterdam)
1965, *General Education in a Changing World,* CESE, London, 1965 (Berlin)
1967, *The University within the Education System,* CESE, London, 1967 (Ghent)
1969, Brian Holmes and Raymond Ryba (eds), *Curriculum Development at the Second Level of Education,* CESE, London, 1969 (Prague)
1971, Brian Holmes and Raymond Ryba (eds), *Teacher Education,* CESE, London, 1971 (Stockholm)
1973, Brian Holmes and Raymond Ryba (eds), *Recurrent Education – Concepts and Policies for Lifelong Education,* CESE, London, 1973 (Frascati)
1975, Denis Kallen and Raymond Ryba (eds), *School and Community,* CESE, London, 1975 (Sevres)
1977, Brian Holmes (ed.), *Diversity and Unity in Education,* Allen & Unwin, London, 1980 (London)
Compare, journal of the British Comparative Education Society, Carfax, Oxford.
P. H. Coombs, *What is Educational Planning?,* International Institute for Educational Planning, Paris, 1970.
U. Dahllof, 'Relevance and fitness analysis in comparative education', *Scandinavian Journal of Educational Research,* vol. 15, no. 3, 1971.
M. Debeauvais, 'The development of education in Latin America since the Santiago Plan', in J. A. Lauwerys *et al.* (eds), *The World Year Book of Education, 1967*, Evans, London, 1967, pp. 358–74.
Maurice Debesse and Gaston Mialaret, *Traité des sciences pédagogiques,* 3 *Pédagogique comparée,* Presses Universitaires de France, Paris, 1972.
M. A. Eckstein and Harold J. Noah, *Scientific Investigations in Comparative Education,* Macmillan, London, 1969.
R. Edwards, 'The dimensions of comparison and of comparative education', *Comparative Education Review,* vol. 14, no. 3, October 1970, pp. 239–54.
R. Edwards *et al*. (eds), *Relevant Methods in Comparative Education,* Unesco Institute for Education, Hamburg, 1973.
Lionel Elvin, 'The philosophy of Unesco', in *The Yearbook of Education, 1957*, Evans, London, 1957, pp. 294–314.
J. Fischer, *The Social Sciences and the Comparative Study of Educational Systems,* International Textbook Company, Scranton, Pa, 1970.
R. Freeman Butts, 'New future for comparative education', *Comparative Education Review,* vol. 17, no. 3, October 1973, pp. 289–94.
K. E. Gezi, *Education in Comparative and International Perspectives,* Holt, Rinehart & Winston, New York, 1971.
W. D. Halls, 'Comparative education: explanations', *Comparative Education,* vol. 3, no. 3, June 1967, pp. 189–93.
W. D. Halls, 'Culture and education: the culturalist approach to comparative education', in R. Edwards *et al*. (eds), *Relevant Methods in Comparative*

Education, Unesco Institute for Education, Hamburg, 1973.
N. Hans, *Comparative Education: A Study of Educational Factors and Traditions,* 3rd edn, Routledge & Kegan Paul, London, 1958.
Franz Hilker, *Vergleichende Pädagogik,* Max Huebner, Munich, 1962.
Brian Holmes and S. B. Robinsohn (eds), *Relevant Data in Comparative Education, Report of an Expert Meeting, March 11–16, 1963,* Unesco Institute for Education, Hamburg, 1963.
E. Hopper, 'A typology for the classification of educational systems', *Sociology,* vol. 2, no. 1, January 1968, pp. 29–46.
M. Huberman, *Understanding Changes in Education: An Introduction,* Unesco/IBE, Paris, 1973.
Torsten Husén, *International Study of Achievement in Mathematics: A Comparison of Twelve Countries,* Wiley, New York, 1967.
Torsten Husén, *The Learning Society,* Methuen, London, 1974.
Torsten Husén, *The School in Question*, Oxford University Press, London, 1979.
Ph. J. Idenburg, *Theorie van het onderwijsbeleid,* Wolters-Noordhoff, Gröningen, 1971.
International Association for the Evaluation of Educational Achievement, 1970 (IEA), Wenner-Gren Center, Stockholm, 1970.
International Review of Education, vol. 15, no. 2, 1969. This issue is devoted to the International Project for the Evaluation of Educational Achievement.
International Standard Classification of Education (ISCED), abridged version, Unesco, Paris, 1975.
P. E. Jones, *Comparative Education,* University of Queensland, St Lucia, 1971.
D. Kallen, 'The present status of comparative education in Europe', *Comparative Education Review,* vol. 7, no. 2, October 1963, pp. 108–12.
Isaac L. Kandel, *Comparative Education,* Houghton Mifflin, Boston, Mass., 1933.
Isaac L. Kandel, *Studies in Comparative Education*, Harrap, London, 1933.
Isaac L. Kandel (ed.), *International Yearbook of the International Institute* (1924–44), Teachers College, Columbia, New York, annually.
Andrew M. Kazamias and B. G. Massialas, *Tradition and Change in Education,* Prentice-Hall, Englewood Cliffs, NJ, 1965.
Andrew M. Kazamias, 'Woozles and wizzles in the methodology of comparative education', *Comparative Education Review,* vol. 14, no. 3, October 1970, pp. 255–61.
Andrew M. Kazamias, 'Comparative pedagogy: an assignment for the seventies', *Comparative Education Review,* vol. 16, no. 3, October 1972, pp. 406–11.
W. Kienitz, 'On the Marxist approach to comparative education in the German Democratic Republic', *Comparative Education,* vol. 7, no. 1, August 1971, pp. 21–31.
Edmund J. King, 'The purpose of comparative education', *Comparative Education,* vol. 1, no. 3, June 1965, pp. 147–59.
Edmund J. King, 'Comparative studies and policy decision', *Comparative Education,* vol. 4, no. 1, November 1967. pp. 51–63.

Edmund J. King, *Comparative Studies and Educational Decision,* Bobbs-Merrill, New York, 1968.
Edmund J. King, *Other Schools and Ours,* Holt, Rinehart & Winston, London, 1970.
Edmund J. King, 'Analytical frameworks in comparative studies of education', *Comparative Education,* vol. 11, no. 1, March 1975, pp. 85–103.
Edmund J. King *et al., Post Compulsory Education,* vols 1 and 2, Sage, London, 1974 and 1975.
K. C. Land, 'Theories, models and indicators of social change', *International Social Science Journal,* vol. 27, no. 1, 1975, pp. 7–37.
J. A. Laska, 'The future of comparative education', *Comparative Education Review,* vol. 17, no. 3, October 1973, pp. 295–8.
Joseph A. Lauwerys, 'The philosophical approach to comparative education', *International Review of Education,* vol. 5, no. 3, 1959, pp. 281–98.
Joseph A. Lauwerys, 'General education in a changing world', *International Review of Education,* vol. 11, no. 3, 1965, pp. 385–403.
Joseph A. Lauwerys *et al.* (eds), *The (World) Year Book of Education*, Evans, London, 1948 to 1970, subsequently under different editors to 1974. Among the volumes edited by Lauwerys and others the following broke new ground.
1954, *Education and Technological Development*
1956, *Education and Economics*
1957, *Education and Philosophy*
1959, *Higher Education*
1961, *Concepts of Excellence in Education*
1963, *The Education and Training of Teachers*
1964, *Education and International Life*
1966, *Church and State in Education*
1967, *Educational Planning*
1968, *Education within Industry*
1970, *Education in Cities*
M. B. Lourenço-Filho, *Educação comparada*, Edições Melhoramentos, São Paulo, 1961.
Vernon Mallinson, *An Introduction to the Study of Comparative Education,* 4th edn, Heinemann, London, 1975.
Angel Diego Marquez, *Educación comparada, teoria y metodogia,* 'El Atoneo' Pedro Garcia, Buenos Aires, 1972.
A. H. Moehlmann and J. S. Roucek, *Comparative Education,* Holt, New York, 1951.
K. C. Muhkerjee, *A Comparative Study of Some Educational Problems,* Lalvani, New York, 1971.
Harold J. Noah, 'Defining comparative education: conceptions', in R. Edwards *et al.* (eds), *Relevant Methods in Comparative Education,* Unesco Institute for Education, Hamburg, 1973.
Harold J. Noah, 'Fast fish and loose fish in comparative education', *Comparative Education Review,* vol. 18, no. 3, October 1974, pp. 341–7.
Harold J. Noah and M. A. Eckstein, 'A design for teaching comparative education', *Comparative Education Review,* vol. 10, no. 3, October 1966, pp. 511–13.

Harold J. Noah and Max A. Eckstein, *Towards a Science of Comparative Education,* Macmillan, London, 1969.

Organisation for Economic Co-operation and Development, *Reviews of National Policy for Education* (various), OECD, Paris. For example, Japan, 1971; United States, 1971; Germany, 1972.

Organisation for Economic Co-operation and Development, *Case Studies of Educational Innovation* (4 vols), 1 *At the Central Level,* 2 *At the Regional Level,* 3 *At the School Level,* 4 *Strategies for Innovation in Education,* OECD, Paris, 1973.

George W. Parkyn, 'Aims and results: problems in comparative education', *London Educational Review,* vol. 2, no. 3, 1973, pp. 20–6.

George W. Parkyn, *Towards a Conceptual Model of Lifelong Education,* Unesco, Paris, 1973.

R. Poignant, *Education in the Industrialised Countries,* Nijhoff, The Hague, 1973.

T. N. Postlethwaite, 'International programme for evaluation of educational achievements (IEA)', *International Review of Education,* vol. 12, no. 3, 1966, pp. 356–69.

Saul B. Robinsohn, *Schulreform in gesellschaftlichen Prozess: ein interkultureller Vergleich,* vol. 1, Klett, Stuttgart, 1972.

Pedro Rossello, *La Teoria de las Corrientes Educativas,* Unesco, Paris, 1960.

Pedro Rossello, 'Concerning the structure of comparative education', *Comparative Education Review,* vol. 7, no. 2, 1961, pp. 1–3.

P. Sandiford, *Comparative Education,* Dent, London, 1918.

F. Schneider, *Triebkräfte der Pädagogik der Völker,* Muller, Salzburg, 1947.

F. Schneider, *Vergleichende Erziehungswissenschaft,* Quelle & Meyer, Heidelberg, 1961.

A. R. Trethewey, *Introducing Comparative Education,* Pergamon, Rushcutters Bay, NSW, 1976.

Juan Tusquets, *Teoria y Pratica de la Pedagogia Comparada,* Magisterio Español, Madrid, 1969.

Robert Ulich, *The Education of Nations, A Comparison in Historical Perspective,* Harvard University Press, Cambridge, Mass., 1961.

Unesco, *World Survey of Education* (5 vols), 1 *Handbook of Educational Organisation and Statistics,* Evans, London, for Unesco, 1955; 2 *Primary Education,* Evans, London, 1958; 3 *Secondary Education,* Unesco, Paris, 1961; 4 *Higher Education,* Unesco, Paris, 1966; 5 *Education Policy, Legislation and Administration,* Unesco, Paris, 1971.

Unesco, *In the Minds of Men: Unesco 1946–1971,* Unesco, Paris, 1972.

Unesco, *Learning To Be,* Unesco, Paris, 1972.

John Vaizey, *Education in the Modern World,* Weidenfeld & Nicholson, London, 1975.

A. Vexliard, *La Pédagogie comparée,* Presses Universitaires de France, Paris, 1967.

World Congress of Comparative Education Societies, Douglas Ray and Jacques Lamontagne (eds), *Cultural Diversity and Political Unity,* abstracts of papers presented at the Third World Congress, London, 1977, University of Western Ontario, Canada, 1977.

Published Works by the Author

BOOKS, MONOGRAPHS AND REPORTS

1 *American Criticism of American Education,* College of Education, Ohio State University, Columbus, Ohio, 1957.
2 with S. B. Robinsohn, *Relevant Data in Comparative Education: A Report of an Expert Meeting, 11–16 March, 1963,* Unesco Institute for Education, Hamburg, 1963.
3 with T. Bristow, *Teaching Comparative Education, Unesco Abstracts* (annotated bibliography with introductory essay), vol. XV, no. 4, 1963.
4 *Problems in Education: A Comparative Approach,* Routledge & Kegan Paul, London, 1965 (translated into Italian and Japanese).
5 *Educational Policy and the Mission Schools* (ed. and contributor), Routledge & Kegan Paul, 1967.
6 with T. Bristow, *Comparative Education through the Literature,* Butterworth, London, 1968.
7 with R. Ryba (eds), *Curriculum Development at the Second Level of Education,* Comparative Education Society in Europe, Proceedings of the Fourth General Meeting, Prague, 1969, The Society, London, 1971.
8 *A Cross-National and Interdisciplinary Analysis of Secondary Educational Change in England, France and Sweden* (report of a conference at Kent State University), US Office of Education (Bureau of Research), Washington, DC, 1970.
9 with R. Ryba (eds), *Teacher Education,* Comparative Education Society in Europe, Proceedings of the Fifth General Meeting, Stockholm, 1971, The Society, Stockholm, 1971.
10 with David G. Scanlon (eds), *The World Year Book of Education, 1971/72: Higher Education in a Changing World,* Evans, London, 1971.
11 with Reginald Edwards *et al.* (eds), *Relevant Methods in Comparative Education, Report of a Meeting of International Experts,* Unesco Institute for Education, Hamburg, 1973.
12 with R. Ryba (eds), *Recurrent Education: Concepts and Policies for Lifelong Education,* Comparative Education Society in Europe, Proceedings of the Sixth General Meeting, Frascati, The Society, London, 1973.
13 with J. A. Lauwerys (*et al.*), *Present Problems in the Democratisation of Secondary and Higher Education,* Unesco, Paris, 1973.

14 'Curriculum innovation at the second level of education, educational documentation and information', *Bulletin of the International Bureau of Education,* 4th year, no. 190, 1st quarter, 1974, IBE, Geneva, 1974 (annotated bibliography).
15 *Ivory Towers, the Glass Bead Game and Open Societies: the Social Functions of Comparative Education,* University of London, Institute of Education, London, 1979.
16 *International Guide to Education Systems, ibedata,* Unesco, Paris, 1979.
17 (ed.), *Diversity and Unity in Education,* Allen & Unwin, London, 1980.
18 *Comparative Education: Some Considerations of Method,* Allen & Unwin, London, 1981.

ARTICLES AND REVIEW ARTICLES

1954

'The teacher of teachers', *Education for Teaching,* no. 32, May 1954.
'UK: education and development', in *The Year Book of Education, 1954: Education and Technological Development,* Evans, London, 1954.

1956

'Teacher training and the science curriculum', in *Science Curriculum* (a report of a meeting of experts), Unesco Institute for Education, Hamburg, 1956.
'The reform of English education under the 1944 Act', in *The Year Book of Education, 1956: Education and Economics,* Evans, London, 1956.
with J. A. Lauwerys 'Der aufgabenbereich der vergleichenden erziehungswissenschaft' in Hans Espe (ed.) *Vergleichende Erziehungswissenschaft*, ORBIS Verlag, Berlin, 1956.
'Some writings of William Torrey Harris', *British Journal of Educational Studies,* vol. V, no. 1, November 1956.

1957

'Education as a profession', *Education for Teaching*, no. 44, November 1957.

1958

'Social change and the curriculum', in George Z. F. Bereday and J. A. Lauwerys (eds), *The Year Book of Education, 1958,* Evans, London, 1958.
'Comparative education and the administrator', *Journal of Higher Education,* vol. 24, no. 5, May 1958.
'The problem approach in comparative education', *Comparative Education Review,* vol. 2, no. 1, June 1958.
'Martin Langeveld: sympathy as method', from a correspondent in the *Times Educational Supplement,* 22 August 1958.
'The nature of scientific truth', in *Art, Science and Education*, Joint Council for Education through Art, London, 1958.

1959

'Research in England', in *Research in Education,* report of an educational conference, Tokyo, 1959.

1960

'Methodology in comparative education', *Education Libraries Bulletin,* no. 9, Autumn 1960.

'Soviet education in transition', in *Phi Delta Kappa,* vol. 42, no. 2, November 1960.

(ed.), 'New media and the promotion of international understanding', in *The Year Book of Education, 1960: Communication and the School,* Evans, London, 1960.

1961

'Polytechnical education in the USSR', *Bulletin of the Institute of Physics and the Physical Society,* March 1961.

1962

'Education in the United States of America', in *Annual Report 1961–2,* University of Southampton, Institute of Education, Southampton, December 1962.

1963

'Teacher education in a changing world', in *The Year Book of Education, 1963: Education and Training of Teachers,* Evans, London, 1963.

'Organisation of teacher training', in *The Year Book of Education, 1963: Education and Training of Teachers,* Evans, London, 1963.

'From McNair to Robbins', *Journal,* Newcastle-upon-Tyne, University Institute of Education, no. 75, November 1963.

'The explosion of expectations and racial problems', *The Link* (Espergaerde, Denmark), December 1963.

1964

'The education of teachers: the Conant Report', *Education for Teaching,* no. 63, February 1964.

'Higher education in Britain', *Journal of Higher Education,* vol. 35, no. 7, October 1964.

'Education as a human right in depressed areas', *The New Era,* vol. 45, no. 10, December 1964.

1965

'The reflective man: John Dewey', in P. Nash *et al.* (eds), *The Educated Man: Studies in the History of Educational Thought,* Wiley, New York, 1965.

'Rational constructs in comparative education', *International Review of Education,* vol. 11, no. 4, 1965.

(with Ann Dryland), 'The role of examinations in an expanding educational system', in *Aspects of US and UK Examination Systems,* Association of Technical Institutions, London, 1965.

1966

'Comparative education and the education of teachers', *Bulletin,* University of London, Institute of Education, no. 10, Autumn Term, 1966.

1967

'Lawrence A. Cremin's "The genius of American education" ', *History of Education Quarterly,* vol. VII, no. 1, Spring 1967.

'Idealism in education', *Studies in the Philosophy of Education,* vol. V, no. 1, Winter 1966–7.

'Education in Western Europe', in John Calmann (ed.), *Western Europe: A Handbook,* Blond, London, 1967.

1968

'Curriculum reform in the USA', in *The Changing School Curriculum,* report of the CESE (British Section) Conference at Bolton, University of Reading, 1968.

1969

'A look to the future and a brief plea for the comparative approach', in Guy Benvenista and Warren F. Ilchman (eds), *Agents of Change: Professionals in Developing Countries,* Praeger, New York, 1969.

'Comprehensions and apprehensions concerning American educational philosophy', in S. E. Fraser (ed.), *International Education: Understandings and Misunderstandings,* Peabody International Center, Nashville, Tenn., 1969.

'A European view of American educational philosophy', in S. E. Fraser (ed.), *American Education in Foreign Perspectives,* Wiley, New York, 1969.

1970

'Educational change in Europe', in *Educational Leadership,* vol. 27, no. 4, January 1970.

'International education in Great Britain', in *Phi Delta Kappa*, vol. 51, no. 5, January 1970.

'The contribution of history to a science of education', in Paul Nash (ed.), *History and Education,* Wiley, New York and London, 1970.

'Education in Eastern Europe', in G. Schöpflin (ed.), *The Soviet Union and Eastern Europe: A Handbook,* Blond, London, 1970.

'Education in cities', in J. A. Lauwerys and David Scanlon (eds), *The World Year Book of Education, 1970: Education in Cities,* Evans, London, 1970.

'Health education – a required subject in schools and colleges', *The Health Education Journal,* vol. 29, no. 3, September 1970.

1971

'The future of teacher education in England and Wales; a comparative view', *Education for Teaching,* no. 85, Summer 1971.

'Universities, higher education and society', in *The World Year Book of Education, 1971/72: Higher Education in a Changing World,* Evans, London, 1971.

'General education: some comparative guidelines', *General Education,* no. 17, Autumn 1971.

'Movements to liberalise the schools in different countries', in *Towards a Freer School,* Loccumer Protokolle 3/71, Loccum, 1971.

'The politics of teacher education', in B. Holmes and R. Ryba (eds), *Teacher Education,* Comparative Education Society in Europe, Proceedings of the Fifth General Meeting, Stockholm, 1971, The Society, Stockholm, 1971.
'Cambio social y educacion', in *Educacion y Cambio Social* Jornadas Adriano Olivetti de Educacion; Ediciones Cultivales Olivetti, Buenos Aires, 1971.
'Politicia de la educacion de profesor', *Perspectivas Pedagógicas*, no. 28, 1971.
'Storm signals, this time from the Grandes Ecoles', *New Academic,* no. 1, 6.5.71.
'Comparative education', in *The Encyclopedia of Education,* Vol. 2, Macmillan, New York, 1971.

1972
'Concepts of culture and society in education research', in *Philosophical Redirection of Educational Research,* 71st Year Book of National Society for the Study of Education, NSSE, University of Chicago Press, Chicago, 1972.
'Universities and the James Report: a case for two year awards', *Times Higher Educational Supplement,* 17 March 1972.
'Examinations – a comparative view', *Compare,* vol. 3, no. 1, 1972.

February 1972.
'Nursing as a profession', *Nursing Times,* 25 May 1972.
'The development of higher education: a comparative survey', in S. J. Eggleston (ed.), *Diversifying Post-secondary Education in Europe, Paedagogica Europaea,* Vol. VII, 1972.
'Teacher education in Europe', *Secondary Education,* vol. 2, no. 3, Summer 1972.
'Saul B. Robinsohn: in memoriam', *International Review of Education,* vol. 18, no. 3, 1972.
'Life and work', in A. R. Pemberton (ed.), *Life and Work,* Proceedings of the Comparative Education Society in Europe (British Section), Sixth Conference, 1971, University of Reading, 1972.
'L'éducation en Angleterre et en Pays de Galles', in M. Debesse and G. Mialaret (eds), *Traité des sciences pédagogiques, Vol. 3, Pédagogie comparée,* Presses universitaires de France, Paris, 1972.
'Comparative education as a scientific study', *British Journal of Educational Studies,* vol. XX, no. 2, June 1972.
'Education in Japan', *Guardian,* 28 June 1972.
'Los "constructos" teóricos en la educación comparada', in Angel Diego Marquez (ed.), *Educación comparada: teoria y metodologia,* El Atoneo, Buenos Aires, 1972.
'Can James be made to work?', *Education for Teaching,* no. 88, Summer 1972.

1973
'Teacher education in England and Wales: a comparative view', in D. E. Lomax (ed.), *The Education of Teachers in Britain,* Wiley, London, 1973.
'Towards a general education', in Joseph Lauwerys and Graham Tayar (eds), *Education at Home and Abroad,* Routledge & Kegan Paul, London, 1973.

'Leicestershire, United Kingdom', in *Case Studies of Educational Innovation, Vol. 2, At the Regional Level*, OECD, Paris, 1973.

'Recurrent and lifelong education in comparative perspective', in *Recurrent Education: Concepts and Policies for Lifelong Education,* Proceedings of the Sixth General Meeting, Comparative Education Society in Europe, Frascati, The Society, 1973.

'Comparative education as a scientific study', in H. J. Krause, E. Neugebauer, J. H. Sislian and J. Wittern (eds), *Orientierungspunkte Internationaler Erziehung, Essays und Fallstudien zur vergleichenden Erziehungsforschung*, Fundament-Verlag Dr Sasse, Hamburg, 1973.

1974

'Metoder i den comparative paedogogik', in *Paedagogiske problemes i Komparativ Belysung,* Festschrift for Professor K. Grue-Sørensen, Jul Gjellerup Forlag, Copenhagen, 1974.

'The World Year Book of Education: a postscript', in P. Foster and J. R. Sheffield (eds), *The World Year Book of Education, 1974: Education and Rural Development,* Evans, London, 1974.

'*Vergleichende Erziehungswissenschaft als Wissenschaftliche Disziplin', in A.* Busch *et al.* (eds), *Vergleichende Erziehungswissenschaft: Texte zur Methodologie – Diskussion*, Verlag Dokumentation, Pullach bei München, 1974.

1975

'The contribution of comparative education to educational research', *Paideia*, (Akademia Nauk, Warsaw), vol. 4, 1975.

'*In memoriam Nicholas Hans',* Robert Williams (ed.), University of London, Institute of Education, London, 1975.

'The problem approach in comparative education: some methodological considerations', in Cliff Bennett (ed.), *Comparative Studies in Adult Education: an Anthology,* Publications in Continuing Education, Syracuse University, Syracuse, NY, 1975.

'School and community', in R. Ryba and D. Kallen (eds), *School and Community,* Proceedings of the Comparative Education Society in Europe, Seventh General Meeting, Sevres, The Society, 1975.

'Comparative education and the philosopher', *Przeszkość Przyszlosci*, Państwowy Instytut, Wydawneczy, Warsawa, 1975.

1976

'Examinations and assessments and European co-operation', in *Trends in European Education,* Jordan Hill College, Glasgow, 1976.

'Methodology in comparative education', in D. J. Foskett (ed.), *Reader in Comparative Librarianship,* Information Handling Services, Englewood, Colo, 1976.

'Comparative education and educational innovation', *Newsletter,* World Council of Comparative Education Societies, vol. 4, no. 3, September 1976.

'American and English education compared', *Trends in Education,* no. 3,

1976, September 1976, Department of Education and Science, HMSO, London, 1976.

'Diversidad y unidad por medio de la educación', *Perspectivas Pedagógicas,* vol. X, nos. 37–8, 1976.

1977

'The positivist debate in comparative education: an Anglo-Saxon perspective', *Comparative Education,* vol. 13, no. 2, June 1977.

'Una mirada retrospectiva a la Conferencia de Londres', *Perspectivas Pedagógicas,* vol. XI, nos. 41–2, 1978.

'Diversity and unity in education: a conference report', *International Review of Education,* vol. 24, no. 1, 1978.

'Comparative education and the philosopher', *Paideia*, 1977 (Festschrift for Professor B. Suchodolski).

'Science education: cultural borrowing and comparative research', *Studies in Science Education,* vol. 4, 1977.

1979

'Education in Japan', in *The Year Book of World Affairs,* Vol. 33, The London Institute of World Affairs/Stevens, London, 1979.

'Thoughts on education in the Third World', *Review of Education*, vol. 5, no. 3, Summer 1979.

'Analyses that fall short', *Times Educational Supplement,* 7 December 1979.

'Neo-Hegelians in education: a warning to Marxists', *Review of Education,* vol. 5, no. 4, Fall 1979.

'Los precursores de la educación comparada', *Revista de Educación*, no. 260, April 1979.

A Selected Guide to Ancillary Reading

Theodor W. Adorno *et al.*, *The Positivist Dispute in German Sociology,* Heinemann, London, 1976.

M. Albrow, *Bureaucracy,* Macmillan, London, 1970.

G. A. Almond and J. S. Coleman, *Politics of the Developing Areas,* Princeton University Press, Princeton, NJ, 1960.

Raymond Aron, *Main Currents in Sociological Thought 2,* Penguin, Harmondsworth, 1967.

Raymond Aron, *The Elusive Revolution: Anatomy of a Student Revolt,* Pall Mall, London, 1969.

Joseph Ben-David, *Centers of Learning,* McGraw-Hill, New York, 1977.

Basil Bernstein, 'Education cannot compensate for society', in D. Rubenstein and C. Stoneman, *Education for Democracy,* 2nd edn, Penguin, Harmondsworth, 1972.

Mark Blaug, *An Introduction to the Economics of Education,* Allen Lane, London, 1970.

Jean Blondel, *Comparing Political Systems,* Weidenfeld & Nicholson, London, 1972.

T. Bottomore, *Elites and Society,* Penguin, Harmondsworth, 1964.

M. Carnoy, *Education as Cultural Imperialism,* McKay, New York, 1974.

James C. Charlesworth (ed.), *Contemporary Political Analysis,* The Free Press, New York, 1967.

M. R. Cohen and E. Nagel, *An Introduction to Logic and Scientific Method*, Routledge, London, 1934.

James S. Coleman, *Education and Political Development,* Princeton University Press, Princeton, NJ, 1965.

John Dewey, *How We Think,* Heath, Boston, Mass., 1910.

John Dewey, *The School and Society,* 2nd edn, University of Chicago Press, Chicago, 1915.

John Dewey, *Democracy and Education,* The Free Press, New York/Collier Macmillan, London, 1966.

R. P. Dore, *The Diploma Disease: Education, Qualification and Development,* Allen & Unwin, London, 1976.

E. Durkheim, *Education and Sociology,* The Free Press, New York/Collier Macmillan, London, 1956.

David Easton, *A Framework for Political Analysis,* Prentice-Hall, Englewood Cliffs, NJ, 1965.
Amitai Etzioni, *A Comparative Analysis of Complex Organizations,* The Free Press, New York/Collier Macmillan, London, 1961.
Amitai and Eva Etzioni, *Social Change: Sources, Patterns and Consequences,* Basic Books, New York, 1964.
Amitai Etzioni, *A Sociological Reader in Complex Organizations,* 2nd edn, Holt, New York and London, 1969.
Paulo Freire, *Pedagogy of the Oppressed,* Sheed, London, 1972.
J. Goldthorpe, *The Sociology of the Third World,* Cambridge University Press, Cambridge, 1975.
Alvin W. Gouldner, *The Coming Crisis of Western Sociology,* Heinemann, London, 1971.
Andrew W. Halpin (ed.), *Administrative Theory in Education,* University of Chicago, Midwest Administration Center, Chicago, 1958.
F. Harbison, *Educational Planning and Human Resource Development,* International Institute for Educational Planning, Paris, 1967.
F. A. von Hayek, *The Road to Serfdom,* Routledge, London, 1944.
E. Hopper (ed.), *Readings in the Theory of Educational Systems,* Hutchinson, London, 1971.
Robert T. Holt and John E. Turner (eds), *The Methodology of Comparative Research,* The Free Press, New York/Collier Macmillan, London, 1972.
Max Horkheimer and Theodor Adorno, *Aspects of Sociology,* Heinemann, London, 1973.
Ivan Illich, *De-schooling Society,* Calder, London, 1971.
Christopher Jencks and David Riesman, *The Academic Revolution,* Doubleday, New York, 1968.
Thomas Kuhn, *The Structure of Scientific Revolutions,* 2nd edn, University of Chicago Press, Chicago, 1969.
C. Levi-Strauss, *Cultural Anthropology,* Penguin, Harmondsworth, 1963.
Myron Lieberman, *Education as a Profession,* Prentice-Hall, Englewood Cliffs, NJ, 1956.
K. Lynch, *Growing up in Cities,* Cambridge University Press, Cambridge, 1978.
Karl Mannheim, *Freedom, Power and Democratic Planning,* Routledge & Kegan Paul, London, 1965.
Robert M. Marsh, *Comparative Sociology,* Harcourt Brace & World, New York, 1967.
Karl Marx and Frederic Engels, *Manifesto of the Communist Party,* Progress, Moscow, 1952.
Peter H. Merkl, *Modern Comparative Politics,* Holt, Rinehart & Winston, New York, 1970.
J. S. Mill, *A System of Logic, Ratocinative and Inductive,* 8th edn, Longman, London, 1970.
Gunnar Myrdal, *An American Dilemma: The Negro Problem and Modern Democracy,* Harper, New York and London, 1944.
William F. Ogburn, *On Culture and Social Change: Selected Papers, Chicago University Press,* Chicago, 1964.
Vilfredo Pareto, Sociological Writings, selected by S. E. Finer, Blackwell, Oxford, 1976.

Talcott Parsons, *The Structure of Social Action: A study in Social Theory with Special Reference to a Group of Recent European Writers,* 2nd edn, The Free Press, New York/Collier Macmillan, London, 1966.
Talcott Parsons, *Social Systems and the Evolution of Action Theory,* The Free Press, New York/Collier Macmillan, London, 1977.
Karl R. Popper, *The Logic of Scientific Discovery,* Hutchinson, London, 1959.
Karl R. Popper, *The Poverty of Historicism,* 2nd edn, Routledge & Kegan Paul, London, 1960.
Karl R. Popper, *Conjectures and Refutations,* Routledge & Kegan Paul, London, 1963.
Karl R. Popper, *The Open Society and its Enemies,* 5th edn, Routledge & Kegan Paul, London, 1966.
Karl R. Popper, *Objective Knowledge: An Evolutionary Approach,* Clarendon Press, Oxford, 1972.
Karl R. Popper and John C. Eccles, *The Self and Its Brain*, Springer, New York and London, 1977.
Joseph Ratner (ed.), *Intelligence in the Modern World, John Dewey's Philosophy,* The Modern Library, New York, Random House, 1939.
John Rex, *Key Problems of Sociological Theory,* Routledge & Kegan Paul, London, 1961.
Bertrand Russell, *A History of Western Philosophy,* Allen & Unwin, London, 1946.
A. Ryan, *The Philosophy of the Social Sciences,* Macmillan, London, 1970.
Israel Scheffler, *Science and Subjectivity,* Bobbs-Merrill, Indianapolis, Ind., 1967.
Israel Scheffler, *Four Pragmatists,* Routledge & Kegan Paul, London, 1974.
P. A. Schlipp, *The Philosophy of Karl Popper,* Open Court, La Salle, Ill., 1974.
Alfred Schultz, *The Phenomenology of the Social World,* Heinemann, London, 1972.
Andre Siegfried, *The Character of Peoples,* Cape, London, 1952.
William Graham Sumner, *Folkways: A Study of the Sociological Importance of Usages, Manners, Customs, Mores and Morals,* Ginn, London, 1906.
William Graham Sumner, *Social Darwinism,* Prentice-Hall, Englewood Cliffs, NJ, 1963.
Ted Tapper, *Political Education and Stability,* Wiley, London, 1976.
F. Tonnies, *Community and Association,* Routledge & Kegan Paul, London, 1955.
R. Turner, 'Modes of social ascent through education: sponsored and contest mobility', in E. Hopper, op. cit.
Max Weber, *The Theory of Social and Economic Organization* (ed. Talcott Parsons), The Free Press, New York/Collier Macmillan, London, 1964.
K. C. Wheare, *Modern Constitutions,* 2nd edn, Oxford University Press, London, 1971.
Peter Winch, *The Idea of a Social Science and Its Relation to Philosophy,* Routledge & Kegan Paul, London, 1958.

Author Index

Addams, Jane 9
Adorno, Theodor 13, 17
Aiken, W. 141
Albert, Hans 13
Altbach, P. 35
Anderson, Archie 9
Anderson, C. A. 56, 74
Andreski, Stanislav 55
Anweiler, Oskar 73, 75
Aristotle 38, 56, 121, 122, 124, 133, 140, 142, 157
Armstrong, H. E. 2, 16
Arnold, Matthew 19, 89, 90
Austin, Sarah 58
Ayer, A. J. 4, 16

Bache, Alexander Dallas 22
Bacon, (Sir) Francis 38, 144
Barnard, Henry 21, 23, 34, 58, 73, 89
Barnett, H. G. 75
Basset, C. A. 39
Bereday, George Z. F. 35, 40, 55, 57, 59, 62, 63, 67, 72
Berger, P. L. 74, 132
Bestor, A. E. 134, 141
Blonsky, P. P. 162
Bode, Boyd H. 9, 16, 134, 141
Bourdieu, P. 71, 74
Bowman, Mary Jean 56, 74
Braithwaite, R. B. 4
Brezhnev, L. I. 169
Brickman, W. W. 39, 55
Broudy, Harry S. 9, 16
Buffon, George-Louis Leclerc de 38, 40, 55
Buisson, Ferdinand 90, 109
Busch, A. 87

Carlson, R. O. 75
Childs, John 9
Chin, R. 75
Clarke, (Sir) Fred 6, 16
Cohen, Morris 3, 63, 70, 74
Comenius 21, 121
Comte, Auguste 39, 41
Condorcet, M. J. A. N. Caritat, Marquis de, 27, 31, 121, 124
Confucius 123
Crosser, Paul 145, 160
Counts, George 9
Cousin, Victor 19, 23, 34, 58, 73, 109

Dahloff, Urban 70
Dahrendorf, Ralf 13
Dalin, P. 75
Darwin, Charles 8, 42, 44, 147
Dawson, N. H. R. 58, 73
Democritus 135
Descartes, Rene 124, 144
Dewey, John 2, 7, 8, 10, 13, 14, 16, 45, 80, 121, 124, 131, 134, 139, 142–61
Dingle, Herbert 4, 13, 43, 44, 46, 56
Dongerkery, S. R. 35
Duke, Benjamin C. 35

Eaton, John 58, 73, 90
Eccles, (Sir) John 4
Eckstein, Max 57, 63, 64, 68, 69, 70, 7£, 74
Edding, Friedrich 7, 16
Eddington, (Sir) Arthur 3, 4, 16
Einstein, Albert 4
Ekuban, B. B. 55
Elbers, Doris 74
Engels, F. 132, 162–75
Evans, (Sir) Robert 5

Faure, Edgar 32, 35

Fellenberg, Phillipp von 23
Fernig, Leo 60, 73, 95
Ferry, Jules 90, 109
Filmer, Paul 56
Findlay, J. J. 9
Floud, Jean 7, 16
Fraser, Stewart E. 22, 34, 40, 55
Froebel, F. 121

Gandhi, Mahatma 30
Garfinkel, H. 71, 74
Ginsberg, Morris 26
Goetz, H. 40, 55
Gouldner, Alvin 13, 69
Green, Nicholas St. John 8
Griscom, John 22
Guba, E. G. 75

Habermas Jürgen 13, 71, 132
Hall, Robert King 5, 7, 35
Hans, Nicholas 1, 2, 3, 5, 6, 12, 14, 16, 26, 39, 57, 61, 62, 64, 65, 73, 74, 89
Harris, William Torrey 8, 19, 24, 25, 34, 37, 46, 58, 59, 73, 90, 109
Hartlib, Samuel 21
Havelock, R. G. 75
Hayek, F. von, 3, 16
Hegel, G. W. F. 3, 8, 41, 56, 124
Hempel, Carl 4
Herbart, H. 121
Hilker, Franz 38, 55, 60, 101, 109
Hitler, A. 137
Holmes, Oliver Wendell, Jnr. 8
Horner, Leonard 24, 58
Huhse, Klaus 74
Hullfish, H. Gordon 9, 16
Husserl, E. 71, 112, 132
Hutchins, Robert Maynard 133, 134

James, William 8, 145, 147
Jayaweera, S. 28, 35
Jefferson, Thomas 27, 143, 144, 146, 148
Jullien, Marc Antoine, de Paris 38, 39, 40, 41, 53, 59, 61, 69, 89

Kahn, Gisela 74
Kalb, Werner 74
Kandel, Isaac L. 6, 14, 26, 32, 35, 57, 62, 64, 74
Kaunitz, Prince 21
Kelly, Gail 28
Kerschensteiner, Georg 30
Kilpatrick, William H. 9
King, Edmund J. 57, 59, 70, 71, 72, 73, 75
Krupskaya, N. K. 162, 171
Krushchev, N. S. 171
Kuhn, Thomas S. 4, 16, 50, 51, 52, 56

Lange, F. A. 3
Langevin, Paul 31
Lapchinskaya, Vera 74
Laski, Harold 133
Lauwerys, Joseph A. 1, 2, 3, 5, 6, 12, 30, 35, 57, 60, 62, 73, 79
Lenin 124, 167, 171
Leonarduzzi, Alessandro 55
Locke, John 121, 124, 146
Lourenço-Filho, M. B. 39, 55
Luckman, T. 74
Lunacharsky, A. V. 162

Macaulay, Lord 28
McCarthy, Joseph 134
Mach, Ernst 3
Machiavelli 137
McLean, Donald 5
McLean, Martin 35
Madariago, Salvador de 26
Makarenko, A. S. 162
Malkova, Zoya 74
Mallinson, Vernon 26, 35, 71, 75, 83, 113
Mann, Horace 22, 23, 34, 58
Mannheim, Karl 3, 9, 10, 45, 56, 133
Maria Theresa of Austria 21
Marx, Karl 9, 10, 13, 39, 41, 42, 56, 68, 121, 123, 162–75
Mead, George H. 8, 9
Medawar, (Sir) Peter 4, 49, 56
Meyer, Adolphe E. 34
Michelson, A. 43, 46
Miles, M. B. 75
Mill, J. S. 2, 39, 40, 42, 50, 56, 59, 61, 63, 65, 68, 75, 124, 132
Mohammed Ali 28
Montesquieu, Charles Louis de 38, 40
Montessori, Maria 121
Moor, Christine 71, 75
Morley, E. W. 43, 46
Mosca 9
Muller, Peter 74
Mumford, Lewis 146
Mundy, Jennifer 71, 75
Myrdal, Gunnar 9, 132

Nagel, Ernest 3, 63, 70, 74
Neurath, Otto 4, 46, 56, 79

Newton, (Sir) Isaac 41, 59
Nidditch, P. H. 4
Noah, Harold J. 57, 63, 64, 68, 69, 70, 72, 74, 110
Nunn, (Sir) Percy 6

Ogburn, William F. 9, 10, 84
Ortega, Jose y Gasset 26

Padover, S. K. 159
Pareto, Vilfredo 9, 112, 132
Parsons, Talcott 17, 82
Passeron, H. 74
Pavlov, I. 169
Peirce, C. S. 8, 9
Pepper, S. C. 156
Percy, (Lord) Eustace 5
Pericles 140
Perry, Ralph Barton 143, 159
Pestalozzi 21, 22, 23, 121
Peter, the Great, of Russia 21
Pilot, Harald 13
Piskunov, A. I. 34
Plato 2, 20, 38, 121, 131, 134–41, 143, 163, 167, 170
Popper, (Sir) Karl R. 2, 3, 4, 9, 10, 13, 14, 16, 42, 45, 49, 50, 52, 53, 56, 68, 69, 70, 76, 77, 78, 85, 87, 119, 139
Protagoras 45, 135, 140, 142, 144, 149

Ratner, Joseph 160
Riesman, David 14, 17
Robinsohn, Saul B. 70, 73, 74, 82
Rossello, Pedro 39, 55, 60, 62, 73, 109
Rousseau, J. J. 144, 159
Rugg, Harold 9
Runciman, W. G. 132
Russell, (Lord) Bertrand 3, 8, 145, 150

Sadler, (Sir) Michael 24, 25, 33, 34, 37, 46, 58, 59, 60, 83, 90
Saint-Simon, Claude Henri de 39
Salvador de Madariago, *see* Madariago
Schairer, Reinhold 6
Scheffler, Israel 4
Schlipp, Paul A. 4, 16, 160
Schneider, Friedrich 14, 57, 62, 75
Schutz, A. 71, 74, 112, 132
Shapere, Dudley 4
Shapovalenko, S. G. 171
Shatsky, S. T. 162
Siegfried, André 27, 35
Silliman, Benjamin 22
Sislian, Jack Heinz 87
Smith, B. O. 9, 16
Socrates 140
Spencer, Herbert 8, 42, 124
Stanley, W. O. 9, 16
Stebbing, Susan 3
Steward, John Hall 35
Stowe, Calvin 22, 23
Sumner, William Graham 41, 42, 56, 83

Tawney, R. H. 31, 35
Taylor, J. Orville 23, 34
Thorndike, E. L. 137
Tscharakarov, N. 62, 74
Turner, Roy 132
Tusquets, Juan 26

Ulich, Robert 62
Ushinsky, K. D. 25
Usill, Harley V. 6

Vaizey, (Lord) John 7, 16
Vygotsky, L. S. 162, 169

Ward, Lester F. 42, 44, 56
Weber, Max 80, 112
Wheare, K. C. 132
Whewell, William 3, 38, 55
Wiener, Philip P. 8, 16, 44, 56
Wittern, Jorn 87
Woodbridge, William C. 22
Wright, Chauncey 8

Place Index

America 19, 31, 32, 37, 44, 122, 123, 139, 143, 145, 146

Britain 8, 13, 22, 69, 72, 133
Bulgaria 62, 72

Centre for Educational Research and Innovation (CERI) 70, 71
Ceylon 29
Chicago, University of 133
Council of Europe 11, 37

Eastern Europe 125
Egypt 28, 29
England 19, 20, 21, 24, 29, 79, 121, 130
Europe 11, 22, 25, 30, 31, 33, 124, 134, 139, 140, 142
European Economic Community 128

Federal German Republic 130
France 19, 20, 22, 23, 27, 28, 31, 32, 72, 79, 89, 90, 94, 106, 121, 122, 125, 130, 131
Frankfurt 13, 69

Germany 23, 24, 57, 72, 93, 137
German Democrtic Republic 33, 72
Greece 122, 138, 142, 171

Hamburg 93, 111
Holland 22, 24, 58
Hungary 21

India 28, 84, 94, 130, 131
Institute of Education, London 3, 133
Institute for International Education, Frankfurt 70
International Bureau of Education, Geneva 11, 60, 71, 82, 95, 96, 111
International Educational Achievement Association 95
Italy 20, 22, 130

Jamaica 28
Japan 32, 49, 130, 131

Kandy 28
Karachi 32
Kashmir 28, 29
King's College, London 1, 3
Kuwait 84

Latin America 27, 33
London 79
London School of Economics 2

Malaysia 29
Massachusetts 23
Max Planck Institute, Berlin 70
Michigan 31
Musée Pedagogique, Paris 60

Netherlands 20
New York City 22
Nigeria 28, 29
North America 11, 22, 33, 124, 131

Organisation for Economic Co-operation and Development (OECD) 12, 17, 57, 65, 70, 71, 89, 90

Poland 21
Prussia 21, 22, 23, 58

Russia 21, 170

Santiago 32
Saudi Arabia 84

Scotland 29
Spain 28, 72
Sparta 20
St Louis 19
Sweden 21, 32, 79
Switzerland 20, 22

Tanzania 32
Teachers' College, Columbia 3, 5, 6, 8, 57, 133
Tokyo 32

UNESCO 2, 11, 30, 32, 37, 46, 60, 95, 111, 127
UNESCO, Institute for Education, Hamburg 13, 60, 82, 89, 91
United Kingdom 98, 111, 127
United Nations 11, 31, 77, 127, 128
University of London 1
US Office of Education 58, 90
USA 8, 9, 22, 23, 24, 27, 31, 72, 77, 79, 81, 84, 93, 94, 98, 111, 125, 127, 131, 13, 133, 139, 142
USSR 32, 72, 125, 130, 131, 132, 162, 169, 170, 171, 172

Virginia 31

Wales 130
Western Europe 22, 57, 124, 131, 140
West Indies 29